# Quality Function Deployment

Also available from Quality Press

*Benchmarking: The Search for Industry Best Practices that Lead to Superior Performance*
Robert C. Camp

*Management by Policy: How Companies Focus Their Total Quality Efforts to Achieve Competitive Advantage*
Brendan Collins and Ernest Huge

*Policy Deployment: The TQM Approach to Long-Range Planning*
Bruce M. Sheridan

*Breakthrough Quality Improvement for Leaders Who Want Results*
Robert F. Wickman and Robert S. Doyle

To request a complimentary catalog of publications, call 800-248-1946.

# Quality Function Deployment

*Linking a Company with Its Customers*

*Ronald G. Day*

*ASQ Quality Press*
*Milwaukee, Wisconsin*

*Quality Function Deployment: Linking a Company with Its Customers*
Ronald G. Day

Library of Congress Cataloging-in-Publication Data
Day, Ronald G.
    Quality function deployment: linking a company with its customers
/ Ronald G. Day
        p.   cm.
    Includes bibliographical references and index.
    ISBN 0-87389-202-X (alk. paper)
    1. Quality function deployment.    2. Production management—Quality
control.    3. New products—Management.    I. Title.
TS156.D387    1993
658.5'62—dc20                                           93-4479
                                                          CIP

10    9    8    7    6    5

ISBN 0-87389-202-X

Acquisitions Editor: Susan Westergard
Production Editor: Annette Wall
Marketing Administrator: Mark Olson
Set in Times by Montgomery Media, Inc.
Cover design by Montgomery Media, Inc.
Printed and bound by BookCrafters, Inc.

ASQ Mission: To facilitate continuous improvement and increase customer satisfaction by identifying, communicating, and promoting the use of quality principles, concepts, and technologies; and thereby be recognized throughout the world as the leading authority on, and champion for, quality.

For a free copy of the ASQ Quality Press Publications Catalog, including ASQ membership information, call 800-248-1946.

Printed in the United States of America

 Printed on acid-free recycled paper

American Society for Quality

Quality Press
611 East Wisconsin Avenue
P.O. Box 3005
Milwaukee, Wisconsin 53201-3005

# Contents

# Preface

The author's experience over many years in industry has served as a constant reminder that most companies have not made an aggressive effort to understand their customers' wants and needs. Many companies depend on their warranty programs, customer complaints, and inputs from their sales staffs to keep them in touch with their customers. The result is a focus on what is wrong with the existing product with little or no focus on what the customer wants and expects in new product offerings. Furthermore, without the benefit of customer surveys, companies have little idea about how customers rate their company and how they rate the performance of their competitors. In these companies, new products are planned and brought to market without a real firsthand knowledge of the potential customers' wants and needs. Simple logic says that products designed without knowledge of the potential customers' requirements will frequently fail to satisfy their needs. Sales will not meet their potential. Competitors who listen to the customer and bring out products that respond to their needs will compete more effectively and gain market share.

The methodology of quality function deployment (QFD) employs the customers' wants and needs as its basic input. It was this aspect of QFD that first attracted the author's attention to the process. If companies could be encouraged to use QFD as a methodology during product development, it would force them to listen to their customers. Thus, for the first time, many companies would be put in touch with existing and prospective customers and the knowledge gained would help them develop more competitive, state-of-the-art products for their markets. This is the aspect of QFD that continues to hold the author's attention—it is a process that puts companies in touch with their customers and helps them develop products that are more customer oriented and responsive. It is a process to increase competitiveness and develop a base of satisfied customers. For many industries threatened by global competition, this level of customer focus and response is necessary for survival.

This is a pragmatic book. It is intended as a guide for practitioners. It captures much of the pertinent experience gained during the last 8 years since the author first investigated and started working with the concept. It is intended to give users an insight into the use of the QFD matrix in a variety of applications. It presents the author's experience and ideas on how to handle some of the typical problems experienced in using the QFD matrix concept.

QFD was introduced to the United States in the early 1980s. Several articles and translations of Japanese examples appeared shortly after its introduction which were based largely on observations of Japanese applications.

The American Supplier Institute (ASI) in Dearborn, Michigan, and GOAL/QPC in Methuen, Massachusetts, have been the primary organizations offering an overview and workshop-type training since that time. Beginning in 1989, ASI and GOAL/QPC have jointly sponsored annual seminars to update the level of QFD knowledge.

The recent emphasis on company-wide processes to improve internal operations and competitiveness has caused many companies to examine the ideas of total quality management, the ISO 9000 standards, and the Malcolm Baldrige National Quality Award requirements. Many companies have been introduced to the importance of knowing their customer through their investigation of these company-wide program concepts.

Typically, as the QFD experience has increased and the knowledge base has expanded, many new ideas and approaches have emerged for handling the data and numerical portions of the matrix. Software has been developed to facilitate the construction of QFD matrices. This process of exploration and refinement will continue, as it does in all disciplines.

The real challenge, however, is a much more pragmatic one. American companies still need to come to grips with the fact that they must be in touch with their customers, that they must fund programs for customer research, and that the process must be a continual one. They must use some organized method to examine these customers' wants and needs and translate them into action within their companies. This is the challenge. It is the intent and purpose of this book to explore issues germane to this focus.

The examples used in the book are generic. They are based on the experience of many companies. Companies that have invested funds to determine the "voice" of their customers typically find a number of issues that are important to their customers and that they will incorporate into their next product developments. From a competitive viewpoint, the opportunity offered through this customer knowledge would be lost if it were published. In recognition of the confidential and proprietary nature of every QFD study, the information and data used in this book have been altered substantially. Some examples were developed strictly to help enhance an understanding of certain aspects of the process.

One of the principal ideas behind this book is to provide insight into the use of QFD in nonproduct applications. The author believes there is a major opportunity for application in these areas and hopes that this text will encourage people to investigate this potential.

# Acknowledgments

In developing this book, I found how deeply indebted I was to a number of friends and associates for their contributions, encouragement, and support. In particular, I extend my personal thanks to:

Bill Eureka of the American Supplier Institute, who gave me the opportunity to work with him and other members of ASI in developing QFD workbooks and acting as a QFD instructor.

Bob Schaefer of General Motors Corporation, who encouraged me to become involved in the development of specialized QFD workshops for the corporation and who was instrumental in my decision to work as instructor in those workshops.

Wayne Forehand and Bill Biondo of General Motors, who taught with me in the General Motors QFD workshops and who spent many hours with me discussing concepts and ideas about QFD applications.

Kurt Hofmeister of the American Supplier Institute, with whom I have taught and exchanged ideas and whose spirit of enthusiasm and dedication are infectious. I am especially indebted to Kurt for his agreement to review this book prior to its publication.

Dr. D. L. Landen, Ph.D. of Landen and Associates, with whom I have worked over many years, for his friendship and encouragement and his agreement to review this book prior to its publication.

My wife, Ginny, without whom this endeavor would have never been completed. She edited all the material. She encouraged me to keep working when I would rather have been fishing. She is as much a part of this book as I am.

# The Quality Function Deployment (QFD) Concept

*chapter one*

## Linking a Company with Its Customers

Businesses are usually started because their founders recognize a customer need and believe that they can satisfy it better than other companies. This is often because they have a new and distinctive approach. They may offer a highly innovative service or product. At the time of its introduction, it may be essentially unique to the industry. Initially, the product or service they offer is highly competitive because of this advantage. *No matter how effectively a company meets the initial needs of its customers, it must remain constantly alert and responsive to its customers' continuing wants and needs. If the company is not responsive to these changing needs, the passage of time will erode its early advantages.*

Most companies understand the need for continuing customer contact. They establish systems for customers to register and receive responses to their complaints. They challenge their sales and marketing people to be cognizant of customer satisfaction with their products and services and of any changing customer needs. Some companies utilize questionnaires to develop measures of customer satisfaction.

These are typical measures in the majority of U.S. businesses. However, they often fail to reveal the reality of the customers' real wants and needs. Determinations made from sales and marketing inputs are usually based on conversations rather than any structured and consistent questioning approach. They are essentially random responses and can be highly misleading. Complaints about existing products represent obvious dissatisfaction with the existing product's features, performance, or service. They represent challenges to the company to correct the problems. However, correcting the problems does not provide assurance that the customer will repurchase the product or recommend it to others. *Furthermore, these complaints provide little insight into what the customer really wants and needs in a product.* They simply reflect what the customer dislikes in the present product or service.

The use of questionnaires represents a positive step compared with dependence on salesperson observations and complaints. Questionnaires usually represent a larger sampling using a common format. The data can be tabulated with some level of assurance and reliability. However, they are very dependent on the type of questions and their wording and they can be misleading. One of the most common problems is with the interpretation of the questions. People who write questions have a definite objective in mind. The respondents, on the other hand, may have an entirely different mindset when answering the question. A typical example is a question on an automotive survey: "How satisfied are you with the exterior finish of your car?" The company's objective was to determine the customers' evaluation of the painted finish of the car. A series of follow-up personal interviews with customers revealed that they had used this question to indicate their dissatisfaction with fit, finish, and operational problems with exterior moldings, emblems, headlamp bezels, hood ornaments, and hood latch key covers. It was the only item on the questionnaire that involved the exterior of the car. People used the question to reflect their dissatisfaction with any exterior problems, not just those related to the paint finish. Had the questionnaire been used without supplemental one-on-one interviews, the company could have drawn fallacious conclusions and taken actions that might not have addressed the real customer concerns.

Many industries have experienced the agonizing problem of introducing a new or revised product that did not meet with customer acceptance. In retrospect, most of these failures can be traced to a lack of understanding of the real customer wants and needs. Even when a company has had a successful product, customer expectations change as customers see other products and services with innovative approaches.

To ensure continued business success, every company should have processes in place to constantly monitor and update its knowledge of its customers' wants, needs, and levels of satisfaction. For small companies, this can represent a major investment, one that must be approached with cautious planning. Many large companies have recognized this need for continuing customer awareness. Their resources frequently permit them to establish marketing and marketing research groups in the organization. These groups work to develop effective ways to monitor the customers' wants and needs—the customers' voice. However, a company's size is often a hindrance to the overall effort. Large companies tend to divide into functional groups that guard their information and are reluctant to engage in a cooperative effort. The customers' voice does not find its way effectively throughout the organization and therefore cannot affect new concepts as it should.

Failure to properly understand the customers' voice—their wants and needs—means that any endeavor to develop new or revised products starts with a major handicap. Because it is customers who must buy the product and who must be satisfied with it, the product must be developed with their needs and wants as the principal inputs to the new product development project. When this is not the case, the new product introduction is often disappointing. Corrective action in the form of redesign is expensive and time-consuming and never as effective as the introduction of a well-executed product whose development was based on customers' inputs.

QFD is a process—a methodology—for planning products and services. It starts with the voice of the customer; *this is the input*. The customers' wants and needs become the *drivers* for the development of requirements for the new or revised product or service. The QFD process requires a number of inputs and decisions that are best done through teamwork. Because of this, the process tends to remove many of the functional barriers that develop in large organizations, thereby helping to merge marketing's knowledge of the customer with product engineering's need to know the customers' requirements.

Thus, companies that decide to use the QFD method find that they must (1) determine the voice of their customer and (2) examine the company response to this voice through an organized team approach. In effect, this links the company to its customers. The organization works more cooperatively, and the new product or service has increased potential for satisfying its ultimate customers.

## Tools and Concepts for Improving the Business

There is never a shortage of challenges for people in industry. There are always issues that need attention. Issues are so interwoven in a business that action to improve one issue will have ripple effects on others. For example, improving customer satisfaction results in increases in new and repeat sales. This, in turn, strengthens the company's financial position and provides capital for improving both the business and the economic health of its employees and the community.

Challenges are diverse. They may involve the need to decrease part variability in manufacturing to reduce costs of scrap and rework, or enlisting the help of the machine operators in planning new machining layouts and processes. Other challenges may involve inventory reduction, improved delivery times, or new and better design concepts for the company's products.

Many tools have been developed to help companies work on these challenges more effectively. Businesses in the United States are very familiar with the plethora of such tools and concepts. They are available to help organizations improve their effectiveness in areas such as problem solving, inventory control, quality assurance, variation simulation, and design practices. Figure 1.1 shows a few of these tools that are currently receiving considerable attention.

Many of these tools tend to have a narrow focus. They are designed to address a specific issue. A number of ancillary concerns of major significance may not be

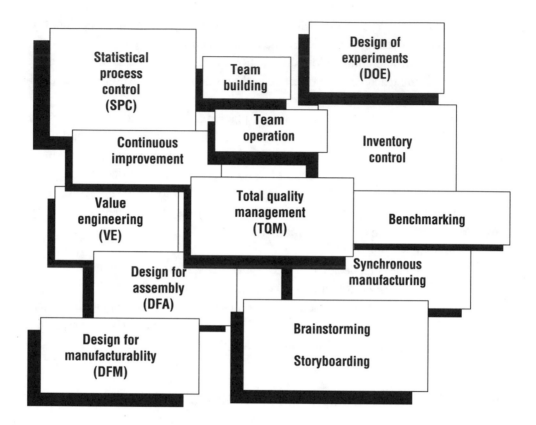

**Figure 1.1**   Some typical improvement tools.

addressed sufficiently when using some of these tools. For example, a tool may address the issue of cost savings and assembly simplification without fully considering the ultimate impact on manufacturing quality or customer perception. For illustration, an assembly plant might currently receive a headlamp, a turn signal lamp, and a transparent lens cover for assembly. Changing this to a purchased unitized assembly might significantly reduce the plant's overall assembly time and cost. However, when a fault occurs during ownership of the product, the owner may be forced to purchase an expensive unitized assembly rather than the less expensive component that failed. The owner's reaction could significantly impact his or her perception of the company and affect repurchase decisions.

People in the United States have a fascination with new ideas and tools. There are problems and challenges in any business, so when a new tool appears on the scene, there is always the hope that it will represent a solution, a panacea for some existing concern. Experience shows, unfortunately, that most of these tools tend to have a half-life of about

2 years. They are tried, frequently with success. However, they are not part of any grand plan for the organization and they are soon replaced by the new "tool of the year." Some tools, such as statistical process control (SPC), do survive and are resurrected many years later, after they are observed to work very well in another industry or country.

Compared with Japanese industries, most U.S. organizations have less fascination with the idea of planning a new project, product, or service. There is an impatience to move ahead, to generate ideas, and to build prototypes for evaluation. The cycle frequently becomes a repetitive one of building a prototype to represent a design concept, testing it, and changing it based on test performance. This continues until there is no more time because the start of production has arrived. Frequently, more changes are made after start-up to correct additional problems encountered in production.

## The Proactive Versus the Reactive Approach

There is ample evidence that the Japanese spend considerably more time in initial planning. Companies that are suppliers to Japanese firms or that have worked with them in joint ventures have experienced this. Figure 1.2 shows the results of a study made by a U.S. company involved in a joint venture with one of the better Japanese companies. Both were involved in the design, development, and ultimate production of similar products. The curve labeled "reactive" represents the U.S. company's experience; the curve representing the Japanese company is labeled "proactive." The "reactive" curve shows that there were few changes in the early stages of the product's development cycle. As the company began generating concepts and building and testing prototypes, problems occurred. Parts and assemblies failed test requirements. Part variability was encountered, which affected performance, appearance, or fit. Changes were necessary to react to these issues. As the curve shows, the number of changes started to increase as the product cycle moved into the prototype and pilot stages.

By contrast, the Japanese company diligently examined the project, evaluated it in detail, and made changes early in the time frame. At this stage, the changes frequently involved plans and concepts rather than materials and parts. Essentially, they represented "paper changes" and were faster and far less expensive to make. The ultimate effect of this attention to every detail at the planning stage is that the Japanese company had far fewer changes in the later pilot and production stages. Changes made during these later stages (prototype and pilot) usually affect tools and involve major time and expense. As the curve shows, these changes were minimal in the Japanese experience.

The dip near the right side of the reactive curve in Figure 1.2 represents a situation that many U.S. companies have experienced. A point is reached where the organization can no longer handle the number of changes required. A restriction, or "freeze," is then placed on certain changes. Only the most important changes are allowed to be

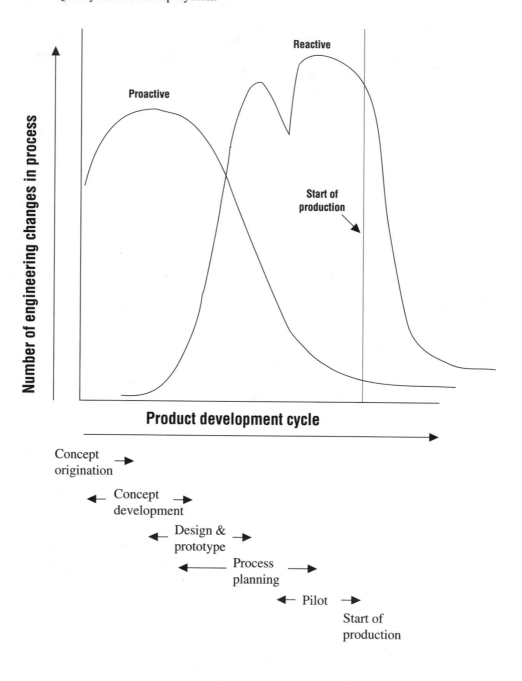

**Figure 1.2**    Number of engineering changes in process versus project timing.

processed. Ultimately, the freeze has to be lifted, and, as noted, the number of changes increases again. Typically, many problems remain at the start of production. As the reactive curve shows, changes continue after start-up. Each of these changes involves the effort of people within the organization. The hours spent in working off these problems would be better spent in planning for the next project. As the proactive curve shows, the Japanese company had few changes remaining at start-up and could therefore better use its personnel to plan the next project. Because the number of changes equates to employee-hours, it is readily apparent that the reactive approach required more people and resulted in additional cost.

In a generic manner, these curves show the difficulty that many U.S. industries experience with the launch of any new endeavor, product, or service. It logically follows that U.S. industries look on new tools, concepts, and ideas as possible ways to help them overcome many of their problems. The use of these tools has generated some major gains for industry. Despite this, evidence shows that much of U.S. industry is still not competing effectively, especially in the areas of customer satisfaction, cost, and development time from concept to delivery.

There is a growing awareness that U.S. industry needs to be more proactive, to get in touch with its customers and to plan products and services with the customer in mind. Similarly, there is a heightened understanding that the tools referred to earlier can have a very beneficial impact when used selectively and in concert with a broader overall approach. Thus, the idea of total quality management (TQM) has received considerable attention. It integrates these tools with people involvement and quality planning. Many discussions of this TQM idea use the illustration of TQM as an umbrella that encompasses the use of these tools, as shown in Figure 1.3.

There is still an inherent danger because of our experience and our fascination with tools. Many efforts to launch a TQM program may still result in a disjointed approach. A number of recent studies have reported that the results of TQM implementation have been disappointing in many companies. In the hands of people whose experience has been reactive, there is a strong move to skip the planning phase and get on with the business of building something tangible that can be tested and perfected.

## Defining QFD

*QFD is not a tool. It is a planning process.* It can help an organization plan for the effective use of the other technical tools to support and complement each other and address priority issues. It can help pinpoint those areas of customer concern where team involvement and the use of specialized tools can be most beneficial.

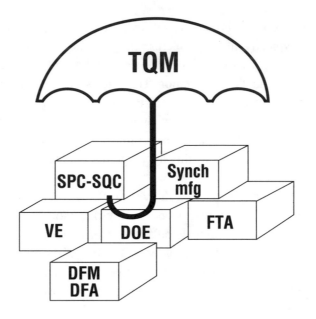

SPC-SQC = Statistical process control–statistical quality control
Synch mfg = Synchronous manufacturing
VE = Value engineering
DOE = Design of experiments
DFM, DFA = Design for manufacturing, design for assembly
FTA = Fault tree analysis

**Figure 1.3**    TQM, a concept for effective use of technical tools.

In addition, because QFD has its origin with the customer, it will assist the organization in gaining a customer focus. It is only through this focus that an organization begins to understand what is needed to increase customer satisfaction.

Figure 1.4 highlights some of the key issues of the QFD concept:

- QFD is a planning process as opposed to a tool for problem solving or analysis.
- The customers' wants and needs—their requirements—are the inputs to the matrix. *The process cannot begin without these inputs.* QFD essentially forces an organization to get in touch with the people who use its products.
- It uses a matrix to display information vital to the project in brief outline format.
- This collection of information in the matrix format facilitates examination, cross-checking, and analysis. It helps an organization set competitive targets and determine the priority action issues.

---

• A planning process

• Inputs: customers' wants and needs

• Matrix format used for recording vital information

• Permits analysis and determination of priority issues

• Output: key action issues for improved customer satisfaction
based on customer inputs

---

**Figure 1.4**   Defining QFD.

• The output resulting from analysis of the QFD matrix is twofold: (1) competitive targets are established for key action items related to the customers' voice and (2) Certain priority issues are selected for special emphasis. Effective response to the targets and to the selected priority issues will result in increased customer satisfaction.

## The Relationship of QFD to Other Quality and Engineering Tools

QFD will help an organization plan for effective application of its quality tools by directing these applications toward issues of importance to customers. Organizations should use the QFD process as one of their principal planning tools in their TQM effort.

The term *quality function deployment* is a translation of the Kanji characters that the Japanese use to describe the QFD process. It would be better defined as a "customer-driven planning process." It causes an organization to stop developing products and services based solely on its own impression of what is required and to turn its attention to what customers require. The results can be impressive.

The selection of priority items for increased customer satisfaction provides a company with a distinct product focus. Those customer requirements that are currently satisfactory to customers can be handled using existing procedures and processes. On the other hand, the QFD process causes the company to focus on customer requirements where the product is not currently competitive. These are the issues that should become the driving force for effective application of the tools associated with TQM.

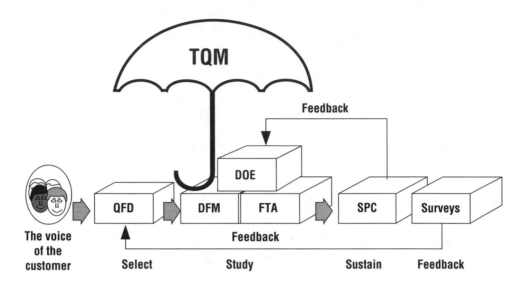

*Note:* Design of experiments (DOE), fault tree analysis (FTA), design
for manufacturing (DFM), and design for assembly (DFA) are typical of the
tools that a company might select to study the product.

**Figure 1.5**   QFD helps the organization plan for the effective use of technical tools.

Figure 1.5 illustrates this idea. The voice of the customer on the left side of the illustration is the *input* to the QFD process. The *output* of the QFD process is the selection of key priority items to improve customer satisfaction. These items should be carefully explored. Applicable tools of the TQM concept should be used to study the product concepts and to provide assurance that quality will be achieved. Statistical process control (SPC) should be used on these product concepts to sustain quality in production, thereby assuring that the customers' requirements have been met. Follow-up surveys should be conducted to help the organization measure the success of its QFD effort. The results can be used as feedback information to strengthen subsequent efforts.

As Joshua Hyatt points out, the experience of Techsonic Industries is an example of the impact of listening to the voice of the customers. Techsonic developed and produced a sonar fish finder that was responsible for almost all of its sales and profits. Hyatt reported that "between 1977 and 1983 the company came out with one new product a year, sometimes two. Nine in all...." Many of them were designed to respond to needs or problems that did not really exist. By 1983, the company had not generated one new product that had found a niche in the market. The old standby, the Super 60, accounted for 97 percent of the company's $11.5 million in sales. The company knew something needed to be done; it was inevitable that another company with a new technology would come along to unseat it from its market dominance (Hyatt 1989: 90–100).

Joshua Hyatt reports that a small advertising agency that had been hired to help with packaging began to ask a number of questions about customer demographics, wants, and needs. Techsonic suddenly realized that it hardly knew its customers at all. All its development work had been based on upgrades of existing products and its own internal ideas about what the company thought customers wanted.

The company began some customer survey work. Its customers—people who enjoy fishing—were interviewed and their comments recorded. Following are some of their responses:

- It should be readable in direct sunlight.
- It should not be complicated. It should be easy to use and not have a lot of buttons to push.
- The buttons should click...so that the customers, even while wearing gloves, could tell if they had hit them.
- It should show the shape of the bottom of the lake or river—like a picture or graph.

These comments were translated into action, and Techsonic worked on a new generation of fish finders that responded to the customers' voice. The customers also put the company on the track of liquid crystals, which could be used to show a picture of the bottom terrain. In 1984, Techsonic introduced the first liquid crystal recorder for showing depth, terrain, and location of fish. Hyatt reports, "They took the industry by surprise. 'It was a tremendously big breakthrough,' recalls Dave Ellison, editor of *Fishing Tackle Retailer.* 'The technology changed overnight.'"

Techsonic's sales jumped to $31 million in 1985, $56 million in 1986, and $70 million in 1988. Talking to the customer had paid off (Hyatt 1989: 90–100).

The voice of the customer is the input to the QFD planning matrix. Companies that decide to use the QFD process must first talk with and listen to their customers to determine their requirements. The result of this experience is that the company, like Techsonic, develops a deeper understanding of its customers' requirements. The new products it brings to market can be designed to satisfy these customer requirements.

## Defining Quality

In the following pages, there will be frequent reference to the concept of *quality*. It is an integral part of QFD. Quality figures strongly in many of the decisions that will be made in the construction of the QFD matrix. It is important, therefore, to have a clear understanding of how the term *quality* is used in this text.

In an article in the *Harvard Business Review,* David A. Garvin discussed the idea of abandoning the historical view of quality as measuring parts and managing defects. He comments:

> To achieve quality gains, I believe managers need a new way of thinking, a conceptual bridge to the consumer's vantage point...high quality means pleasing consumers, not just protecting them from annoyances....But managers have to take a more preliminary step—a crucial one, however obvious it may appear. They must first develop a clear vocabulary with which to discuss quality as *strategy.* They must break down the word quality into manageable parts.... I propose eight critical dimensions or categories of quality that can serve as a framework for strategic analysis: performance, features, reliability, conformance, durability, serviceability, aesthetics, and perceived quality. (Garvin 1987: 101–109)

When companies start their product cycles by first talking with their customers, they find that the customers' comments involve these eight dimensions. When these customer comments are used as the input to product planning, through the QFD matrix, the company's view of quality is significantly broadened.

The concept of quality must go beyond the concept of simply "conforming to requirements." It must have a broader context. *A company's minimum objective should be to satisfy customers.* A broader objective should be to go beyond satisfaction and to create quality that is exciting and differentiates the product from that of its competitors.

For purposes of this text, *quality* will be defined as follows: Goods and services that satisfy customers' requirements. *Quality control* will be defined as the processes that economically produce goods and services that satisfy customers' requirements.

Many readers will recognize these as the basic elements of the Japanese Industry Standard definition of quality control.

## QFD and the Product Development Process

There is great flexibility inherent in the use of the QFD methodology. Planning can be on a major scale or limited in scope. The concept can be used only for the early product planning, or it can be used on subsequent subsystem issues in design or processing. It can be used to help organize production planning issues and to examine service or after-market concerns.

Most industries recognize the need for an established process for bringing products to fruition from their early concept stages. Some industries use a four-phase process;

some use a seven-stage process. Much of the difference arises from the definition of the details involved with each step rather than any major difference in the total set of decisions and actions required.

Most of these product development processes start with a stage in which the customer is defined. The target market is established, and studies are conducted to determine the customers' wants and needs. The general product description and content, its marketing strategies, expected volumes, possible market conquests, demographics, and similar issue are defined. The generation of a series of alternative concepts normally follows the definition stage. This should be followed by a careful assessment of these concepts and by the selection or synthesis of the best concept. These early steps are the point at which the proactive planning idea can produce some of its greatest benefits. Much of this review and determination can be accomplished via simulation and partial prototyping. This helps the organization avoid the pitfall of committing to one concept and beginning the iterative process of prototyping, testing, and changing the design. A study by British Aerospace, a United Kingdom firm, helps illustrate this issue; it suggests that decisions made in the first 5 percent of the design effort determine 85 percent of the product's quality, cost, and manufacturability (Wood 1988: 22–27). Careful weighing of various concept proposals and study of their impact will aim the organization down a proactive path.

In most industries, the remaining steps of the product development process are similar and are well understood by the organizations. Once the concepts are assessed and a best concept selected, product design and process planning can begin in earnest. Requirements can be determined and designs developed. Prototypes are built and tested. Designs are finalized. Products and processes are validated to the established requirements. Production starts and work begins on after-market issues, such as delivery, service, and customer feedback surveys.

The QFD process can be used to assist the planning at any or all of these stages. The decision to use QFD is a team judgment based on the customers' priorities and tempered by any constraints within the organization.

In addition, the QFD matrix idea can be used successfully in other areas not specifically related to products or services, such as business planning, site planning, and test planning. It can also be used selectively for problem solving. The effort should be confined to those cases in which traditional problem-solving approaches have proven ineffective.

QFD was observed in operation in Japan in the early 1980s. The teachings of Akashi Fukuhara of the Central Quality Control Association and Dr. Yoji Akao of Tamaqawa University in Tokyo have been prime sources for Japanese information on QFD experience. Using his experience at Toyota as background, Fukuhara follows a pragmatic approach that moves along a logical path from the customers' voice to the production floor. Based on extensive experience with the Union of Japanese Scientists and Engineers (JUSE), the Japanese Society for Quality Control (JSQC), and other societies and industries, Dr. Akao summarizes the QFD experience, citing use of a number of matrices for a variety of applications. The overall intent is to ensure quality in all stages of the design process. This can involve the use of such diverse deployment applications as overall cost, part cost, fault tree analysis, analysis of a product's functions, and process planning. Both the American Supplier Institute, Dearborn, Michigan, and the GOAL/QPC organization in Methuen, Massachusetts, were responsible for bringing many of the ideas to the United States. The experience of many U.S. industries during the last ten years has greatly increased our knowledge of how to use the concept effectively. This experience is captured in the following chapters.

The many matrices reported in Dr. Akao's work can be summarized in an array or matrix of matrices as shown in Figure 1.6. Many of these can be used for various studies during a product development project. The matrix and table options are denoted by

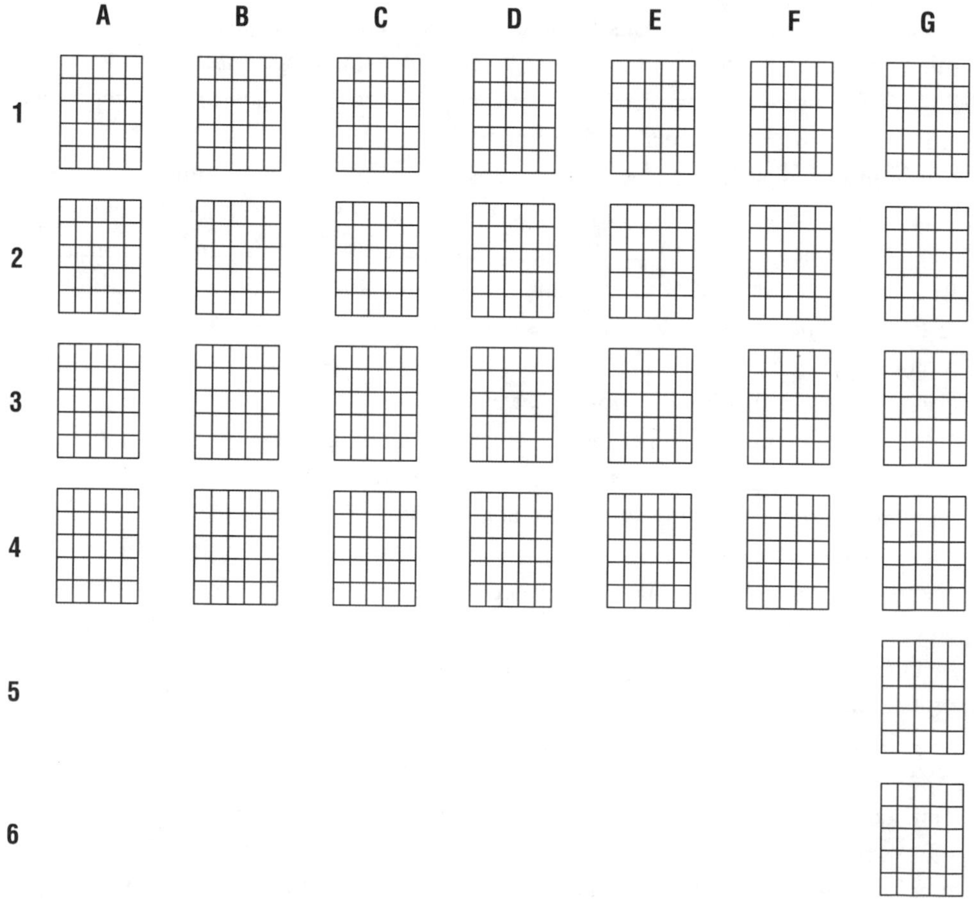

**Figure 1.6**   An array or "matrix" of matrices.

numbered rows and lettered columns. With this approach, each matrix can be identified; thus, table A-1 is the table in the upper left corner and table D-4 is at the intersection of column D and row 4. A wide number of options and processes are represented by this grouping. For example, matrix A-1 is a basic matrix for initial product planning studies. It uses the customers' voice as inputs on the left. The technical requirements that the company must use to satisfy the customers' voice are shown across the top of the matrix. Matrix B-2 represents a basic competitive analysis table in which features such as volume, price, and market share are listed on the left and the competitors are listed across the top. Matrix F-2 is an indicator or reminder that a new product design should be examined for its potential failures using a tool such as fault tree analysis. Matrix G-4 highlights the need to perform this same type of failure examination for the process. Each of these intersections in this overall matrix serves as a reminder of good business practices involved in new product development.

Many of the intersections in the matrix highlight the use of charts, tables, or studies that should be part of a company's normal product development process. For most organizations, it is easier to understand the need and application for many of these tools if they are portrayed in a flow diagram for the development process rather than in a matrix format.

Experience has shown that the approach taken by Fukuhara has more pragmatic appeal. It involves the use of the matrix for examining the customers' voice versus the company's technical requirements as in matrix A-1. Key priority items are selected for examination. The matrix concept is then used for part or process analysis on an as-required basis. The matrix concept can be easily embedded in a company's flow diagrams for product development. Ancillary tools, such as the fault tree analysis, and planning information, such as competitive tables, are also included in the flow diagram at their point of use.

In general, the discussion in this book follows the concepts of Fukuhara. His approach is direct and pragmatic. Observation has shown that this approach is easily understood and applied. It helps a company develop an organized approach for linking its planning with customers. The following chapters describe the QFD process and its application in areas of product and service planning. Its utilization in deploying priority issues to other planning matrices are discussed, and applications in other areas, such as business planning, are reviewed.

# An Overview of the QFD Process

*chapter two*

This chapter will provide an overview of the QFD process. It is intended to provide an understanding of the QFD matrix and its content. The general sequence of events, which typifies the overall process, and the development and deployment of items is shown in flow diagram format.

## The Objective of the QFD Process

*QFD should be viewed from a very global perspective as a methodology that will link a company with its customers and assist the organization in its planning processes.* Often, an organization's introduction to QFD takes the form of "how to build a matrix." A common result is that building the matrix becomes the objective. Companies must avoid this pitfall. *The purpose is not to build matrices; it is to get in touch with the customer and to use this knowledge to develop products which satisfy the customer.* The QFD process will help in the organization and analysis of all the pertinent information associated with a project. The priority items selected from the matrix during its analysis are items that will measurably improve the level of customer satisfaction.

The net effect is that the items that drive the company's actions are driven by the customers' requirements. There is an increased focus on customers and an increased awareness of their wants. Because of this focus, the process leads to improved customer understanding and increased customer satisfaction.

## Understanding the QFD Matrix Concept

Every successful company has always used data and information to help in its planning processes. In planning a new product, engineers have always examined the manufacturing and performance history of the current product. They look at laboratory or field test data, comparing their product to their competitor's product. They examine any customer satisfaction information that might be available.

Unfortunately, much of this information is often incomplete. It is frequently examined as individual data, without comparison to other data that may support or contradict it.

By contrast, QFD uses a matrix format to capture a number of issues pertinent and vital to the planning process. The matrix presents these issues in an outline form which permits the organization to examine the information in a multidimensional manner. This encourages effective decisions based on a team's examination and integration of the pertinent data.

The QFD process can be used for a variety of planning challenges. It is most often defined and taught as a product planning process. However, it has potential application in such diverse areas as service planning, business planning, site selection, and curriculum planning. The introductory chapters of this book will use a product focus for most examples. This will serve as a basis for developing an understanding of the QFD process. Subsequent chapters will address applications in other areas.

## The Two Primary Parts of the QFD Matrix

The QFD matrix has two principal parts. The horizontal portion of the matrix contains information relative to the customer. The vertical portion of the matrix contains technical information that responds to the customer inputs.

Figures 2.1 and 2.2 show the principal components of these horizontal and vertical portions of the matrix. Each of these components will be described in further detail in subsequent flowcharts.

### The Customer Portion

Customers express their wants and needs in their own language. In describing a control on a piece of equipment, customers might state "want the control to be easy to operate." Companies have to change these customers' words into language that they can use internally to describe and measure the item. Thus, a company might translate the customers' voice into "operating effort" or "force to operate."

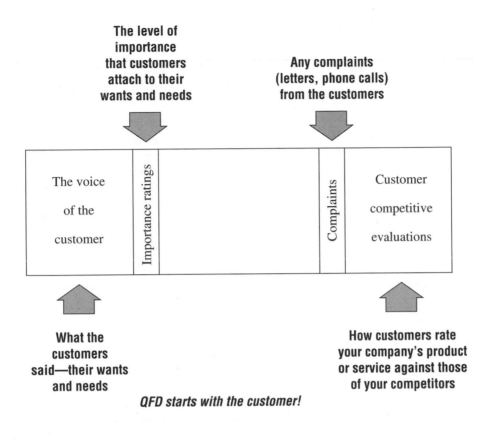

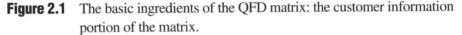

**Figure 2.1**  The basic ingredients of the QFD matrix: the customer information portion of the matrix.

The voice of the customer is the basic input required to begin a QFD project. As shown in Figure 2.1, there are other pieces of customer information that help a company understand the customers' wants and needs. The customers' importance rating is a measure of the relative importance that customers assign to each of the voices. The customers' competitive evaluation of the company's product (or service) permits a company to observe how its customers rate its products on a numerical scale (such as 1 to 5). It can compare this against how its competitors' customers rate their products on a similar scale. Any complaints that customers have personally registered with the company serve as an indication of dissatisfaction. Thus, they help punctuate the importance of a specific voice. This information is examined by the team developing the matrix to determine which of the customers' voices are the priority issues for the company.

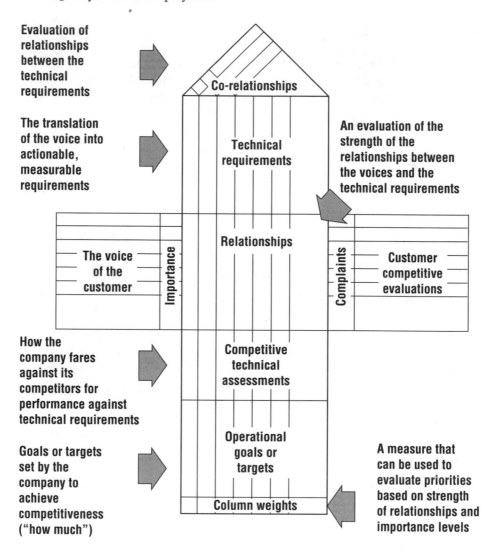

**Evaluation of relationships between the technical requirements**

**The translation of the voice into actionable, measurable requirements**

**An evaluation of the strength of the relationships between the voices and the technical requirements**

**How the company fares against its competitors for performance against technical requirements**

**Goals or targets set by the company to achieve competitiveness ("how much")**

**A measure that can be used to evaluate priorities based on strength of relationships and importance levels**

Co-relationships

Technical requirements

Relationships

The voice of the customer

Importance

Complaints

Customer competitive evaluations

Competitive technical assessments

Operational goals or targets

Column weights

**Figure 2.2**    The basic ingredients of the QFD matrix: adding the technical information portion of the matrix.

### The Technical Portion

Once the customer portion of a matrix has been determined, the next step is to develop
the technical information portion of the matrix (Figure 2.2). The first step is to determine how the company will respond to each voice. The technical or design requirements that the company will use to describe and *measure* each customer's voice are

placed across the top of the matrix. Thus, for the customer voice "want the control to be easy to operate," the technical requirement would be "operating effort." Other technical requirements might be "hand clearance" and "tactile force." The technical requirements represent *how* the company will respond to the customers' wants and needs, the *whats.*

The center of the matrix where the customer and technical portions intersect provides an opportunity to record the presence and strength of relationships between these inputs and action items. Symbols are used to indicate the strength of these relationships.

Each of the technical requirements can be examined in the laboratory or proving grounds to evaluate the performance of the company versus that of its chief competitors. The results are plotted in the section of the matrix entitled "competitive technical assessments" in Figure 2.2.

The information in the matrix can be examined and weighed by the QFD team. Goals or target values can be established for each technical requirement. These represent *how much*—the targets required to respond to the customers' wants and needs and to meet or exceed the competition.

The items *what, how, relationships,* and *how much* are the four parts of the *basic QFD matrix.* QFD applications in areas such as business planning, part and process planning, and problem solving generally employ the four-part basic matrix.

Tradeoffs can be examined and recorded in the triangular matrix at the top of Figure 2.2. This is accomplished by comparing each technical requirement against the other technical requirements. Each relationship is examined to determine the net result that changing one requirement has on the other. The triangular shape of this co-relationship matrix gives the overall QFD matrix the appearance of a rooftop. As a result, the QFD matrix is sometimes referred to as the *house of quality.*

Organizations may choose to add other ingredients to their matrices, such as field experience and expense, regulatory issues, and measures of potential organizational difficulty related to a technical requirement. Column weights can be calculated. These are developed using the customers' importance levels in conjunction with weights assigned to the relationship symbols. The resultant numbers provide a method of judging the relative importance of each of the technical requirements. These column weights can be used to reinforce judgments about issues of priority.

## An Overview Flowchart of the QFD Process

The following pages provide a brief overview of this process that will lay a foundation for subsequent chapters. A flowchart diagram format is used. The chapters that follow provide a detailed description of the development of a QFD matrix, its analysis, and the further deployment of selected items using additional matrices.

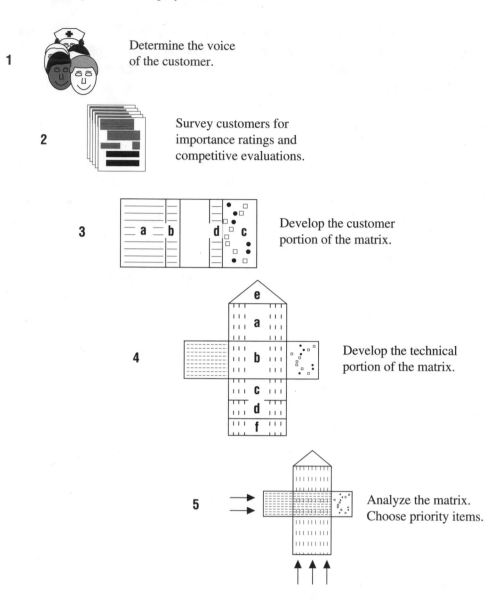

**Figure 2.3**    The QFD process: a simple flow diagram.

In planning a new venture or revisions to an existing one, companies need to be in touch with the people who buy and use their products and services. They need to determine the voice of their customers (see step 1 in Figure 2.3). This is vital for hard issues, such as a product whose sales are dependent on the customers' evaluation of how well their needs and wants are satisfied. It is equally crucial for softer issues, such as site selection and business planning. In these cases, the customers are the people in the organization who are responsible for determining how to accomplish the task.

Once the customers' wants and needs (voices) are known, the company can obtain other pertinent customer information. Through surveys, it can establish how its customers feel about the relative importance of the various wants and needs. It can also sample a number of customers who use its product and competitors' products. This provides the customers' evaluation of both the company's performance and that of its chief competitors (see step 2 in Figure 2.3).

Records can be examined to determine the presence of any customer complaint histories. This can be the result of letters of complaint, 800-number complaints, or other inquiries and comments.

Once this information is available, it can be organized and placed in the horizontal customer information portion of the QFD matrix. The voices of the customers represent their wants and needs—their requirements. These are the inputs to the matrix (see step 3, box a in Figure 2.3). The customers' importance ratings are placed in area b. The customers' competitive evaluations are placed in area c. Any complaints are recorded in area d.

The QFD team can then begin developing the technical information portion of the matrix. The customers' voice must be translated into items that are *measurable and actionable within the company*. Companies use a variety of names to describe these measureable items, such as design requirements, technical requirements, product characteristics, and product criteria. The term *technical requirements* will be used in this text. As an example, for the customers' desire that "controls should be easy to reach," one technical requirement might be "reach distance." This is measurable and can be related to anthropomorphic data. This would be entered as a technical requirement in area a, step 4 in Figure 2.3.

The relationships between the inputs (customer requirements) and the action items (technical requirements) can then be examined. Each technical requirement is examined to determine if action on the item will affect the customers' requirements. The typical question is: "Would the organization work on this technical requirement to respond favorably to the customers' requirements?"

For those items in which a relationship is determined to exist, the QFD team then must decide on the strength of the relationship. Symbols are normally used to denote a strong, moderate, or weak relationship. The common symbols are a double (concentric) circle, a single circle, and a triangle, respectively. The symbols provide a quick visual impression of the overall relationship strengths of the technical requirements and the customers' wants and needs. These are placed in area b in step 4.

The QFD team must instigate testing to develop technical data showing the performance of the parent company and its competitors for each of the technical requirements. This competitive technical data is plotted in the vertical portion of the matrix, area d.

Once this information is available, the team can begin a study to determine the target value that should be established for each technical requirement. The objective is to ensure that the next-generation product will be truly competitive and satisfy its customers' wants and needs. A comparison of the customers' competitive ratings and the competitive technical assessments helps the organization determine these targets. This is also the point where the ability to examine information in a multidimensional fashion becomes most apparent. A comparison of customers' evaluations against technical competitive assessments of the product may show conflicts that need to be resolved to ensure customer satisfaction. Target values are placed in area c of the matrix.

The co-relationship of the technical requirements can be examined. The objective is to highlight any requirements that are in conflict with each other. If action on one item will harm another item, this negative effect needs to be resolved. On the other hand, action on one item can benefit another. These positive and negative co-relationships are shown through the use of symbols. They are recorded in area e of Figure 2.3. One common approach is to use a double circle for a positive co-relationship and an X for a negative one.

Additional information can be added to the matrix depending on the team's judgment of value. Significant internal and regulatory requirements may be added. Measures of organizational difficulty can be added. Rows are often used to record field experience.

Column weights can be calculated as previously mentioned. These can serve as an index for highlighting those technical requirements that have the largest relative effect on the product (see area f, step 4 in Figure 2.3).

Once this matrix is complete, the analysis stage begins. The chief focus should be on the customer information portion of the matrix. It should be examined to determine which customer requirements need the most attention. This is an integrated decision involving the customers' competitive evaluation, their importance ratings, and their complaint histories. The number of priority items selected will be a balance between their importance and the resources available within the company. The arrows in Figure 2.3, step 5, indicate the selection of two priority voices. This resulted in the selection of three related technical requirements to be worked on to satisfy the two priority voices.

Items selected for action can be treated as special projects to improve customer satisfaction. They may be handled by the organization following normal procedures for high-priority issues. They can also be handled by use of the QFD matrix at the next level of detail. Any items so selected can become the input to a new matrix.

For example, the customer voice "should be easy to operate" was mentioned earlier. A strongly related design requirement (a measurable item) would be "operating effort." If the team selected this customer voice as a high priority issue for company attention, the technical requirement "operating effort" and its associated target value would be deployed as the input to a new matrix.

Whereas the first matrix was a planning matrix for the complete product, this new matrix is at a lower level. It concerns the subsystem (or assembly) that affects the operating effort.

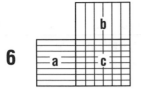

**6** Compare proposed design concepts, synthesize the best.

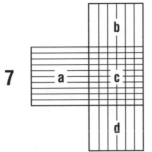

**7** Develop a part planning matrix for priority design requirements.

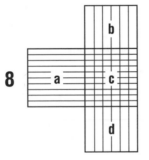

**8** Develop a process planning matrix for priority process requirements.

Develop a manufacturing planning chart.

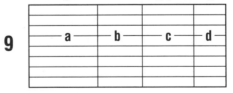

**9**

**Figure 2.4** The QFD process: a simple flow diagram.

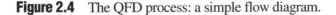

The challenge in this second-level matrix is to determine the concept that best satisfies the deployed requirement—operating effort. This requires evaluation of some design concept alternatives. Several techniques are available for this type of comparative review. A matrix format (see Figure 2.4, step 6) can be used. The criteria (or requirements) for the product or service are listed at the left in area a; concept alternatives are listed across the top (area b). The results of the evaluation of each concept versus the criteria can be entered in the center portion (area c) of the matrix. Because the team membership includes processing and manufacturing people, the effect of processing will enter this concept selection discussion. The final concept selection will be based on the best combination of design and processing alternatives.

Once the best concept alternative is selected, a QFD part planning matrix can be generated for the component level. The development of this matrix follows the same sequence as that of the prior matrix. Generally, less comparative information is available at this level, and the matrix is simpler. The technical requirements from the prior matrix are the inputs (see area a, step 7 in Figure 2.4). Each component in the selected design concept is examined to determine its critical part requirements. These are listed in area b. Relationships are examined, and symbols are entered in area c. The specifications are then entered for these selected critical part requirements in area d.

The part planning matrix should then be examined. Experience with similar parts and assemblies should be a major factor in this review. The analysis should involve the issue of *which of the listed critical part requirements are the most difficult to control or ensure continually.* This review will likely lead to the selection of certain critical part requirements that the team believes deserve specific followup attention.

As in the case of selected technical requirements in the initial product planning matrix, the selected critical part requirements from this matrix can be handled in several ways: through normal channels, by special project teams, or through another level of QFD matrix.

If the team believes that the selected critical part characteristics are best handled through the QFD process, it should proceed to step 8. A matrix should be developed for process planning. The critical part concerns from the part planning matrix should be used as inputs in area a. The critical process requirements (the operating windows in which the process must be maintained) are listed across the top in area b. Relationships are developed and examined in area c. The specifications for operating levels for each process requirement are recorded in area d. For example, if a critical part requirement was spot-weld strength, one critical process requirement would be weld current. The amount of current would be a critical process parameter to ensure proper spot-weld strength. The specification for this critical process requirement would be the amperes of current required to ensure the weld strength.

On completion of the planning at the part and process levels, the key concerns should be deployed to the manufacturing level, as indicated in step 9. Most organizations have detailed planning at this level and have developed spreadsheets and forms for recording their planning decisions. The determinations from the prior matrices should become inputs to these documents. Often, the primary document at this level is a basic planning chart (see step 9 in Figure 2.4). Items of concern are entered in area a. Frequently, the risk associated with these items is assessed. This is recorded in area b.

In typical risk assessments, the level of the concern and the probability of its occurrence are listed, as are the severity of any developing problems and the probability of detection. These items, along with other concerns, can be used to develop an index to highlight items of significant concern. Areas such as c and d can then be used to indicate issues such as the general types of controls, frequency of checking, measuring devices, responsibility, and timing.

This chapter provided an overview of the QFD process that will be amplified in subsequent chapters. Some of the key points to be remembered are as follows:

- The input to the QFD planning matrix is the voice of the customer. The matrix cannot be started until the customers' requirements—their wants and needs—are known. This applies to internal planning projects as well as products and services that will be sold to marketplace customers. Use of the QFD process leads an organization to develop a vital customer focus.
- The initial matrix is usually the product planning matrix. The customers' requirements are inputs. Subsequent matrices may be used to deploy or "flow down" selected requirements from the product planning matrix for part planning and process planning. Some form of manufacturing planning chart or matrix can be used to enter critical product and process requirements from prior matrices.
- The principal objective of the QFD process is to help a company organize and analyze all the pertinent information associated with a project and to use the process to help it select the items demanding priority attention. All companies do many things right. The QFD process will help them focus on the areas that need special attention. For those areas in which performance has been good, the company can continue its normal procedures and methods.

# The Voice of the Customer

*chapter three*

T his chapter will address some of the key issues involved in determining the voice of the customer, the customers' levels of importance, and their competitive evaluation of products.

## Determining Which People to Survey

The objective of the survey process is to determine the wants and needs of the customers. This may be referred to as the customers' wants and needs, customer requirements, or simply the voice of the customer.

The first step is to establish the target market. This will dictate who should be surveyed. This is a complex issue. Persons with knowledge and experience in market research should be involved. Figure 3.1 lists some of the major points to be considered.

- The target market must be established before any survey work is undertaken. It is important to talk to owners of products similar to those planned for introduction. For example, if the company plans to introduce a new sports car, the audience should include people who own or have interest in sports cars. Surveying an audience of large luxury sedan owners would not disclose the voice of the real sports car enthusiast. When plans involve introducing a new or updated version of an existing product, the surveys will typically involve existing customers. Companies wishing to expand their market will want to interview people who represent potential customers. Surveys should include some of the competitors'

---

• Determine the target market.

• Determine the demographics.

• Determine the geographical distribution.

• Use a nonaffiliated survey organization.

• Survey people external to the organization.

• Survey with or without samples of the current product.

---

**Figure 3.1**     Determining which people to survey.

customers to gain insight into any differences in expectations between them and the company's customers.

In many cases, there will be more than one customer whose wants and needs are important in the development of a new product or service. For example, in examining the customers' voice for disposable diapers, the primary customer is the parent who purchases the diaper. Parents have certain wants and needs regarding the product, such as level of absorption, leak prevention, reappliable tape, and form-fitting shapes. The child also has needs and wants, but children can't be their own spokespersons. Information of concern to the child, such as comfort and allergies, will have to be elicited from the parent. In addition, the distributors and marketers of the product will have concerns about issues such as shelf space and package size and strength. The primary customer is the parent. It is the parent who will make the decision about which brand best satisfies his or her wants and needs. However, other customers, such as distributors and retailers, are important to the company, and their wants and needs should also be known.

• Demographics need to be established. The sampling should represent a good cross section of the expected buyers. This requires a knowledge of such issues as the age distribution, income level, marital status, geographical differences, and current or prior ownership of the product.

• The geographical distribution needs examination because location may affect the customers' expectations of a product or service. Expectations are often affected by the customs or environment of the geographic location. The customers' wants and needs for items such as clothing, furniture, packaged foods, and building supplies will vary depending on their geographic location. For example, in the 1970s, owners of cars and trucks in the northeastern quadrants of the United States and Canada had major concerns about product corrosion. Customers in the western states did not experience this problem but had concerns resulting from heavy exposure to sunlight and ultraviolet degradation. A sampling restricted to just one of these geographic areas would not have determined the full extent of the customers' wants and needs.

- It is important to consider the use of a nonaffiliated organization for the actual survey. Experience has shown the need for confidentiality. When people know the survey is being conducted for the benefit of company X, some bias will be introduced. Use of an outside group helps to ensure that the company will not be identified during the interview process. In addition, these groups have a level of knowledge and expertise that is valuable in setting up survey sites, developing the survey method, organizing the survey logistics, and tabulating the data.

    Use of a market-survey organization should be undertaken as a joint endeavor. The outside organization needs an understanding of the company's product or service to obtain the maximum benefit from the customer interviews. The opportunity for maximizing knowledge of a customer's wants and needs occurs only once—during the interview process. If the survey organization does not understand the company's products, it cannot be expected to probe sufficiently to get at the real underlying customer wants and needs.

    Companies should have representatives present during surveys—especially those who will be involved in the product development process. This gives them the opportunity to hear the customer's comments firsthand. There is no substitute for listening to the customer. Some of the company representatives should also work with the survey organization. Opportunity should be provided for them to talk with customers after the interview process to probe critical customer issues in greater depth.

- Survey people who are external to the organization, not people within the company. Surveys are expensive. Usually, people are asked to spend a significant amount of time during the interview process. They may be asked to come to a specific site. It is frequently necessary to offer some monetary incentive. In the desire to contain expenses, companies often propose using their own people to obtain the voice. This usually leads to a biased set of wants and needs because the employees are closer to the product or service and have an idea of the company's expectations. For example, a survey of car door interiors on midsized cars provided respondents the opportunity to choose from a variety of trim concepts. The survey showed that customers preferred the presence of carpet on the lower portion of the injection-molded plastic door-trim pad. They believed it was important to soften and accent the plastic panel. When the same survey was conducted within the product engineering organization, the choices were significantly different. The engineers' decisions were influenced by their knowledge of cost, management expectations, manufacturing capabilities, past practices, and pride of ownership in current designs.

• Surveys can be conducted either with or without samples of the current product present. Survey results that involve examination of a specific product or service will differ from those obtained when no product was present. Both approaches provide useful information. It may be desirable to combine both in a single survey to take advantage of the respondent's presence and of any incentives that were involved. For example, in talking about fish finders with people who fish, if no product is present they may make comments like "Should be able to read in direct sunlight and at night" or "I'd like to see the shape of the river bottom like on a paper strip recorder but without the paper." However, when an actual product is present, it usually triggers thoughts related to product experience, such as "Don't ever design that kind of attachment again because it's too hard to fasten and unfasten and it doesn't turn easily; besides, this piece came off after just one season." Sometimes the interview process can be accompanied by a small ancillary survey of product concepts and proposals to develop information about customer reaction and acceptance.

## Obtaining the Voice of the Customer

An organization can obtain the voice of the customer in a number of ways once the issues of segments, demographics, and methods have been decided. Figure 3.2 shows the most common approaches.

---

• Focus groups

• Interviews
  — Telephone
  — One-on-one

• Mail questionnaires

• Product clinics

• Murmurs, observations

• Root wants

---

**Figure 3.2**   Obtaining the voice of the customer.

- Focus groups usually involve eight to 12 people. A number of discussion issues are agreed on in advance. A facilitator works with the group to develop conversation on the attitudes, wants, and needs of the participants relative to each discussion issue. The facilitator needs to exercise care to keep the discussion moving, to avoid domination by more vocal members, and to take advantage of the natural synergy developed in group discussion.

A number of articles have been written about the customer focus that drives Stew Leonard's Norwalk, Connecticut, food store. Michael Barrier reported:

> But the Leonards also probe for customer attitudes that might not lie so close to the surface. Stew Sr. cites the customer focus groups that Stew Jr. has started. At least once a month he meets with about 12 customers for a one-time, one-hour session in which they say what changes they'd like to see in the store; each participant receives a $20 store certificate. "Some of the ideas that have come out of that have been incredible," says Stew Sr. The Leonards learned, for example, that customers thought that fish wasn't as fresh if it came in plastic supermarket packages; they preferred to buy it on ice.
>
> "We have carpenters here in the store," Stew Sr. says, "and we went down the next morning and built a counter and put ice in the darned thing, then we put all the fish on it. And before you know it, we were selling twice as many fish, on ice. I don't know how many years it might have been before I thought of that— maybe a hundred." (Barrier 1991: 16-22)

Many of the subjects that surface in a focus group are the same ones that will come up in one-on-one interviews. For this reason, focus groups are a good precursor to more intensive interviews because they give the interviewers insight into typical responses. This helps in the development of the questions and approach to be used in the interviews.

- Interviews represent one-on-one conversations with customers. They may be conducted by telephone or in person. Personal interviews conducted eye-to-eye have potential for being the most effective method. When respondents are contacted and agree to come to a site for the process, they are aware of their time commitment. Thus, the interview can be more probing and the information obtained will be more detailed. The interviewer can gain insight into the emotional concerns as well as the practical concerns. Onsite, person to person interviews usually take 45 to 60 minutes. Questions are open-ended, and the interviewer can continue to ask questions until the real customer want (the root want) is determined. Company representatives should attend these interviews, listen to the audio of the interviews, or view the interviews through one-way glass. These interviews are expensive. They are time-intensive for the interviewer and company members who assist in the process. Also, because of their length, it is common practice to provide a monetary incentive. Thus, they are usually limited to 75 to 200 persons at two or three geographic locations.

Because the customer is present and remuneration is usually involved, many companies combine the interview with an opportunity to examine concept proposals or the respondent's personal product. Car companies frequently follow this practice. After the personal interview, the respondent may be accompanied to his or her car for some additional questioning. As pointed out earlier, different sets of observations result from the different approaches. For example, during the interview, issues will surface, such as "Want a comfortable seat—one with lower back support—lots of adjustment fore and aft with a tilt back." In the review of the car, typical comments are "I think this material will stain and won't clean up," "This control operates hard," and "This lever is too hard to reach."

- Mail questionnaires can be sent out in volume at nominal expense. The return rate will vary, for example, from 15 percent to 50 percent, depending on questionnaire length, respondent interest, and presence of incentives. The usual practice is to use questions accompanied by a set of response categories. These require some sort of checked response. This approach lends itself to ease of tabulation. However, there is no scientific way to ensure that the respondent views the question the same way as its author does. Thus, there is no way to ensure that the respondent's answers truly address the issue the questioner sought to explore. For example, respondents may reply that they are satisfied with the performance of a company service. When these same respondents are questioned during a one-on-one interview, they will often make comments that indicate a level of dissatisfaction with aspects of the service. Because the original question was not open-ended and did not give them a chance to enumerate their concerns, they simply checked a box on the form indicating a level of satisfaction.
- Product clinics are an excellent way to develop perspective on how people feel about a specific proposal or concept. They have application where questions alone will not suffice, such as "Which of these beverages or foods taste best?" "Which of these power screwdrivers feels the best?" "Which works best on these sample screws?" and "Which of these serving temperatures is preferred for a cup of coffee?"

Clinics provide an organization the opportunity to get customer opinions on a variety of proposed concepts that have been developed for observation and/or use. Respondents are provided questionnaires on which they record their viewpoints. The organization and analysis of the questionnaire lend it to statistical evaluation techniques.

- Personal observation is another effective approach. The Japanese use the term "murmurs" to describe this simple process of listening and observing. While this is not a scientific process, it can provide some interesting insights into customer issues. Stationing people at a product show to listen to customers' comments about product offerings may reveal likes and dislikes with both the company's products and those of its competitors. Watching children at school might reveal problems with the force required to open drink packages and to insert straws. Observing people using almost any product, such as hand-operated power tools, automatic teller machines, computers and computer software, or fish finders can reveal customer difficulties. Respectively, these observations might reveal problems such as difficult to hold and operate, hard to read in sunlight, poor keyboard layout, time consumed by multiple menus, and difficult to operate with gloves on. Each of these represents a built-in potential for product dissatisfaction.

When observers see the users experiencing difficulty with products, it signals a real opportunity for improvement. It may encourage some creative changes that can give the company a competitive edge—an advertising or sales opportunity. For example, a number of young mothers walk for exercise in the mall when it is open for early-morning walking. Many push their children in strollers. Observation of this might raise a question about the ability of the stroller to sustain long-term operation at these speeds and about the comfort and safety of the child under these operating conditions. Redesign to incorporate features aimed at stroller longevity and child safety might be considered. Observation of elderly people shopping in supermarkets might raise questions about product placement, shelf angulation, and labeling for people who have restricted vision and physical limitations. Observation of people loading packages and other articles into their cars in parking lots at supermarkets and builder supply stores might encourage action to lower the lift-over height for loading articles into a car trunk. Observing that more than half of the population drink beverages in their cars while driving might encourage the addition of cup holders. Creating a drip-free dispenser cap for laundry products might result from the observation of rings on the appliances in the laundromat resulting from containers that dripped.

It is important for interviewers to determine the root want associated with customers' comments. Customers frequently comment on their preferences for a product or service. Sometimes they even tell the interviewer how the manufacturer or provider should design the service or product. Comments of this type are interesting; they may even spark an imaginative idea within the company. However, they do not fulfill the real objective of the survey, which is to determine customers' basic wants and needs. For example, a customer being interviewed about expectations for a sport locker executive-type padlock might comment that its "U" bolt should be 1/4 inch in diameter. If the interviewer goes further and asks why the bolt should be 1/4 inch, the respondent will likely comment about how some lockers have small holes and the lock bolt won't pass through them or how the width of the hasp is such that the padlock can't be rotated through it. The real issue is the ability of the padlock to be used in conjunction with mainstream lockers, hasps, and other devices that are commonly padlocked. It is the responsibility of the padlock manufacturer to develop the appropriate diameter and shape for the padlock bolt.

In interviews about automobiles, people frequently comment about seat comfort. Simply knowing that a customer is concerned does not help a company in its search to determine a response to the customers' needs and wants. The questioning process must be continued until the *root want* is determined. The interviewer needs to ask the customer to comment further on this issue of seat comfort. The discussion may center around the range of adjustability of the seat back or the total fore and aft adjustment range. It may involve the shape of the seat or the amount of support in the lower back for long trips. The probing process must be continued until the real root want is determined. Once the respondents are gone and the company personnel are back home trying to figure out what the customer meant, it is too late.

## Understanding the Voice

The process of questioning people will not reveal everything involved in understanding the customers' wants and needs. The work of Noritaki Kano provides a model that helps us understand the overall spectrum of customer expectations and satisfaction. Figure 3.3 illustrates the Kano observations. The horizontal axis shows how well the customers think the company's product or service met their expectation. The vertical axis shows the degree of actual customer satisfaction with the product or service.

The lower curve will serve as an example for explanation. The arrow tip at the extreme right of this curve represents customers who feel that the manufacturer of the product (or the provider of the service) fully met their expectations. Note, however, that the level of satisfaction for these customers does not reach the maximum represented by the top of the vertical axis. This is because this lower curve represents issues that are basic functions or "givens" for the product or service. These are things that customers have learned to expect. Their presence does little to promote major satisfaction. Their absence, on the other hand, will lead to dissatisfaction. Failure to provide a basic functional requirement represents a built-in dissatisfier.

During the interview process, customers seldom mention basic issues. They take for granted that there will always be a dial tone on the phone system and that the hotel will honor their reservations. They expect the carton of cream from the supermarket to be neither toxic nor sour. They do not expect the busboy to clatter dishes in the restaurant. They expect that the car will always start.

**The Kano Model**

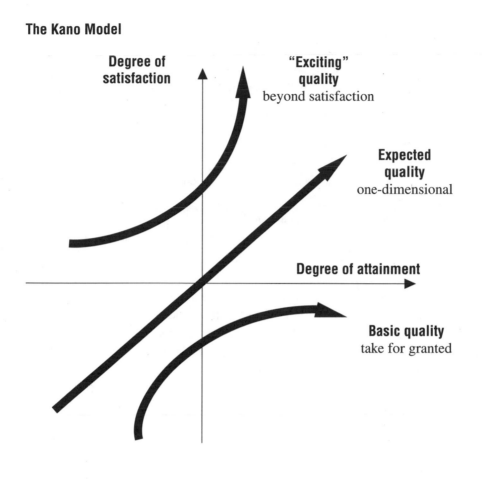

**Figure 3.3** Listening to the customer.

In value-engineering terms, these basic issues are the product's functions. For example, a cup for carry-out coffee has basic functions: hold liquid, fit hand, and restrict heat transfer. A phone service also has basic functions: provide communication linkage and provide volume.

Unless there has been a personal encounter with a recent incident of failure, customers will not normally mention issues of basic quality in an interview. Because these basics are expected and are normally provided, they do not come to mind in the interview process.

The middle curve represents issues that typically arise during customer interviews. These are the things customers talk about:

- "The coffee should be freshly brewed—within 20 minutes of serving."
- "There should be designated smoking and nonsmoking areas."
- "There should not be any smoking allowed."
- "The person I'm dealing with (clerk, businessperson) should be courteous and not brusque."
- "The directions should be clear and easy to follow."
- "The door should close easily and solidly."
- "The restaurant should be quiet."
- "The airline sound system needs to be improved so I can hear the music and the movie."
- "No baggage delay or loss at airport."
- "I expect quick resumption of electrical service after a disconnect in a storm—no more than six hours."

Failure to meet these expectations moves an organization down the curve toward dissatisfaction. This is why it so important to know the real needs of the customer. When Techsonics Industries talked to customers about their wants and needs in a fish finder, it discovered what had to be done to respond. Effective response moved the company toward the arrowhead on this curve.

This middle curve dramatically reinforces the idea brought out in Chapter 1. One of the principles of the QFD process is that it forces companies to talk with their customers. In the process, they learn what customers want and need and can plan their strategy for increasing customer satisfaction.

The upper curve involves things that represent exciting quality. Customers seldom mention these directly in the interview process. These are things that go beyond the customer's expectations. Many industries today talk about their desire to go "beyond customer expectations," to go "beyond satisfaction," or to create "exciting quality." Exciting quality is generated by making a "creative leap" based on some customer comment or some observation of customer behavior.

The concept embodied in the upper curve is extremely significant. As companies listen to their customers, they should search very carefully for clues that may spark a creative idea that produces exciting quality. Some examples are as follows:

- Antilock brakes that respond to the customer concern for stopping straight in bad weather or in panic situations.
- The funeral director who takes a Polaroid camera shot of each floral display and notes the sender's name and address on the back, as a memento for the family.
- Kao Corporation in Japan recognized the small living quarters of typical Japanese families and developed a soap with a seven-to-one concentration over other soaps. The box was smaller and took less storage space. Within a year after

introduction of the concentrate, one major soap supplier's market share dropped from 20 percent to 8 percent while Kao's share climbed to 30 percent (Swasy 1989: B6).

- Permanent press fabrics
- Twist-off bottle caps
- Wide-slot toasters
- Hotel bathroom mirrors with hidden heated panels to prevent fogging
- Refrigerator doors that can be opened from either side
- Fish finders with liquid crystal displays that allow people fishing to see river and lake bottom contours and to locate fish

These creative ideas generate a level of product excitement. They create an increased level of interest. They attract customers. They also attract the attention of the competitors, who seek to emulate the idea in their product or service as soon as possible. As a result, a company that develops an exciting quality feature can expect it to be emulated by its competitors and to move eventually from the exciting category to the expected category.

Colby H. Chandler, chairman and chief executive officer of Eastman Kodak Company, commented on the significance of this issue in his keynote remarks to the National Quality Forum IV in 1988.

> As the theme for this forum suggests, we must take quality beyond customer satisfaction to customer delight. Customer delight is the delivery of products and services that exceed expectations. Customer delight represents excellence in every respect....Let me help you with a few personal examples. I would be delighted if commercial airline flights departed and arrived on time, every time. I would be delighted if delivery or repair service people could provide an estimated arrival time at my home, say within a given hour, and meet schedule. Finally I would be delighted if all the clothing I buy looked as good after the first washing or cleaning as it did in the store. (Chandler, 1989: 30–32)

## Handling the Voice

Some key issues involved in working with the customers' voice are shown in Figure 3.4.

- The idea of determining the root want involved in customers' comments is crucial to the success of the interview process. Customers tend to mix needs, solutions, and problem concerns. They will frequently tell the interviewer what they

- Determine root wants.

- Capture "verbatims."

- Abbreviate the voices as necessary.

- Consolidate the voice.

**Figure 3.4**  Handling the voice.

want without stating why they want it. For example, in early surveys of car owners, one common response was "I want the carpet in my car to look like it does in my house." Further exploration of the issue revealed that the concern was not one of material or texture. It involved having the carpet lay flat, with no apparent seams or overlap, and having it fit well in all areas with no raw edges showing. This knowledge led to the development of the one-piece molded carpets currently used in most cars.

If the questioning process does not aim at this root want, the value of the data suffers measurably. Once the interview is over and the customer has left, it is virtually impossible to determine what was meant by a comment that was not fully understood. For example, in a survey about toasters, a frequent comment was "I want the toaster to be small or compact—to have a small footprint." When customers were asked "Why?" the real root want was identified as "because I have small counters and limited space and I want a toaster that takes up as little space as possible." Similarly, the initial comment "It should be heavy and not move around easily" turned out to be a concern for the toaster's stability and not its weight. "I want more room in the theater seat" can refer to a desire for a roomier seat or for more leg room or to the issue of having to stand for people who are moving to a seat farther in the row.

Survey organizations must be aware of the need to get at root wants. This is another reason why a survey group needs to understand the company's product well. Good product knowledge helps the interviewer know what questions to ask to determine the root wants.

- At the completion of each interview, the interviewer and a company representative should go over the survey notes and tapes to document the actual verbatim comments of the customer. For example, a typical automotive verbatim comment might be "I want a comfortable seat. I've had a lot of car seats that give me a backache in the lower back after about 30 to 45 minutes." A typical verbatim comment for the fish finder might be "Make the buttons or switches big enough so I can operate them with gloves or mittens on in cold weather. Give them a sound so I know when I turned them on or off."

- Voices need some level of brevity for use as inputs to a matrix. Customer comments are usually lengthy, such as "I'd like to get a problem resolved without being switched around to a dozen people and taking half an hour to get it done. Makes me feel like I'm lost in a bureaucracy." These have to be shortened to enter them in a matrix. The previous statement, for example, might be shortened to "want quick/direct problem solution." However, too much condensation can lead to a loss of the real customer input. It is common for many people to consolidate and to use terms such as *responsive*, *attractive*, and *easy to use*. The problem is that the content of the customers' voice has been lost. The term *responsive* doesn't really convey the full emotion of a customer who wants a problem resolved quickly and effectively without having to talk to a number of people. *Attractive* doesn't really capture the essence of the voice "I want it to look good in my kitchen." Teams working on voice consolidation and abbreviation should work to retain the essence—the flavor of the customers' verbatim voice. When they do so, the matrix will read as if the customers were talking to the company, and readers will get the *feel* of the customers' voice. Phrases such as "Looks good in kitchen, operates quietly, and is comfortable to hold" sound more like a customer talking than do terms such as *appearance*, *quiet*, and *functionality*.

- In a review of the verbatims, it will also become apparent that many people said the same things in slightly different words. Where possible, these should be consolidated into one voice. The difficulty of managing a matrix is magnified as the number of customer voices increases. The fewer the total number of voices, the easier it will be to work with the remaining information requirements of the matrix.

## Organizing the Voices into Natural Groups

Customers' voices develop in a random manner. The comment "Coffee is freshly brewed" may be followed by one involving the cup, such as "The cup keeps the coffee hot" or "Needs a lid to help keep the coffee from spilling." In working with a QFD matrix, it is helpful if items of a similar nature are grouped together. If all the items involving the cup, for example, are grouped together, the process of examining and

---

- Using the affinity diagram approach:
  — Use one card per voice.
  — Use team action.
  — Develop natural groupings.
  — Group the groups.
  — Title the groups using customer words.

---

**Figure 3.5**    Organizing the voice.

translating them into technical requirements is greatly facilitated. The discussion centers on one subject, and synergy develops in the discussion.

One effective way to group the voices is to use the affinity diagram process. This is a simple and straightforward team process. Some key points are shown in Figure 3.5. The process is as follows:

- Put each voice on a card. 3 x 5 inch index cards work well.
- Have one team member place the cards one at a time on a table in groups that seem "natural" to the member. Other members can move cards to other groups if they feel they fit better with that group.

  An alternative approach is to lay all the cards on the table in the beginning and give all the team members an opportunity to move them into natural groups. The cards should be moved by team members until it is apparent that most movement has stopped. Discussion is then useful.

  In either approach, it is effective to work in silence for the first few minutes until a number of cards have been placed on the table. Early discussion can slow the process. During the silent period, team members can see which cards are being moved. These become the obvious cards for later discussion and consensus.

- Once the cards are grouped and the team members are satisfied with the groups, category titles can be developed for each group. Care should be exercised to keep these titles in customer language. There is a tendency to try to find one-word titles, such as *convenience*, *durability*, *performance*, and *options*. The matrix will convey a more convincing customer presence if the team will use words similar to those used by customers.

  Thus, a team might use "lasts a long time" rather than "durability," "looks good" instead of "appearance," and "is easy to use" instead of "convenient."

- Once the group titles are completed for the voices, the next step should be to see which of these can be grouped into larger groups. For example, if we consider the voices to be at a tertiary level, the first group titles would constitute the secondary level. The last step is to arrange secondary groups that have natural linkages into primary groups. These should also be titled with customer language. As a guideline, the number of primary group headings typically varies between three and seven.

## Obtaining Additional Customer Information

Once the voices have been determined and consolidated, a determination of the customers' level of importance and their competitive evaluation can be undertaken. Some key points are captured in Figure 3.6.

- Surveys are normally conducted using mail questionnaires. These are sent to people who own the company's products or use its services. They are also sent to owners and users of competitive products. For example, if company A had made the voice determination and companies B, C, and D were its principal competitors, questionnaires would be sent to customers of companies A, B, C, and D.

    The questionnaires would ask respondents to rate the level of importance for a group of voices and to rate how well they thought their product was performing for each of the voices. Here again, the value of using a survey organization that is experienced in customer opinion surveys is apparent. Its knowledge of such issues as sample size, questionnaire language, and length of questionnaire will be invaluable.

---

- Customer importance levels and competitive evaluations:
  — Mail questionnaires
  — Importance ratings
  — Competitive evaluations
    - Several competitors
    - One major competitor
    - No existing product

---

**Figure 3.6**    Additional customer information.

It is not necessary to ask each respondent to address all voices. This may make the questionnaire too large and may discourage people from responding. A group of smaller questionnaires can be developed. Each questionnaire can cover a portion of the total number of voices. Collectively, the response to the whole group of questionnaires will cover the spectrum of voices.

It is important that the questions involving levels of importance be properly handled. People have difficulty assigning measures of priority to a list of voices. If given a list of voices and asked to note the level of importance by a checkmark on a numerical scale (for example, 1 to 5 or 1 to 9), they soon lose objectivity, and their base for comparison will change. Survey organizations can help through the design of paired questions, where respondents are asked "How do you rate A relative to B?" After they have been asked to rate B relative to C, it is then possible to rank A, B, and C.

- When reviewing customer responses, it is evident that there is variation. Not everyone has the same opinion about importance. Typically, these values are examined and averaged. Sometimes the histogram of the data will show a cluster of customers with low levels of importance and one of customers with high levels. A bimodal distribution of this type may indicate the value of two offerings. For example, in response to a question about a feature on a toaster to hold and warm toast, some respondents might favor it and some might not. Thus, it might be offered as a desirable addition on an upper-level product but not on the standard toaster.

Questionnaires for levels of importance and competitive evaluations normally use scales with odd numbers, such as 1 to 3, 1 to 5, and 1 to 9. When the responses are averaged, they will develop numbers such as 7.8 and 6.2. These can be used as calculated or rounded off to the nearest whole number.

- When customer evaluation data is obtained for a group of competitors, it is usually plotted on the right side of the matrix in a format similar to that shown in Figure 3.7, example A. In this example, the performance of the surveying company is compared with that of one or more principal competitors using a 1 to 5 scale with 5 representing "excellent."

There may be cases in which this type of data cannot be generated. For example, a company making a special machine might have one principal competitor. Its customers would likely cooperate to determine the key customer wants and needs to be considered in a proposed machine redesign. The company might also be able to get their customers to compare their machines to those of their competitors to give them some insight into competitive evaluation. For simplicity, it might be best simply to ask, "For this voice, does the competitor perform the same as, worse than, or better than our company? Data might be plotted as shown in Figure 3.7, example B. In this case, the circles indicate the competitor's position relative to the surveying company as worse

**Key:**

- ■ **Surveying company**
- ◇ **Competitor A**
- ○ **Competitor B**
- ▲ **Objective for new product**

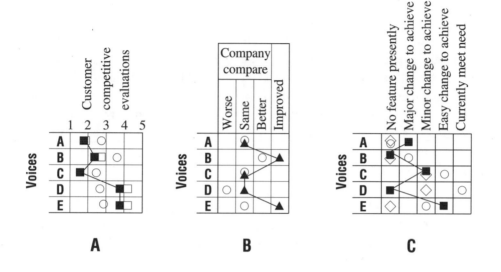

**Figure 3.7**   Customer competitive evaluations.

than, same as, or better than. The surveying company can then examine its position for each voice and decide if its current competitive level is satisfactory or if higher objectives should be set. These decisions are represented by triangles in this graph.

When companies are planning innovative concepts, no products may be available for customers' competitive evaluations. One approach that can be used is to conduct the evaluations in-house. The customers' wants and needs should be determined for the general type of product or service being planned. The surveying company can then examine products or services currently available that come closest to the planned offering. Each of these can be examined using some evaluation scale, such as that shown in Figure 3.7, example C. This examination will reveal whether anyone has a product that comes close to the proposed concept and whether there is a strong competitive opportunity. In essence, this type of review is part of a business case study of the potential for the product. For example, software developers who are planning a major new market entry or working to produce a breakthrough in technology find that customer wants and needs have limitations. Users of current software programs of the same genre can respond with their wants, needs, likes, and dislikes based on their current level of experience, but usually there is no effective way to generate comments involving visions about future ideas. Because customers cannot give competitive evaluations, the in-house review of the best current offerings is often the best avenue to develop the initial knowledge of the market opportunity for the new product.

No company should rely on a single approach to understanding its customers. Focus groups help companies develop an awareness of general customer concerns. They are excellent precursors to personal interviews. Phone interviews can be used to follow up and enlarge on wants and needs that surface in personal interviews. Tracking observations or murmurs should be a regular part of a company's program to understand its customers. Nintendo provides an excellent example of the use of a variety of methods to keep in constant touch with its customers. Christopher Boehme reported the following:

> Nintendo America excels by making decisions based not on retailers' opinions of buying trends but on direct contact with the customer. Bar code data from some 600 retailers giving hard-sell, thorough data—who bought what, where, and when—lands on the desks of executives at Nintendo America on Monday of each week.
>
> Added to that is information from warranty cards coming in. For instance, marketing had always had a theory that adults were fooling with Junior's Nintendo after bedtime....When warranty cards from their new Gameboy product came in...the cards demonstrated that 40 percent of the players were adults....Armed with this information, marketing fine-tuned its advertising mix, producing...[a] television spot targeted to adults.
>
> Howard Phillips (game master) strolls over to the game counseling area. Here, the loop of direct marketing, customer service, data collection, and ultimately, product development can be seen in all its glory.
>
> In this modular barracks, 140 young people field phone calls from befuddled Nintendo players....Counselors are fielding some 50,000 calls a week....If a player wants the tips, he can look in *Nintendo Power!* or call the counselors.

Boehme points out that Nintendo America purposely omits certain game tips from its software manuals. These do not affect the casual player. Advanced players, however, may find it necessary to call for tips. This gives the counselors an opportunity to talk with them, to exchange knowledge, and to get ideas for exciting quality (Boehme 1990: 22–30).

Companies may learn about techniques for listening to and observing customers by benchmarking other companies who have good track records in these fields. Union Pacific Railroad used this approach to get a better understanding of the dimensions to explore in improving its customer service. Andrew Kupfer reports

> ...UP looked outward to see how other companies excelled. Then it surveyed their customers: those of American Express in customer service. Marriott in telephone processing. American Airlines in reservations. Hertz in vehicle preparation. Florida Power and Light in overall quality of service....These companies are notable not only for the service they deliver—which competitors can see and copy—but for the way they managed to reach their objectives, which is not so apparent.
>
> Companies are more satisfied; company surveys show they judge UP first or second against such competitors as Burlington Northern and Southern Pacific. Three years ago it ranked near the bottom of the heap. On a scale of one to ten, Boise Cascade, for example, gives *UP* a strong six or seven up from three just last year. (Kupfer 1989: 133–146)

Voices change over time. People are influenced by a variety of items. New products with new technologies appear on the market. Television advertising suggests new ideas and new standards of performance or excellence. Magazine and newspaper articles compare products and extol their positive features. Friends discuss their experiences, especially those that are unfavorable. Environmental concerns increase, affecting product decisions. These and many more factors cause customers' ideas and attitudes to change. Ultimately, these affect the customers' expression of wants and needs.

The disposable diaper represents an excellent example. This product met a significant customer need when it was introduced in the 1960s. Based on initial success, companies went on to make the product more responsive to customer needs and to introduce "exciting" features. Diapers came in different sizes. Colored sketches of favorite characters were added. Improved deodorants were developed. Reusable tape was added. Customers learned to expect an array of products to meet their needs and wants. The advent of strong interest in environmental concerns has changed that outlook during the past few years. Magazine and newspaper articles and television news programs have highlighted concerns with landfills and biodegradability. In the early 1990s there was an obvious move by many parents to use cloth diapers and diaper laundry services. Usage of these services increased approximately 15 percent in both 1990 and 1991.

Keeping in touch with the customers' voice must, therefore, be an ongoing process. The voice will change. Its importance level will change. The perception of competitive performance will change. Only by continual surveys can a company keep in touch with its customers' current wants and needs.

In summary, companies should do the following:

- Plan the survey carefully. Study the issues, such as target markets, demographics, sampling methods, and data tabulation. Document plans and timing.
- One-on-one interviews will provide the greatest insight into the customers' wants and needs. Typically, a monetary incentive is required for the survey participants.
- Search for root causes in the interviews. Keep asking "Why?" until the real want is determined.
- Record the customers' comments verbatim and retain these as a key reference.
- Carefully examine each response for clues to "exciting quality." Remember that aggressive competitors are working to go beyond satisfaction and create excitement.
- Organize the customers' wants and needs into natural groups for ease in handling and discussion.
- Determine the customers' levels of importance and their competitive evaluations of the product (or service) and those of principal competitors.
- Continue the survey process on an ongoing basis for feedback on accomplishments and for determination of trends and changing voices.

# Developing a QFD Matrix:
# The Customer Information Portion

*chapter four*

Chapter 3 discussed the key issues in developing and conducting surveys to determine the customers' voice. The information collected in these surveys is the input—the starting point for the QFD matrix. This chapter will review the basic steps involved in transferring the customer information to the matrix. Use of a preplanning chart will be discussed as an effective way to screen customer information prior to transferring it to the QFD product planning matrix.

The QFD matrix has two major components: one captures the customer information and one contains technical information, as illustrated in Figure 4.1. Each of these components is a separate table. The customer table captures the information pertinent to the customers' wants, needs, and evaluations. The technical table contains information relative to the company's determination of the actionable issues and the information that amplifies and delineates these issues. Together, these two tables combine to produce the QFD product planning matrix. In the following chapters, these two QFD matrix components will be referred to as the "customer table" and the "technical table."

## A Team Process

QFD is a team process. The size of a typical QFD matrix, the scope of the information required, and the need for synergistic discussion dictate that it be a team project. The team should be formed at the initiation of the project, in its earliest stages of market research planning.

- **The customer information portion**
- **The technical information portion**

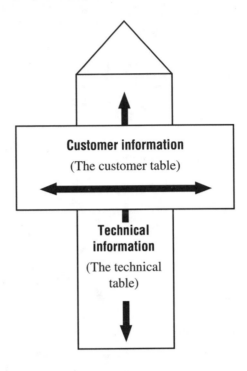

**Figure 4.1**    The two main aspects of the QFD matrix.

Organizations that have used team processes have learned the value of team training early in the process. It is especially important for the team to develop a level of comfort with the team process, to agree on the rules for team operation, and to plan the project well before launching into action. In the case of QFD projects, some workshop training in the methodology should also be considered as a prerequisite. Additional information is presented in Chapter 17.

## Developing the Customer Information Table

Experience with workshop sessions to help people understand the QFD process has demonstrated the value of using simple products as examples. Complex products develop large matrices that are difficult to read when reduced to book size. In addition, as the QFD matrix moves to levels of greater detail, the complexity interferes with the learning process. Because the basic intent is to describe the process, it is the process and not the product that is important. For this reason, the examples used are simple products, such as coffee cups, clothespins, theater seats, and toasters.

Figure 4.2 shows typical examples of "verbatims" from people who were asked about their expectations, wants, and needs for clothespins and take-out coffee. Even in these few examples, it is apparent that customers' voices follow no order. Customers do not deliver their comments in an organized manner. In the coffee example, the first comment concerns the cup, the second concerns the lid, the next states preferences for types of coffee material, and the fourth voice again concerns the cup. This illustrates the need to sort these voices into groups of similar concerns to help a team concentrate on like items. This is the purpose of the affinity diagram process described in Chapter 3.

Figure 4.3 shows these voices abbreviated and organized into natural groups. The primary items are shown on the left, the secondary next, and the tertiary (actual voices) on the right.

---

### Clothespin verbatims

"Grips the laundry tightly so it doesn't fall or blow off the line"
"Doesn't stain or leave dirt marks on laundry"
"They last a long time—at least 2 years"
"Can use to hang skirts, scarves, etc. on hangers"
"Can write on them for use in classroom or to note
    what papers they are clipping together"
"Can use to close flour, pretzel, potato chip bags, etc."
"They don't get all tangled up in the bag"

### Coffee verbatims

"Cup should be insulated—cool— so it doesn't burn my hand"
"Lid should have a drink opening, one that is easy to remove
    and doesn't leave sharp edges "
"Should have both decaf and regular coffee"
"Should be hard to spill or tip over"
"Shouldn't be flimsy so it squeezes in my hand and spills
    the coffee or pops the lid or collapses"
"The lid ought to fit tight—not come off easily"

---

**Figure 4.2**  Typical verbatims from surveys.

**Wants and needs for clothespins**

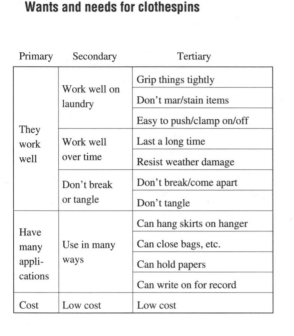

| Primary | Secondary | Tertiary |
|---------|-----------|----------|
| They work well | Work well on laundry | Grip things tightly |
| | | Don't mar/stain items |
| | | Easy to push/clamp on/off |
| | Work well over time | Last a long time |
| | | Resist weather damage |
| | Don't break or tangle | Don't break/come apart |
| | | Don't tangle |
| Have many applications | Use in many ways | Can hang skirts on hanger |
| | | Can close bags, etc. |
| | | Can hold papers |
| | | Can write on for record |
| Cost | Low cost | Low cost |

**Wants and needs for a cup of coffee**

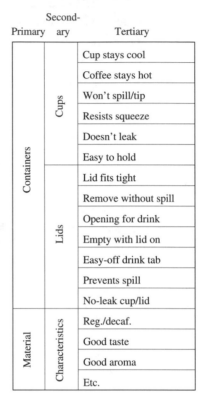

| Primary | Secondary | Tertiary |
|---------|-----------|----------|
| Containers | Cups | Cup stays cool |
| | | Coffee stays hot |
| | | Won't spill/tip |
| | | Resists squeeze |
| | | Doesn't leak |
| | | Easy to hold |
| | Lids | Lid fits tight |
| | | Remove without spill |
| | | Opening for drink |
| | | Empty with lid on |
| | | Easy-off drink tab |
| | | Prevents spill |
| | | No-leak cup/lid |
| Material | Characteristics | Reg./decaf. |
| | | Good taste |
| | | Good aroma |
| | | Etc. |

**Figure 4.3**    Voices abbreviated and arranged in natural groups.

No two teams will organize a group of customer voices in exactly the same way. The affinity diagram process is not a precise process, nor does it need to be. The purpose is to group like items in a manner satisfactory to the team. For example, in the cup table, this team put the voice "Doesn't leak" in the secondary group entitled "Cups." Another team might have decided to put this in the secondary group for lids because, in its judgment, the issue of leaks was related more strongly to the lid than to the cup. Another team might feel that it actually belonged in both groups. If so, it would have created a second card in the affinity diagram and placed it in both the cup and the lid categories. These minor differences should not become a matter of concern. The team organizes and works with the grouped voices. As long as these groupings satisfy the team, the objective is accomplished.

Figure 4.4 shows the customer table. Voice information from the previous illustration is combined with the importance and competitive evaluation information developed during surveys. The first three columns on the left are the primary, secondary, and

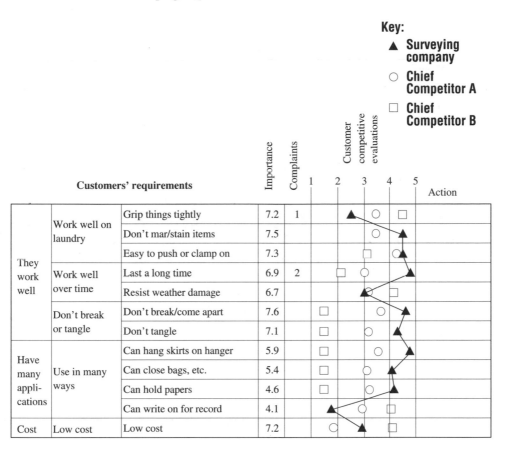

**Figure 4.4**    The customer portion of the matrix: the customer table.

tertiary groupings for the voices. This is followed by the importance column showing the averages of owners' inputs. A scale of 1 to 9 was used, with 1 representing low importance and 9 representing high importance. Some organizations prefer a scale of 1 to 5. Some prefer letter codes to identify item priorities. For example, the code letter "A" might represent numerical importance levels of 8 and 9, the code letter "B" might represent numerical levels of 6 and 7, and the code letter "C" might be used for all levels 5 and below. The use of letters can be valuable in certain situations. It focuses attention on macrodifferences between customer levels of importance and minimizes the tendency to argue about whether a 7.8 is really more important than a 7.6.

Customer complaints are shown in the adjacent column. These represent cases in which customers have taken time to write or call the company to express their dissatisfaction with the product or service. Repair and warranty data should not be used in this column. It can usually be associated with technical requirements and should be placed in the technical portion of the matrix. *Complaints from customers are like exclamation marks for their voice. They represent people who have taken the time to call or write and to say "You did not perform well for my concern, for this voice, and I mean it!"* A study by the Technical Assistance Research Program in Washington, D.C., of products in the $100 to $300 price range showed that 50 percent of customers who had a problem never complained to anyone. Forty-five percent complained to the retailer or a sales representative. Only 5 percent went to the manufacturer or to management. The possibility is strong, then, that for every complaint received at the company, there are 19 other customers who are similarly dissatisfied. Thus, the written or verbal complaints constitute major negative exclamation marks for the voice in question (Goodman 1989: 37–40).

The customer competitive evaluations are shown in the next columns as a graph. The surveying company is shown as a darkened triangle. Companies A and B are chief competitors and are shown as a circle and a square. It is a good practice to leave room on the far right of the customer matrix for issues that the team may find useful in its decision process. For example, this table shows a column for action that can be used to check off items of priority for customer satisfaction.

Figure 4.5 shows a typical customer table for an automatic teller machine (ATM) based on an IBM study. Two customers are shown. The first 13 items represent individual users of the ATMs. Item 14 represents the voice of a commercial user (bank or store) (Sharkey 1991: 379–416).

## Using the Customer Information Table as a Preplanning Chart

The *initial* customer information table usually needs some review before it is used as the horizontal portion of the product planning matrix. This is a sort of "sanity check" to make sure that the table does not contain voices that do not have a direct application in the first-level QFD matrix.

When the initial customer information table is used for the purpose of screening the voices, it is usually referred to as a preplanning chart. The term is logical because the chart is being used to screen voices prior to transferring them to the product planning matrix. *This preplanning chart terminology will be used in the discussion that follows.*

Figure 4.6 illustrates the use of a preplanning chart to evaluate and sort voices into categories. The preplanning chart example in the illustration is related to voices collected for a car QFD product planning matrix.

- For example, a voice such as "Should blend easily in expressway traffic. Good passing capability" obviously refers to a customer expectation for the whole

| Customers' wants and needs | | Customer importance rating 1 = least 9 = most | Customer competitive perception | | | | |
|---|---|---|---|---|---|---|---|
| | | | 5 Very good | 4 Good | 3 OK | 2 Bad | 1 Very bad |
| **Ease of use** | | | | | | | |
| 01 | Can access all accounts | 9.0 | | | * | A | |
| 02 | Easy-to-follow instructions | 9.0 | | * | | A | |
| 03 | Machine in weatherproof environment | 7.0 | | | * | A | |
| 04 | Legible at any height | 7.0 | | A | | * | |
| 05 | Clear and readable screen | 7.0 | | A | | * | |
| 06 | Easy to correct | 9.0 | A | * | | | |
| 07 | Access account through any ATM | 8.0 | | | | * | A |
| **Function** | | | | | | | |
| 08 | Any bill/coin denomination | 6.0 | | | | * | A |
| 09 | Accurate | 9.0 | A | * | | | |
| **Performance** | | | | | | | |
| 10 | Fast transactions | 7.0 | | A | | * | |
| 11 | Fast response | 8.0 | A | | * | | |
| 12 | Always available | 9.0 | | A | | * | |
| **Security** | | | | | | | |
| 13 | Can change PIN at any ATM | 3.0 | | | | * | A |
| 14 | Security from misuse | 8.0 | A | * | | | |

Key: * = ours   A = competitor's

**Figure 4.5**   Customer information table for automatic teller machine.

• **Where they should be directed?**

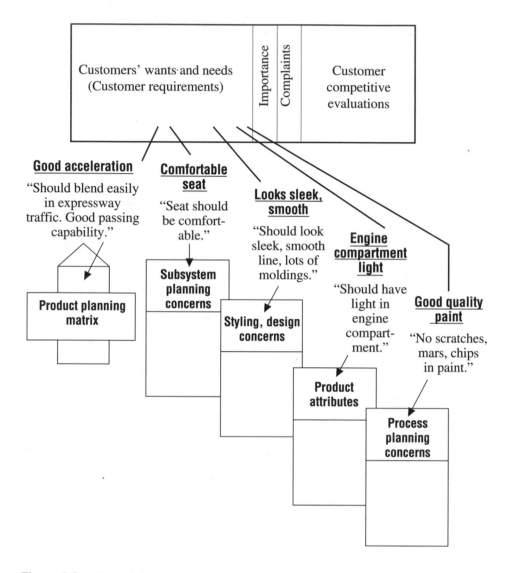

**Figure 4.6**    Examining the voices in the preplanning chart.

car. It involves a number of systems that must work collectively to satisfy the customer. Thus, it is shown as a voice which should be included in the car QFD product planning matrix.

• A customer voice commenting that "The seat should be comfortable" refers to a subsystem of the car as a whole. Issues involving the seat and its comfort can be studied using a subsystem planning matrix.

- Some items concern styling. They cannot be handled effectively in a QFD matrix. They are important, however, and the people responsible for the design should be aware of these attitudes. Items of this type should be listed and provided to the design group. Such issues as "Should match my kitchen decor," "Should look sleek, low, and tapered," and "Should have smooth lines" are typical voices that should be removed from the customer table and listed for design group consideration.

- Some items require yes or no responses. They represent attributes. The company must decide early in the planning stage whether these are to be included. In the car example, the voice "Want a light in the engine compartment of my car" is a yes/no decision for the company. If it is decided that it is a desirable attribute that should be present in the next product, then it should be included in the product plan. Some other examples of attribute issues are "Want a softener dispenser on my washing machine" and "Want an electric clock that doesn't need resetting when I unplug and move it."

- Some customer comments concern items that require a certain level of manufacturing control and may not be items for design consideration. An item relating to automotive paint finish on a product such as "no scratches, mars, chips in paint, or dull paint" should be forwarded to the paint processing group. A comment on newsprint such as "Should be easy to read—legible—shouldn't be like dull ink on the paper" may concern both the material design requirements and the printing process. If experience shows this to be the case, this item should be considered for inclusion in the product planning matrix and added to the list of process planning concerns as well. For a coffee cup, the comment "Doesn't leak" is usually related to a product concern and to probable process variation.

When the preplanning chart is used to screen voices, the number of voices that ultimately will be transferred to the QFD product planning matrix will be reduced. There is value in keeping this matrix size as small as possible. Huge matrices involve the collection of so much data and the determination of so many interrelationships that they can be self-defeating. Ideally, matrices should have between 25 and 50 entries in the customer requirements area. The subject of controlling the size of the matrix is addressed in further detail in Chapter 12.

During the preplanning chart screening process, items that belong to other groups or lower levels of detail are removed and listed separately with their applicable groups. The items that remain constitute the customer portion of the QFD matrix. Thus, the item "Should blend easily in expressway traffic. Good passing capability" shown in Figure 4.6 would be one of the items transferred to the QFD product planning matrix.

At this point, the team should also take time to confirm that it is satisfied that the voices are all clearly understood. If care was exercised in determining root wants during the interview process, this should not constitute a problem. However, an occasional item may be spotted for which there is no certainty concerning what the customer meant. If the team proceeds without exploring this issue, it will have to decide and define the real root want. This puts the team in the position of guessing what the customer meant. If any of the voices are in question, this is the time to resample some respondents. This can be done by phone with people who were part of the original interview group.

Once the above screening and examination process is complete, work to develop the product planning QFD matrix can begin. These steps are described in Chapter 5.

## Using the Preplanning Chart for Project Management and Priority Item Selection

There are times when an organization finds it impossible to continue beyond the development of the customer information table. Factors such as timing and expense may make it necessary to stop action at this point. Even if the process stops at this stage, it will have contributed immeasurably to the company. The company will be in touch with its customers. Their wants and needs will be known. In such cases, the team should use the customer information table as a preplanning chart for determining the priority voices which should receive attention as part of the project management process.

Figure 4.7 is an example of a preplanning chart (for a cup of take-out coffee) used for priority planning purposes. The action column on the right shows the team's determination of items that should be investigated for improvement. The first item, "Cup stays cool," is highly important to the customer, registering 8 on a scale of 1 to 9 (with 9 indicating very important). There have been three complaints (per 1000 sales). The customers' competitive evaluation of the surveying company is poor relative to competition. Basically, the surveying company is in a poor competitive position. The team has designated this as an item requiring attention. The team's comment is "Examine concepts." Initially, this could involve an examination of competitors' cups. Alternative cup designs should then be considered and evaluated. The ultimate objective is to develop a concept that will move the surveying company to a superior position, as judged by the customer.

For voice number 3, "Won't spill/tip," the comment in the action column, "Competitive opportunity," means that the team sees no company responding effectively to this important customer requirement. The action column comment is intended to note this item as one worthy of some research and development action. Similarly, for voice number 15, "Good taste," if the surveying company can develop a coffee with superior taste, it will have developed exciting quality and can gain a competitive advantage.

Most companies hold periodic project reviews. These are often referred to as design reviews. These reviews often serve as "toll gates" or simply "gates" in the company's overall product development process. When the preplanning chart is used to highlight the action items as shown in Figure 4.7, these items can be discussed in gate

- **Examine the information before proceeding**
  - **—Establish that all necessary customer information is known and understood.**
  - **—May be used to set priorities for action to improve customer satisfaction.**

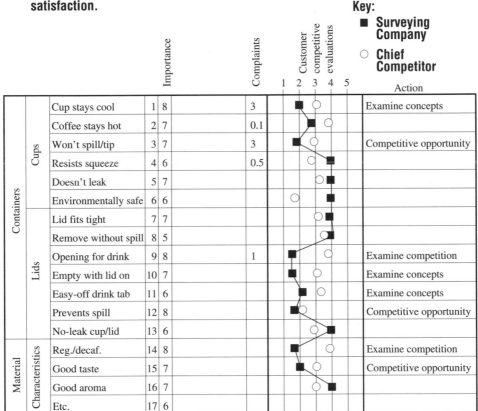

| | | | Importance | | Complaints | Customer competitive evaluations | Action |
|---|---|---|---|---|---|---|---|
| | | | | | | 1  2  3  4  5 | |
| Containers | Cups | Cup stays cool | 1 | 8 | 3 | | Examine concepts |
| | | Coffee stays hot | 2 | 7 | 0.1 | | |
| | | Won't spill/tip | 3 | 7 | 3 | | Competitive opportunity |
| | | Resists squeeze | 4 | 6 | 0.5 | | |
| | | Doesn't leak | 5 | 7 | | | |
| | | Environmentally safe | 6 | 6 | | | |
| | Lids | Lid fits tight | 7 | 7 | | | |
| | | Remove without spill | 8 | 5 | | | |
| | | Opening for drink | 9 | 8 | 1 | | Examine competition |
| | | Empty with lid on | 10 | 7 | | | Examine concepts |
| | | Easy-off drink tab | 11 | 6 | | | Examine concepts |
| | | Prevents spill | 12 | 8 | | | Competitive opportunity |
| | | No-leak cup/lid | 13 | 6 | | | |
| Material | Characteristics | Reg./decaf. | 14 | 8 | | | Examine competition |
| | | Good taste | 15 | 7 | | | Competitive opportunity |
| | | Good aroma | 16 | 7 | | | |
| | | Etc. | 17 | 6 | | | |

**Key:**
- ■ **Surveying Company**
- ○ **Chief Competitor**

**Figure 4.7** Evaluating inputs using a preplanning table.

reviews. Managers will be present and agreement can be reached on the items that will be the priorities for product revision. This is a key issue. Resource constraints often dictate that only a few of the items initially selected become finalized product improvement projects. The preplanning chart level is the proper time to review and agree on top priorities and the plan of attack.

There is another alternative which is gaining favor in many companies. If the organization does not have time to develop a complete product planning matrix *using all the voices, it can use the preplanning chart as a method of screening customer voices and developing an abbreviated or "short form" product planning matrix.* In this approach, the preplanning chart is used to sort out the priority items and to *use only these* in developing the QFD product planning matrix. In effect, this helps a team keep its focus on the critical issues and significantly reduces the overall time involved in developing the product planning matrix.

There is a potential problem in using this approach; it should be comprehended and action should be taken to minimize its effect. For example, when an organization develops a full QFD product planning matrix, it examines and discusses the relationships between voices and technical requirements. When a voice is chosen for priority action, the technical requirements that are strongly related to it become the actual items that the company will work on. For a voice such as "Good pick-up, gets away from the stoplight, and blends easily in traffic," one strong technical requirement would be "Good acceleration 0 to 60 mph." In the co-relationship matrix, the items "Fuel economy" and "Driving range" would be apparent negative co-relationships. If action is taken to improve acceleration, fuel economy and range will be diminished.

*If an organization decides to use the preplanning matrix to select priority items, this same sort of reasoning must apply.* Figure 4.8 is a copy of the preplanning chart

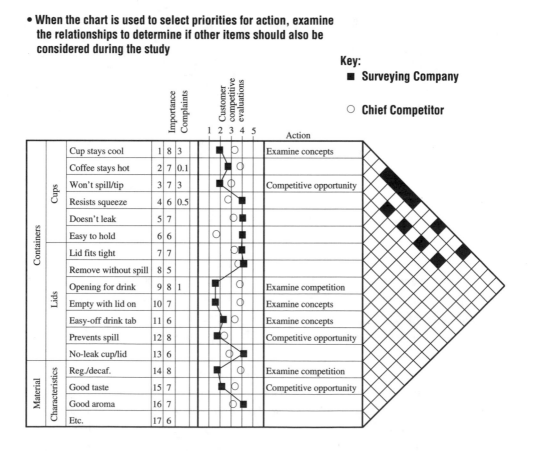

**Figure 4.8** Using a preplanning chart.

shown in Figure 4.7. The actions to be taken that were noted in Figure 4.7 represent the voices that would be selected as the priority voices to be transferred to the "short form" product planning matrix. Note that a horizontal co-relationship matrix has been constructed at the right side of the chart. This is used to compare each of the selected priority voices against all others. As shown, when the team examined the selected priority voice "Cup stays cool" in conjunction with every other voice on the chart, a number of relationships were noted. For example, it was decided that action to improve the cup for heat transfer to keep it cool might affect the ability to hold the cup comfortably. The team reasoned that changes in material, shape, or surface texture might harm the cup for the voice "Easy to hold." Currently, customers are satisfied with the company's performance. Any proposed changes should be compared with the present cup to make sure no degradation has occurred. This co-relationship concern is shown by the darkened box at the intersection of these two voices in the triangular matrix on the right. In determining these possible co-relationships, there is no knowledge at this point about the probable design for the cup. Therefore, these co-relationships must be examined in a very general manner. If there is the possibility, for example, that some change in material or cup shape might occur to help keep the cup cool, then its effect on issues such as resisting squeeze, ease of holding, and lid fit must be examined. If there is the possibility that one change will affect another, the co-relationship box should be noted. This is the reason symbols were not used. Until a design concept is established, it is not known whether a change to improve one voice will influence another voice positively, negatively, or not at all.

Note that in Figure 4.8, a total of 16 voices are shown, from "Cup stays cool" to "Good aroma." Six of these were chosen as priority voices as shown by the six entries in the action column. One of these, "Examine competition," is a straightforward action that does not require further QFD examination. The other five voices should be considered as priority voices for transfer to the QFD "short form" product planning matrix. Examination of the co-relationship matrix shows an additional six voices that might be affected (either positively, negatively, or not at all) by action to improve the selected five voices. Thus, 11 voices should be transferred to the "short form" matrix.

Use of the preplanning matrix in this manner has reduced the number of voices to be transferred from 16 to 11, a 31 percent reduction.

The preplanning chart and its use to identify voices for a "short form" product planning matrix is an extremely pragmatic approach. It offers distinct advantages to an organization. On the plus side, the organization will be working on fewer items. Each of these items will represent "priorities" on which the organization has agreed. The resources and time required to develop the matrix is less, and the level of interest is usually higher due to focus on a smaller number of voices.

On the negative side, the organization does not develop a matrix for the *whole product*. As a consequence, the team does not have the chance to work with all the key voices as they relate to the product. There may be areas where the customer likes the current product but it is overdesigned for the level of importance and its intended function. In addition, there may be key interactions (co-relationships) between certain technical requirements that did not surface in the examination of the relationship between voices.

One suggested approach or "bottom line" to this discussion is for an organization to develop a complete product planning matrix the first time it examines its product. There will be value in becoming familiar with all the voices of customers. There will be value in determining and examining the technical requirements necessary to respond to customers. It ensures that the company examines the whole picture. In subsequent developments, the emphasis will be on changing voices and determining opportunities for exciting niche issues. The use of a "short form" product planning matrix based on a selection of priority voices from the preplanning chart can be very suitable at this stage.

In this text, the QFD product planning matrix will be developed based on the assumption that the organization wants to examine its product *using all the customers' voices*. This represents the most common approach. However, the approach that would be taken using only selected "priority" voices as a "short form" method is exactly the same. The matrix would be developed in the same manner. The only difference would be that fewer voices would be used as inputs.

Following is a summary of the key points covered in this chapter:

- The customer table is the horizontal portion of the QFD product planning matrix. It contains four principal items:
  1. The customers' requirements. These are their wants and needs as reflected by their voices.
  2. The customers' level of importance as determined through survey.
  3. Any complaints that customers have registered through letters or phone calls.
  4. The customers' evaluation of the performance of the surveying company and its competitors for each of the customer requirements.
- It is helpful to organize the customers' voices into logical, natural groups using the affinity diagram process.
- Early examination of the voices using a preplanning chart will help limit the number of voices by sorting out those that involve attributes, styling, or items that are on a lower level and should be handled in a subsequent matrix.
- The customer information table can be used as a preplanning chart for project management. It can be used to examine the customers' wants and needs and to determine where the company needs to take action to increase the level of customer satisfaction. If desired, these selected priority voices can then be transferred to a new "short form" matrix. They then represent an abbreviated list of high-priority voices that are used for the product planning process.

# Developing a QFD Matrix:
# The Technical Information Portion

*chapter five*

C hapter 4 discussed the first steps in the development of a QFD product planning matrix. This involved completion of the horizontal portion (customer information table) of the QFD matrix. Voices, importance levels, customer complaints, and the customers' competitive evaluations were placed in the customer information table.

Chapter 4 also discussed the advantage of using the customer information table for certain preplanning actions. These included screening the voices to determine if some voices should be removed from the table for specific action at component level QFD, styling, process, or business decisions studies. The preplanning chart can also be used to evaluate the relative priority of the customer voices either to guide project management or as a method of picking priority voices for transfer to the QFD product planning matrix.

This chapter discusses the technical or vertical portion of the QFD product planning matrix. Normally, companies wait until the customer information table portion of the matrix is completed before starting work on the technical portion. However, if time is a critical factor, work on the technical portion of the matrix can begin after the voices have been collected. They should be arranged in natural groupings and examined to make certain the customers' requirements are fully understood. They can then be used as inputs to the matrix. The technical translation can begin while the questionnaire process is taking place to determine customers' levels of importance and their competitive evaluations.

*There is no specified order in which information is entered into the QFD product planning matrix.* The sequence described is the one most typically followed. The actual sequence will vary from team to team and from project to project and is highly dependent on the availability of information. For example, once a team has translated the voices of the customer into technical requirements, it will usually issue test requests to develop the competitive technical assessment data. This takes time in any organization. While the team is waiting for this data, it may determine relationships, develop organizational difficulty determinations, and research any field service data, such as warranty and frequency of repairs. The sequence described in this chapter should be viewed as a typical approach, one that is often followed by teams but which can be altered depending on time and availability of data.

## Translating Customer Voices into Technical Requirements

The first step in beginning the technical portion of the matrix is the translation of the customers' voices into technical requirements. The voices must be translated into the type of language that the company uses to describe its products for design, processing, and manufacture (Figure 5.1). At the same time, the technical requirements must not represent solutions. The objective is to translate each voice into one or more technical requirements. Each technical requirement should be (1) something that should be worked on to satisfy the voice, (2) measurable, and (3) global in nature, one that does not imply any specific design intent.

It is not the intent of the QFD matrix in the product planning stage to imply any design solutions. Its purpose, instead, is to provide a series of technical requirements that specify a generic design that responds to the customers' voices. This is one of the hardest parts of the QFD matrix for most teams. People have a natural desire to think of solutions. When the customers' voice states "Want to stop straight, especially in emergency situations and on wet or slippery roads," the normal tendency is to think about ways to accomplish this. Teams tend to think about improvements to tires or technologies that can be applied to the brake system to provide more consistent straight stopping. The search has to be for ways to measure a characteristic that satisfies the voice rather than ways to accomplish the response to the voice. Thus, one typical *measurable response* to the voice might be *variation from straight line during stopping*. This is a way to measure the customers' concern. The less the variation, the higher the customer satisfaction. The best concept for providing this absence of variation can be chosen later, and a subsequent matrix—the component level planning matrix—can be used to record the detailed requirements for the selected concept.

Figure 5.1 shows some typical customers' voices and technical requirements. Issues such as force, temperature, cycle life, strength, time to transact or complete an action, readability, porosity, reach distance, and noise level are typical of *measurable* non–design-specific responses.

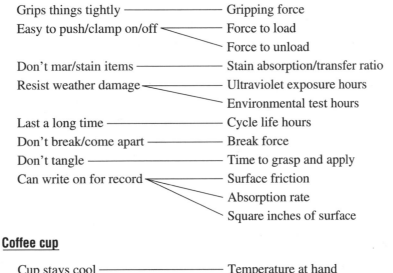

| The Customers' Requirements | Examples of Translations into Technical Requirements |
| --- | --- |

**Clothespin**

Grips things tightly ———————— Gripping force

Easy to push/clamp on/off ———— Force to load

Force to unload

Don't mar/stain items ————————— Stain absorption/transfer ratio

Resist weather damage ————— Ultraviolet exposure hours

Environmental test hours

Last a long time ————————— Cycle life hours

Don't break/come apart ————— Break force

Don't tangle ————————————— Time to grasp and apply

Can write on for record ———— Surface friction

Absorption rate

Square inches of surface

**Coffee cup**

Cup stays cool ———————————— Temperature at hand

Coffee stays hot ————————— Fluid temperature loss over time

Won't spill/tip ———— Tip force at top

Fluid loss vertical impact

Fluid loss horizontal impact

Resists squeeze ———— Indent/force relation

Force/set relation

Doesn't leak ————————————— Porosity

**Figure 5.1** Translating customer requirements into technical requirements.

Figure 5.2 illustrates some customer requirements in nonproduct areas. The voices shown for service are typical customer inputs. Customers expect quick, courteous, and reliable service for their products. Service personnel expect instructions that are clear, readable, and easy to follow for the diagnosis and correction of faults. The technical requirements that respond to these take the form of time to respond, time to service, effectiveness of service, readability of instructions, and number of returns for poor problem correction.

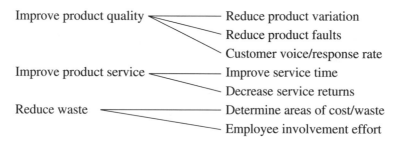

| The Customers' Requirements | Examples of Translations into Technical Requirements |
|---|---|

**Service**

Service is quick ———————— Time to respond
                            Time to service

Service is not expensive ———— Cost to service
Repairs are done right———————— Repair/service effectiveness
Instructions clear, easy ———— Readability of instructions
    to understand               Time to follow instructions
Rooms are clean———————————— Cleanliness standards
Deliveries on time as ———— Variance from schedule
    promised                   Percent on time
Baggage is not lost ———————— Pieces lost per million

**Business**

Improve product quality ———— Reduce product variation
                            Reduce product faults
                            Customer voice/response rate
Improve product service ———— Improve service time
                            Decrease service returns
Reduce waste ———————————— Determine areas of cost/waste
                            Employee involvement effort

**Figure 5.2**    Translating customer requirements into technical requirements in non-product applications.

The customer desire for on-time delivery can be measured by variance from promise or schedule and percent on time. The desire to have baggage delivered on time can be measured by pieces that did not arrive as scheduled per million bags handled.

The lower portion of Figure 5.2 shows some internal company voices typical of those that arise during business planning discussions. The matrix format is an ideal vehicle for examination of items of this type. Measurements can also be developed for these items, as shown in Figure 5.2.

## Recording the Team Decisions for Technical Requirements

The QFD product planning matrix should be viewed as a document that creates a product development history. Every complete QFD product planning matrix documents the relationship between the customers' inputs and the product's technical requirements. It is a valuable historical document that should be the starting point whenever the product is being examined for redesign or new concept development. The value of this history should be enhanced by retention of good notes and good paper trails documenting the decisions and determinations of the team.

The QFD matrix is similar to an outline of the vital information that is normally examined during the development of a product. It is important to keep all entries brief (but understandable) so that the matrix remains easy to examine and interpret. At the same time, provisions need to be made to document the team discussions and decisions. While the results of these discussions cannot be placed directly in the matrix, they should be retained either as footnotes to the matrix or as accompanying documentation. Many organizations have recognized this and use some form of document to record their determinations. Figure 5.3 shows one typical method of recording the determination of technical requirements related to customers' voices. The top of the figure shows a generic example of the use of a fishbone for recording technical requirements. The customers' voice as it appears on the matrix is shown in the box on the left. The actual customers' verbatims are shown below this box as reminders of the detailed customer requirements. The translations into technical requirements are shown in the fishbone diagram on the right side of the illustration. Sometimes these technical requirements can be clarified or amplified by the addition of notes added below the diagram.

Two specific examples are shown in the lower portion of Figure 5.3. It is important to recognize that *the purpose of the fishbone diagram in this application is to develop a record*. Many teams have had the experience of using fishbone diagrams to record the results of brainstorming sessions. This is a common use of the diagram during problem solving team studies. It is important for the team to distinguish between these two types of applications. When the fishbone is used during the translation stage of a QFD study, its purpose is simply to record the team's determination of the technical requirements that are the principal issues for responding to the customers' voice. When used for problem solving, the fishbone diagram is normally used to record all the possible causes of the problem without a value judgment of their impact.

Some teams prefer a simple worksheet, such as the one illustrated in Figure 5.4. This worksheet shows the voice and its row number on the left. The technical requirements determined for the voice are shown in the adjoining column to the right. A column is usually provided for measuring units. This is a reminder to the team that the

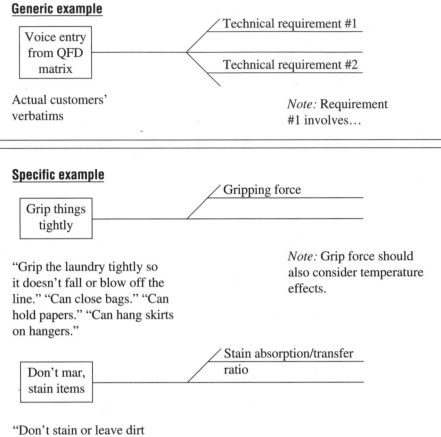

**Generic example**

Voice entry from QFD matrix

Technical requirement #1

Technical requirement #2

Actual customers' verbatims

*Note:* Requirement #1 involves...

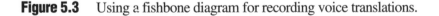

**Specific example**

Grip things tightly

Gripping force

"Grip the laundry tightly so it doesn't fall or blow off the line." "Can close bags." "Can hold papers." "Can hang skirts on hangers."

*Note:* Grip force should also consider temperature effects.

Don't mar, stain items

Stain absorption/transfer ratio

"Don't stain or leave dirt marks on the laundry."

**Figure 5.3**    Using a fishbone diagram for recording voice translations.

technical requirement *must be measurable*. If the team cannot put a measurement such as pounds, seconds, temperature per second, miles per gallon, threads per inch, or pounds per square inch in this column, then the technical requirement should be reexamined. A team can add columns of its choice to this type of worksheet. This example shows columns for the direction of improvement (DIR) arrows and for the strength of the relationships (REL). Determination of these issues can be easily made and recorded at this point if the team desires.

Wherever possible, the technical requirement should be a measure that can be determined through engineering calculation or simulation. In this way, design concept alternatives can be examined without the need to build prototypes or partial prototypes. When a test requirement or a jury is used to measure the technical requirement, an

| Customers' voices | | Technical | Measuring | DIR | REL |
| No. | Tertiary | requirements | units | | |
|---|---|---|---|---|---|
| 1 | Grip things tightly | Gripping force | Pounds | | |
| 2 | Easy to push/clamp | Force to load | Pounds | | |
| | on/off | Force to unload | Pounds | | |

DIR  = Direction of
        improvement
REL = Strength of
        relationship

**Figure 5.4**    Customer requirements translation worksheet.

engineer cannot evaluate design concept alternatives without building and testing samples. When prototypes are developed for test or jury evaluation, there is an inherent danger that the final concept will be determined through a continued revamping of the initial prototype idea rather than through a broader examination of many concept alternatives. A team might choose to add a column that asks the question "Can this be measured without building hardware?"

A third approach that many teams follow is simply to use the matrix as the recording device. Each voice entry is examined, starting with row 1 and continuing through the last row. For each voice, the team determines the technical requirement(s) required to address the voice. These are then entered across the top of the matrix in the space reserved for the technical requirements. Figure 5.5 shows an example of the customer portion of the coffee matrix with technical requirements added. The matrix shown is not complete. Only a portion is shown to permit ease of understanding.

With large matrices, it is usually advisable to arrange the technical requirements into natural groups, as was done for the customers' voices with use of the affinity diagram

**Key:**
■ Surveying Company
○ Chief Competitor

**Technical requirements**

**Customer requirements**

| Containers / Material | | Customer requirement | No. | Importance | Temperature at hand | Fluid temp. loss over time | Tip force at top | Fluid loss vertical impact | Fluid loss horizontal impact | Indent/force relation | Puncture resistance | Porosity | Material life cycle impact | Cup/lid interference | Retention force | Depth drink well to rim | Drink opening area | Evacuate angle | Tab remove force | Complaints | Customer competitive evaluations (1 2 3 4 5) | Action |
|---|---|---|---|---|---|---|---|---|---|---|---|---|---|---|---|---|---|---|---|---|---|---|
| Containers | Cups | Cup stays cool | 1 | 8 | | | | | | | | | | | | | | | | 3 | | |
| | | Coffee stays hot | 2 | 7 | | | | | | | | | | | | | | | | 0.1 | | |
| | | Won't spill/tip | 3 | 7 | | | | | | | | | | | | | | | | 3 | | |
| | | Resists squeeze | 4 | 6 | | | | | | | | | | | | | | | | 0.5 | | |
| | | Doesn't leak | 5 | 7 | | | | | | | | | | | | | | | | | | |
| | | Environmentally safe | 6 | 6 | | | | | | | | | | | | | | | | | | |
| | Lids | Lid fits tight | 7 | 7 | | | | | | | | | | | | | | | | | | |
| | | Remove without spill | 8 | 5 | | | | | | | | | | | | | | | | | | |
| | | Opening for drink | 9 | 8 | | | | | | | | | | | | | | | | 1 | | |
| | | Empty with lid on | 10 | 7 | | | | | | | | | | | | | | | | | | |
| | | Easy-off drink tab | 11 | 6 | | | | | | | | | | | | | | | | | | |
| | | Prevents spill | 12 | 8 | | | | | | | | | | | | | | | | | | |
| | | No-leak cup/lid | 13 | 6 | | | | | | | | | | | | | | | | | | |
| Material | Characteristics | Reg./decaf. | 14 | 8 | | | | | | | | | | | | | | | | | | |
| | | Good taste | 15 | 7 | | | | | | | | | | | | | | | | | | |
| | | Good aroma | 16 | 7 | | | | | | | | | | | | | | | | | | |
| | | Etc. | 17 | 6 | | | | | | | | | | | | | | | | | | |

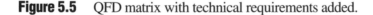

*Note:* For clarity of illustration, some voices, technical requirements, and relationships are not shown.

**Figure 5.5**   QFD matrix with technical requirements added.

approach. In the case of the technical requirements, this is often done by arranging them by functional responsibility.

Technical requirements should be determined with care. Generally, one or two requirements are necessary to satisfy a voice. If a team starts to brainstorm possible responses to each voice, the matrix will have too many technical requirements and too great a level of detail. As the number of technical requirements increases, the complexity of the matrix increases measurably. The number of technical requirements determines the number of columns in the matrix. This, in turn, increases both the number of tests required to develop the competitive technical assessment data and the number of relationship decisions that must be made. *As a rule of thumb, the team should try to keep the ratio of technical requirements to customer requirements somewhere between 1 and 1.5.*

Once the technical requirements are determined, the team should begin the process of initiating test requests to determine the competitive technical assessment data. Testing is a time-consuming process for most companies. While teams are waiting for the test data, they can use the time to determine directions of improvement and relationships and to collect pertinent information on warranty and competitive trends. Once the technical requirements are developed, the sequence of steps that follows is primarily dependent on the availability of data. *The sequence that follows is typical but will obviously vary for each team and each project.*

## Determining Relationships

While a team is waiting for data, such as test results, it can examine the relationship between the technical requirements and the customers' requirements. Its decisions are recorded in the matrix using symbols to indicate the strength of the relationships. The most common symbols are the double circle for a strong relationship, a single circle for a moderate relationship, and a triangle for a weak relationship. Teams have tried using numbers, such as 1, 3, and 5, instead of symbols, but their experience has shown that the symbols are much more easily read. They tend to quickly telegraph the ideas of strong, moderate, or weak relationships. The use of numbers is not nearly as effective.

When determining relationship strengths, it is important to work in columns. Teams should look at each technical requirement and move down the column, asking "Would we work on this technical requirement to satisfy this customer requirement?"

If teams work in rows, they soon discover that they can find a relationship between almost any combination of customer and technical requirements. The purpose of determining relationships is to highlight those technical requirements that have major relationships to customers' voices. Later, when the completed matrix is analyzed to determine the priority customer voices, the relationship symbols are scanned for the selected voices to determine which technical requirements require attention. If teams work across the matrix in rows, the resulting matrix usually contains many symbols that do not indicate true relationships. This will result in the selection of many technical requirements that do not require attention.

Figure 5.6 shows the coffee matrix with relationships added. Note that when the team asked "Would we work on the temperature of the cup at the hand to satisfy this customer requirement?" only the first two voices were related. It was decided that if the company worked on controlling the cup's temperature at the hand, it would have a strong impact on the voice "Cup stays cool." The team also reasoned that a cup that provided insulation from the heat of the coffee would also help reduce loss in coffee temperature. A moderate strength was assigned to this relationship.

When the relationship determinations are complete, the team should take a few minutes to review the relationship portion of the matrix. Each row and column should be examined. There should be none with no relationship symbols or only a weak symbol(s). Absence of symbols or presence only of weak symbols indicates either that a

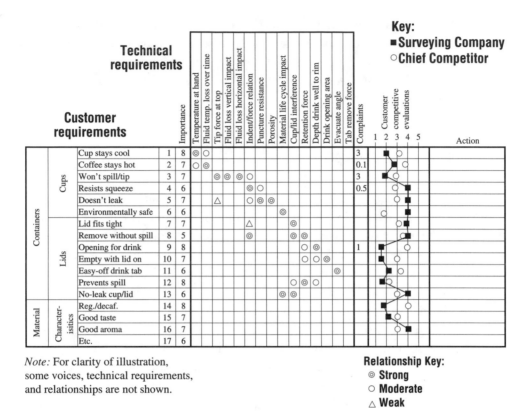

**Figure 5.6**   QFD matrix with symbols added to show the relationships of customer and technical requirements.

customer requirement has not been adequately addressed or that a technical requirement has no significant relationship to the customers' wants.

## Direction of Improvement

It is helpful for a team to record its decisions about each technical requirement to show
the direction that customers prefer. For every technical requirement, there is a direction
that is most favorable for customers, one that will maximize their satisfaction.

    This information can be helpful to teams when they are examining the co-relation-
ship between technical requirements and when they are establishing targets. One effective way to record this is to use symbols to indicate the direction of improvement for
customers. Figure 5.7 shows symbols that are commonly used by many companies. An
arrow pointing up is used to indicate a technical requirement that the customer would

• **For every technical requirement, there is a direction that is most favorable for customers—one that will maximize satisfaction.**

• **Symbols can be used to denote this direction of improvement:**

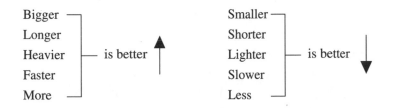

| | |
|---|---|
| ○ | Meeting a definite target is best for customer satisfaction |

A target is the best objective. If there is any difficulty in meeting the target, it should be on the low side of target.

A target is the best objective. If there is any difficulty in meeting the target, it should be on the high side of target.

**Figure 5.7**    Use of symbols to indicate the direction of improvement for customers.

prefer to be larger, bigger, heavier, or in general, more. By contrast, an arrow pointing down indicates that the customer would prefer the technical requirement to be less, slower, smaller, lighter, or shorter. There are many cases in which satisfying the customer can be best achieved by meeting a target. Customers often comment that they "want a control to be within reach" or that they "want the symbols or graphics to be readable." Teams usually consult with the human factors or ergonomic engineers on issues of this type. These customer wants can usually be expressed in terms of a reach zone or a readability distance for a specified population group. Thus, the reach zone might be defined as a zone that will satisfy all persons from the fifth percentile female to the 95th percentile male. This reach zone is a target. If the design is within the zone, the customers' requirements will be met. A circle is often used as a symbol for these target issues.

There are also some cases in which there is a definite customer preference, but only to a point. In most surveys involving mechanical or hardware products, customers will discuss their desire for controls to be easy to operate. Engineers recognize that there is a limit to how little effort is required for most controls. If the operating effort is diminished to an extreme, the control will slide of its own weight or through vibration. Under this condition, it will not hold a setting, and customers will be dissatisfied with the control's operation for a different reason. A modified target symbol can be used for technical requirements of this type by combining the circle for a target with an appropriate arrow. Thus, in the case of the control, a target symbol of a circle with an arrow pointing down was chosen. This indicates that the team felt a target (circle) should be set for the effort reduction. However, if there was any error in meeting the target, it should be in the direction of less effort (pointing down), not more.

The selection of the direction for customer improvement can be made during the discussion of the technical requirement. It can be recorded on the record sheet that the team chooses to use. One example was shown in Figure 5.4. Figure 5.8 shows a second example in which the fishbone diagram was used to record symbols for both the relationships and the direction of improvement.

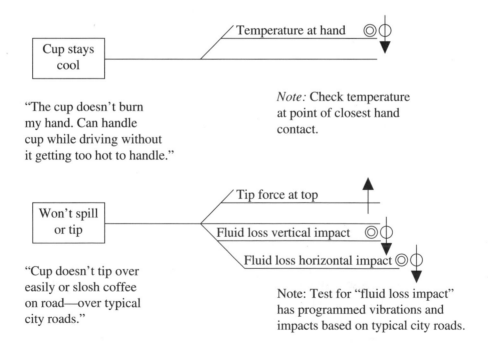

**Figure 5.8**    Use of a fishbone diagram for recording direction of improvement.

The symbols showing direction of customer improvement are usually placed in the matrix above the technical requirements. They have their greatest value when examining the co-relationships between technical requirements. When they are placed across the top of the matrix, they are conveniently located during co-relationship determination. Figure 5.9 shows these symbols added to the matrix.

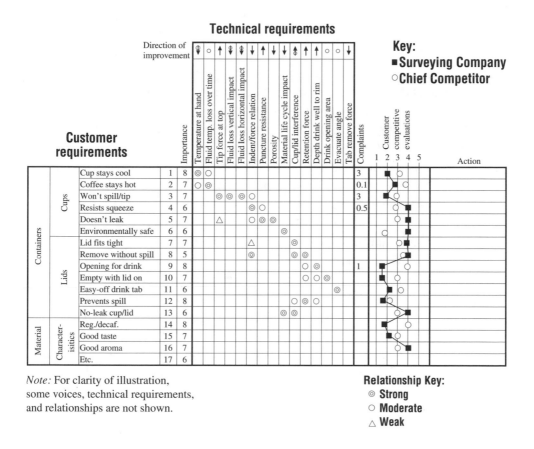

*Note:* For clarity of illustration, some voices, technical requirements, and relationships are not shown.

**Relationship Key:**
◎ Strong
○ Moderate
△ Weak

**Figure 5.9**    Direction of customer improvement added to the QFD matrix.

## Competitive Technical Data

Use of the QFD product planning matrix approach often causes companies to discover deficiencies in their traditional test programs. Frequently, they find that their usual practices have not generated comparative competitive test information *for all the key technical requirements* for themselves and their chief competitors.

Many companies find that they do not have good tests for some of the technical requirements. Many of their tests may be subjective and depend on judgments or use of test juries for decisions. Tests of this type require that prototypes be built for test evaluation. Mathematical or analytical techniques cannot be used. The use of QFD as a planning tool usually causes organizations to face the reality that they need to thoroughly review their test programs and to develop quantitative test approaches for the technical requirements. The matrix approach can be a valuable tool for the comparison of technical requirements and test methods. An example is shown in Chapter 16.

As soon as the technical requirements have been established, the team should begin the process of arranging for the testing. One of the chief determinations affecting test time is the number of competitors' products that will be evaluated. The total test time and expense will increase in proportion to the number of tests scheduled. *Test time and expense can be controlled by carefully managing the number of technical requirements for the matrix and by limiting the number of competitors evaluated.* The organization should review the customers' competitive evaluations obtained during development of the customer portion of the matrix. This information can be used to help determine which of the competitors should be selected for comparative testing. The team should select the number of competitors for the comparative tests that represents a balance between the total test time and cost and the need for information.

When the competitive tests are complete, work can begin to record this data on the matrix in graph form and to begin team discussion about target values. In most situations, some tests take more time than others. Material procurement, setup time, and test time are all variables affecting the final total test time. It is a good practice to have one team member assigned to the task of tracking the competitive testing to determine the overall progress. The team should not wait until all tests are completed and the data is formally reported. Instead, it should make a judgment about the overall progress and scheduled completion dates of testing. Discussion of the target values and plotting the data on the matrix can begin when the team believes that much of the data is available and most of the remaining information will become available during the discussion period.

Test data should be recorded in some tabular form to serve as a paper trail or documentation for the QFD study. Figure 5.10 shows a typical format. This could be expanded to show the log book or test report numbers which are the backup for the data.

The portion of the QFD planning matrix reserved for the results of competitive technical testing can be used in a variety of ways depending upon a team's determination. The competitive assessment data shown in Figure 5.10 can be transferred to the matrix as a series of numerical data. An alternative is to portray the data graphically. Another approach is to show both the data and the graphic portrayal. Observation indicates that most people find the graphic representation easiest to use when analyzing the completed matrix to establish priorities and competitive targets. Therefore, this is the approach discussed in this text.

| Customer requirements | Technical requirements | Competitive assessment | | | Units |
|---|---|---|---|---|---|
| | | A | B | C | |
| Resists squeeze | Indent/force relationship | 0.17 | 0.23 | 0.36 | in. per lb. |
| Coffee stays hot | Temp. loss over time | 4.9 | 4.2 | 3.9 | deg./min. |
| Cup stays cool | Temp. at hand | 150 | 130 | 148 | degrees |
| Easy to operate | Operating effort | 8.6 | 6.8 | 4.6 | ounces |
| Easy to follow instructions | Readability level<br>Time to accomplish | 11.6<br>50 | 10.2<br>42 | 7.8<br>68 | grade level<br>seconds |
| Time to connect to representative | Connect time<br>Transaction time | 5<br>180 | 5<br>260 | 24<br>240 | seconds<br>seconds |
| Quick service | Task completion time | 6.5 | 11.2 | 6.6 | hours |

**Figure 5.10**    Table of test results from technical competitive assessment of typical technical requirements.

The competitive technical assessment graph should be viewed as a pictorial representation of the test data rather than as an engineering portrayal of the data. The graph's purpose is to provide a pictorial view of the competitive position of the QFD company compared with its chief competitors. This is reinforced by the fact that the graph itself has a qualitative scale. Note that in Figure 5.11, the scale runs from 1 to 5 and an arrow indicates that bigger is better. A qualitative scale is necessary because the data to be plotted does not have a common metric. Measures may be in pounds, degrees, inch-ounces, feet, deflection per pound, or pounds per square inch. A generic scale is one way to respond to these vast differences in metrics for the technical requirements.

The technical competitive assessment data can be plotted and the target values can be determined as separate issues. However, experience shows that they are best done conjunctively during discussion of the target values. As team members review the competitive technical data and other associated information to determine the best competitive target value, they develop an understanding of the scale for the graph for each technical requirement. It is a natural followup to plot data after the discussion of target values. This is best illustrated by example.

Figures 5.11 and 5.12 show two approaches to the idea of plotting the technical competitive data independently of the discussion of target values. These are followed by several examples of target value discussions and the resultant determination of

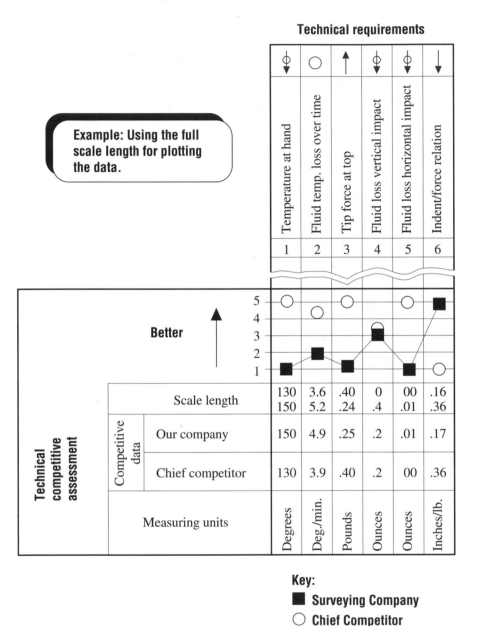

**Figure 5.11**    Plotting technical competitive assessment data.

graphic plotting. Either approach or some combination can be used. In each example that follows, the technical requirement "Temperature at the hand" is used for illustration. The temperature measurements have been exaggerated for purposes of illustration.

Figure 5.11 is an enlargement of the technical competitive assessment portion of the QFD coffee matrix. It illustrates the simplest approach to the issue of plotting competitive technical data. For illustration, the actual test data is shown for the QFD company and its chief competitor in the rows labeled "Competitive Data." For example, for the technical requirement "Temperature at the hand," our company is shown as 150 F° and the best competitor's is shown as 130° F. The direction of improvement at the top of the illustration shows that customers prefer a lower temperature but that there is an optimum or target value for the temperature at the hand. The team can simply allocate a scale length to fit this data. Thus, the scale might be selected as 130° to 150°. The 20° difference is divisible by four scale segments; thus, each of the four segments of the scale would be 5°. Because the customer prefers the lower temperature, the scale would run from 130° at the top to 150° at the bottom. In the data plot, the dark squares represent our company.

This is a straightforward approach to the data plotting. Generally, the scale length is based on the actual data, and the data occupies most of the scale. Some judgment may be used, as is shown in column 4, "Fluid loss on vertical impact." Both companies measured 0.2 ounce of spill. The team, however, felt that the customer would definitely prefer less spillage and elected to make the scale reflect this. The scale was developed as a range of 0.4 ounces. Both companies plot in the middle of the chart.

A major disadvantage of this approach is that the full scale length is generally used to portray the competitive data. In the example discussed of "Temperature at the hand," the graph tends to indicate that the chief competitor is a satisfactory contender, with a 130° temperature. Our company, on the other hand, is not a good competitor, with its cup temperature of 150°. The arrow showing direction of improvement indicates that customers want a low temperature. The circle indicates that there is an obvious target, however, that would be satisfactory to customers.

When the graph is plotted as in this example, a reader can easily interpret that the competitor has met the customers' requirement because the competitor is shown at or near the top of the scale. This may not be the case, however. Other available data that the team might examine could indicate otherwise. As an example, human factors data might support the fact that if the maximum temperature at the hand is 115° F, people will not complain of a "hot cup." If this were established data, then it would be more reasonable to show this in the pictorial plot of the competitive technical data. Thus, the scale length could be changed to run from 80° to 160°. Figure 5.12 shows the competitive data plotted with this scale length. Note that the chief competitor is now closer to the center of the scale rather than near the top, as in Figure 5.11. *Thus, the scale reflects some "built-in reach."* The graph in Figure 5.12 still shows that the chief competitor is better than our

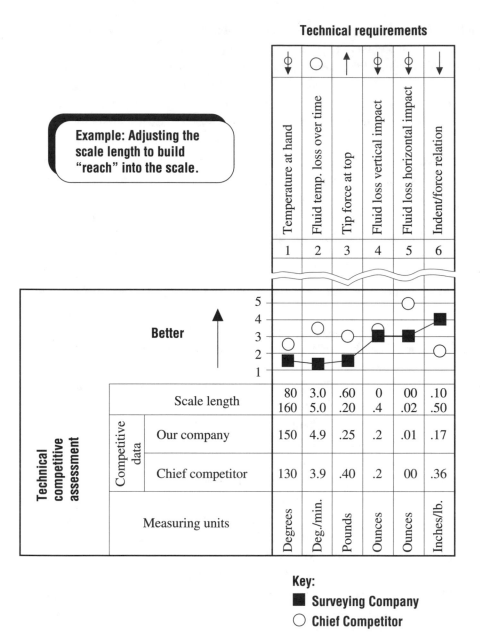

**Figure 5.12** Plotting technical competitive assessment data.

company. However, it reflects the fact that there is room for improvement; there is reach in the graphic representation of the data. A glance at the graph shows that the chief competitor is still the best in columns 1, 2, 3, and 5. However, it also indicates that the team believes that customer satisfaction will be improved by reaching to achieve target values that exceed the current level of performance of the chief competitor.

Many teams prefer this alternative approach and purposely build reach into their graphs. If the team acknowledges that the principal purpose of the graph is to provide a pictorial representation of the data, this approach may have considerable appeal. On the other hand, if the team wants the graph to represent more of a precise representation of the data, it may prefer the approach shown in Figure 5.11.

## Establishing Targets

If the team combines its discussion of target values and graphic plots, the concern for how to plot the data will normally resolve itself. The next four examples will help illustrate this process; *each represents a selected piece of the QFD product planning matrix.* Each shows the customer voice, importance, complaints, and competitive evaluation along with the technical competitive assessment data and the strength of relationship. Each uses the technical requirement "Temperature at the hand." *Different customer competitive evaluations and different competitive test assessment data are used in each figure to help illustrate the team decision process.*

Figure 5.13 shows a situation in which our company is judged by the customer to be better than the two leading competitors. There has been one complaint per thousand sales for our company. The customers' voice is "Cup stays cool." The level of importance for this voice is high, at 7.2, and there is a strong relationship between the voice and the technical requirement "Temperature at the hand." The technical competitive assessment data shows that the laboratory finds our company's cup to have the lowest temperature at the hand. In general, the competitive technical data supports the customers' evaluation.

The question is "What target should be set?" The customers' competitive evaluation data shows that no company is judged to be good. The best company, our company, is only judged as a 2 on a 1 to 5 scale. In addition, the best company (our company) is still receiving one complaint per thousand sales. The customers' evaluation of poor performance of all companies is a strong signal that a competitive opportunity exists. Any other company doing similar customer research will see this same situation and the obvious opportunity. The company that can develop a cup whose temperature at the hand is lower and is in line with human factors data will be able to take advantage of this competitive opportunity. That company will be able to use this development as an advertising opportunity or "sales point."

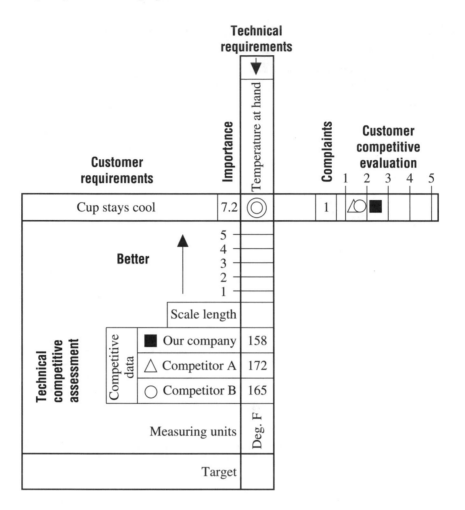

**Figure 5.13**    Determining target values for the technical requirements.

In this case, if the human factors data were to reveal that 115° F was an acceptable temperature, then the company should proceed to develop a cup to satisfy this require-ment. Its outside temperature (at the hand) would be a maximum of 115° when filled with coffee whose temperature represented the most acceptable serving temperature for customers.

Thus, the team discussion needs to involve both how the customers evaluated the products and how the tests evaluated the products. Other data will be needed. In this case, data about acceptable temperatures at the hand and about acceptable serving tempera-tures is required to permit evaluation of various cup concepts that will best satisfy the voice "Cup stays cool." If the team were to establish 115° as the maximum temperature at the hand, this would be recorded on the matrix in the target row. If this were the team choice, then plotting the data is simply a matter of reviewing the selected target value versus the actual competitive test data. In this case, the scale would have to accommodate the data 115°, 158°, 172°, and 165° and might run from 180° to 100°.

Figure 5.14 shows this same voice and technical requirement with different customer evaluation data and competitive technical data. In this illustration, our company is again judged to be the best by customers. The customer evaluation places our company at 4.4 on the 1 to 5 scale. There have been no complaints. The technical competitive data supports this. Our company measures 120°, while the worst competitor, both from a customer viewpoint and technically, measures 172°.

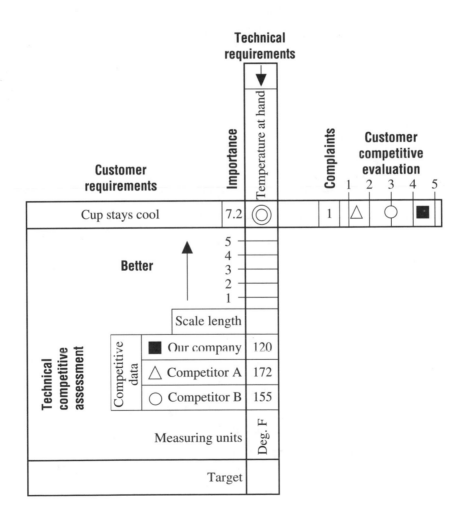

**Figure 5.14**   Determining target values for the technical requirements.

In this case, the team decision might be to set the target value at 120°, representing the current cup design. The 120° value is very close to the 115° human factors data and is currently very satisfactory to customers. There is no apparent value to be gained by working on this item. If plotting is being done in conjunction with the team discussion of target values, a scale length of 180° to 120° might be chosen.

Figure 5.15 shows a situation in which our company is judged by customers to be a very poor performer. Companies A and B are judged to be better. Customer complaints reflect this. The technical competitive data agrees with the customers' evaluation.

This is an obvious case of being a poor competitor from the customers' viewpoint. Our company is in a catch-up position and must take action. The quickest and simplest

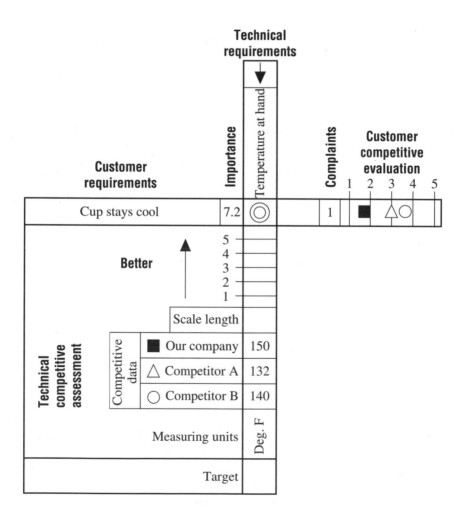

**Figure 5.15**  Determining target values for the technical requirements.

approach for immediate action would be to purchase cups from the supplier of either company A or company B. However, neither of these companies is really superior in the eyes of the customer. The best competitor, company B, is only rated as 3.5 on the 1 to 5 scale. In this case, a competitive advantage would be possible if our company could bring out a cup with a temperature closer to the 115° mark. Thus, the team might set a target for long-range development of a cup with a 115° temperature. It might also move to purchase the best cup currently on the market from the supplier to company B until the development of a better cup was completed.

Organizations cannot expect exact relationships between customer evaluations and competitive test assessments. There will be many cases in which this data appears to be in disagreement. These differences in results should be examined carefully. This opportunity to examine the customers' viewpoint versus the company's test data is one of the highlights of the QFD approach. In general, there should be no major difference between what the customer says and what the tests determine. If major differences exist, it should alert a team to carefully investigate and resolve the difference.

For example, in Figure 5.16, company A was judged the best by customers and company B was judged second best. In laboratory testing, this was reversed: company B was actually better than company A. This disparity should not be dismissed as simply "a small anomaly." Instead, the situation should be examined to determine a possible cause. In testing, for example, it would be logical for the laboratory to fill all cups with liquid at the same temperature (for example, 185° F) and then measure the temperature at the hand. This would ensure comparable test results. Perhaps company A serves its coffee at a lower temperature than company B, explaining the customers' evaluation. If this were the case, then the difference would be explained. If it were not, the question should be examined further. The key point is this: what the customer perceives is reality. If the customer believes company A's cup is superior concerning temperature at the hand, then there must be an explanation. These investigations of significant anomalies may disclose a number of possibilities:

- The test method may not truly reflect the customers' wants and needs.
- There may be some technical requirement other than the one(s) chosen to represent the voice that has stronger bearing on customer evaluation. The matrix should be revised to include such discoveries.
- The customer may use the product differently than expected, thereby creating a need for additional technical requirements and tests.

When these anomalies are observed, the team should reinvestigate when necessary. It may be valuable to do additional customer surveys by phone or questionnaire. Observation of customers' usage of the product may reveal some customers' wants

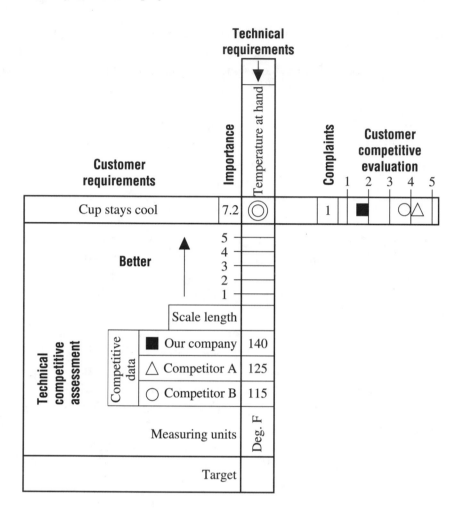

**Figure 5.16**    Determining target values for the technical requirements.

and needs that were not understood. For example, one strong customer voice for office chairs is "Want lots of vertical adjustment ability." One historical measure of this has been the technical requirement "Height adjustment in inches." It is possible, in competitive testing, that a company might find its competitor had the same or less vertical travel but was still judged superior for the voice. Investigation and observation often disclose that the customers' perception is influenced by such issues as the amount of effort involved or the number of operations needed to make the adjustment. Time to adjust might be an important factor. If these were not part of the company's test procedures, then its tests would not reveal the potential for customer dissatisfaction with the chair's adjustment. When the QFD matrix highlights issues of

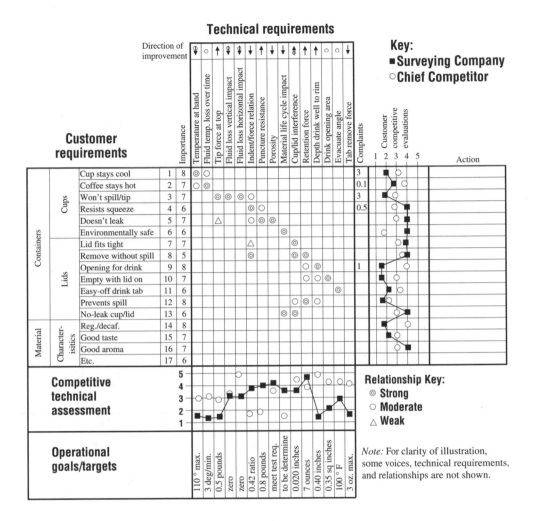

**Figure 5.17**   Direction of customer improvement added to the QFD matrix.

difference between the customers' perception and the test reality, a company must respond. The reason for the disparity must be found. The result of the investigation will help the company understand action required to develop highly competitive products.

Figure 5.17 shows the partial matrix for take-out coffee, with the competitive technical assessment and operational goals and targets entered on the matrix. As stated earlier, the temperatures used for the preceding discussion were exaggerated for purposes of illustration. Note that the target set for the temperature at the hand is 110°F. The actual test results were 135° and 120°, respectively, for our company and our chief competitor.

## Co-relationships

Many technical requirements are related to other technical requirements. Working to improve one may help a related requirement, and a positive or beneficial effect results. On the other hand, working to improve one requirement may negatively affect a related requirement. Improvement of miles per gallon may negatively affect acceleration. Both are customer voices, both are very important, and they are related. The relationship is negative because action to improve either one will have a harmful effect on the other. On the other hand, reduction of the mass of a vehicle will have a beneficial effect both on miles per gallon and on acceleration, assuming the power train characteristics are not altered during the weight reduction effort.

Unlike technical requirements that should be generic and non–design-specific, the determination of co-relationships requires that a specific design be considered. For example, in theater seats, two important technical requirements are the fore and aft distance between seats and the overall theater seating density. The first requirement responds to the voice of theatergoers who want people to be able to get to their seats without the need to stand and let them pass. The second requirement responds to the voice of the theater owner who wants to seat as many people as possible per square foot of space. If the co-relationship determination is made with a conventional seat, these two requirements are negatively related. Because the distance between seats must be increased to improve entry room, the seating density declines. On the other hand, if the design concept is one in which the seats move in some manner to permit entry, the relationship changes. In this case, the customers' want may be satisfied with no increase in the distance between seats and might even be achieved with a slight reduction in distance. Thus, the relationship may change from negative to positive as a result of the consideration of another design concept.

One of the principal benefits of the co-relationship matrix is that it flags the negative relationships. As the product concept proceeds, each of these negative relationships needs careful examination. Each of these is like a red flag telling the organization that any action to improve one requirement can have adverse effects on one or more other requirements. If these issues are not settled satisfactorily, some aspects of the final product will dissatisfy customers. It is important to examine each of these red flags to determine how the design can be changed or desensitized to eliminate or at least reduce the effect of the negative co-relationship.

On a large matrix, the task of developing the co-relationship matrix can be overwhelming. It may be possible for the team to determine whether a relationship exists between each of the technical requirements, but it is often impossible for the team to be knowledgeable enough to know the type of relationship (that is, positive or negative). This often requires consultation with experts and can be a time-consuming process. Therefore, some teams simply use the co-relationship matrix to indicate those requirements that are related and do not indicate whether they are positive or negative.

The reasoning is that as the product development proceeds, the areas of co-relationship are flagged and the experts can make the determination about the positive or negative nature as they examine concept alternatives.

Many Japanese co-relationship matrices show the use of four symbols. A double circle is used to indicate a strong positive co-relationship; a single circle, a weaker but positive relationship; a double XX, a strong negative relationship; and a single X, a negative relationship. Many teams find that use of these four levels of co-relationship further complicates the determination issue and is more time-consuming.

Figure 5.18 shows the coffee matrix with the co-relationship matrix added. Note that, for simplicity, only two symbols are used: a circle to indicate positive and an X to indicate negative co-relationships. Also, note that all four of the negative co-relationships involve the technical requirement "Material life cycle impact." This requirement has a strong relationship to the customers' voice "Environmentally safe." The team felt that the requirements of temperature at the hand, fluid loss over time, indent/force, and puncture resistance were all negatively related to this environmental issue. The reasoning was that the customers' concerns for a cup that stays cool, keeps coffee hot, and resists squeezing is one of material choice. Every material has its own individual life cycle impact and will harm the environment to some extent.

## Other Possible Matrix Entries

There is no recipe for developing a QFD matrix. Certain portions of the matrix are essential and can be considered mandatory. The customers' wants and needs, the technical requirements, relationships, and target values are essentials. In product planning, the targets cannot reasonably be established without competitive technical assessment data. Consequently, this data becomes an essential part of the product planning matrix. Other issues, such as regulatory requirements, management voices, assessment of technical difficulty, column weights, field experience data, and assessments of organizational difficulty, are optional for the team. Many of these represent valuable inputs that help the decision process in product planning. Each team must determine the need and value of these other possible entries and add them to its matrix based on its assessment of value added (Figure 5.19).

### Other Voices

Most companies have some regulatory requirements that affect their operations. These may be the result of federal or state legislation. They may represent a voluntary conformance to certain requirements established through an industry council. Other requirements may involve action to achieve Underwriters Laboratories certification or similar approval from recognized test agencies.

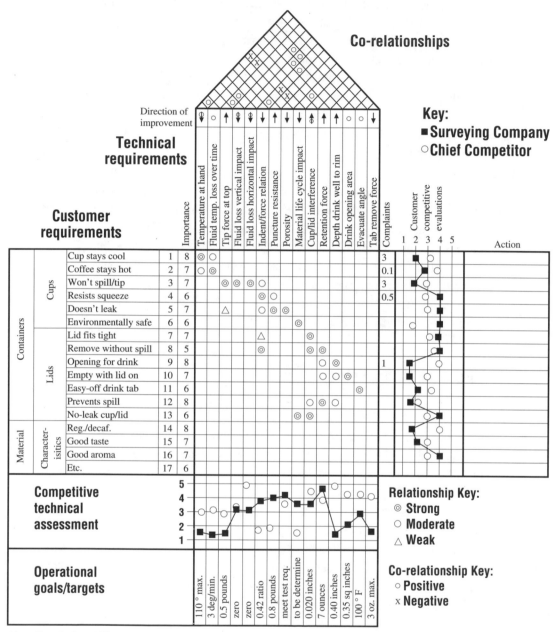

**Figure 5.18**    QFD matrix with co-relationships added.

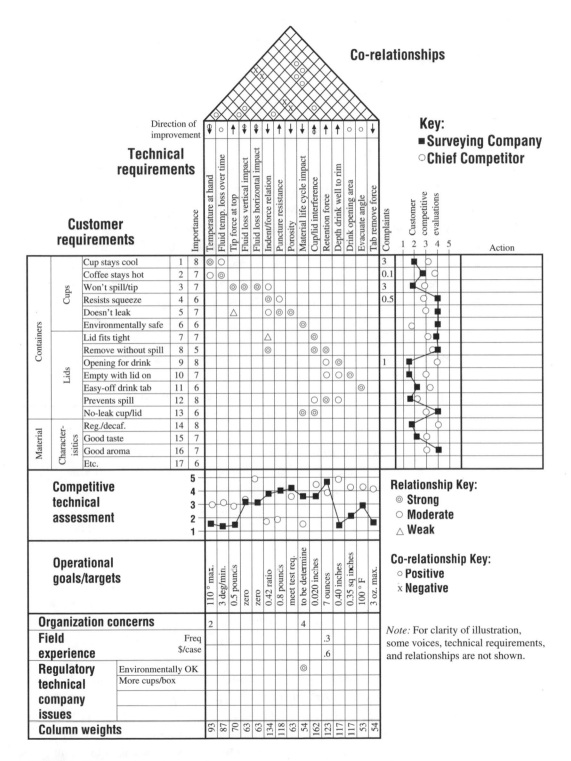

**Figure 5.19** Putting it all together.

Standards of this type represent the voice of a customer who must be satisfied. Even if that customer never buys a single product from the company, the company must meet the requirements.

Similarly, managers within the company may state requirements for a new product that should be considered during the product planning stage. These may involve a concern for use of existing facilities or a proposal for use of a new processing concept. It may involve management's desire to add a feature to the product that it believes is required to meet competition.

Requirements of this type represent needs that must be addressed and satisfied. In the QFD matrix, they are kept separate from the customers' voices determined through interviews and questionnaires. This is done intentionally so they will not dilute or diffuse the voice of real customer, the one who purchases the product.

In Figure 5.19, the area in the lower portion of the matrix entitled "Regulatory, technical, company issues" shows two entries: "Environmentally OK" and "More cups per box." Both of these are internal company voices. Note that when any of these internal voices is related to a technical requirement across the top of the matrix, the appropriate relationship strength symbol is shown. A strong symbol is shown at the intersection of the internal voice "Environmentally OK" and the technical requirement "Material life cycle impact."

Teams may also elect to add a row for any organizational concerns. This represents a team determination of the difficulty that a technical requirement may create within the organization. This is often done using a scale of 1 to 5 for degree of difficulty, with 5 representing a high level of difficulty. If the technical requirement is essentially carry-over in nature and no difficulty is anticipated, the column/row intersection will be left blank. Note that in the partial coffee matrix, only two organizational difficulties are flagged. The company feels that achieving a lower temperature at the hand may require changes in cup material. This could have a detrimental effect on the manufacture of the cup and on the restaurant stacking, handling, and usage of the cup. Similarly, the related requirement concerning life cycle impact of the material is viewed as having potential organizational problems because it may affect manufacturing processes and the recycling and disposal of materials.

When organizations examine their completed matrices to select priority items, one determinant in their decision process should be a concern for items that are new and difficult. The organizational difficulty row can help flag such items.

### Field Experience

Most organizations have some mechanism for collecting information from the field that is related to technical difficulty. Items returned for repair under warranty and 800-number conversations are two common ways to determine service problems with the product. Technical difficulties can usually be related to technical requirements and, therefore, represent an indicator of difficulty with the current product for specific technical requirements.

When this data is placed in the matrix, it helps reinforce the decision process during analysis of the matrix for priority items. For example, a commonly expressed strong customer's voice for many products is "Easy to operate." This is usually translated into a technical requirement such as "Operating effort." If this voice and its associated requirement were chosen as a priority item for action, the presence of any field service data would help reinforce the decision and the need for action. In this case, if there had been a number of instances of service work to replace some component (for example, a spring) to reduce effort, this would be reflected in the matrix and would serve to reinforce the decision to work on operating effort. In addition, the warranty cost might serve as an offset to the cost of changing the product concept.

In Figure 5.19, some field expense is shown under the technical requirement "Retention force" (for the lid). This might be the result of poor retention of the lids that caused some spillage and resultant customer bills for dry cleaning. Thus, frequency and cost are shown.

### Column Weights

A team may elect to add column weights across the bottom of the matrix. This involves arbitrarily assigning weights to the relationship symbols. The most commonly used weights are 9 for a strong symbol, 3 for a moderate symbol, and 1 for a weak symbol. Some organizations use 5, 3, and 1 as weights.

The concept is that a weight can be calculated for each column that represents a combination of both the customers' level of importance and the strength of the relationships. This is accomplished by using the product of the relationship strength and the importance. Thus, in column 1, row 1, in Figure 5.19, the customers' importance level is 8 and the weight for the strong relationship symbol is 9; their product is 72. At the intersection of column 1 and row 2, the product is 7 times 3, or 21. This calculation process is continued wherever there is a relationship symbol in the column. For column 1, the sum of these products is 72 plus 21, or 93. This is recorded across the bottom of the matrix.

The software programs available to help organizations develop their matrices do this calculation automatically. The raw column weights are also converted to percentages to help highlight columns with strong relative column weights.

This chapter discussed the technical portion of the QFD product planning matrix. Each basic entry to the matrix was reviewed to describe its purpose and some of the issues that should be considered in the development and handling of the information for the matrix. Following are some key points related to this chapter:

- A completed QFD matrix represents a product planning history. It records a number of pieces of information that are normally considered but that are seldom organized for ease of analysis and multidimensional review. Organizations should use the completed matrix as a source of planning information for each successive generation of the product.

- Companies that have used the QFD product planning matrix for several product iterations find that the majority of customer wants and needs (voices) are repeated in the subsequent surveys. Voices such as "Easy to operate," "Easy to reach," "Quick response time," "Easy to understand instructions," "Tastes good," "Has a good aroma," and "Lasts a long time" will be heard over and over in subsequent surveys. This fact is a boon for organizations. It means that the survey attention can be focused on those voices that are new or where subtle changes in wants and needs are expressed. It also means that the competitive assessment test program can begin early in the planning stage for each of those voices that are judged to be generic to the product. Because those voices have already been translated into technical requirements in the prior QFD studies, the items for testing are easy to determine.

- Development of a QFD matrix is a flexible issue that is dependent on the type and extent of the data, the type and complexity of the product, the team, time constraints, and organizational readiness. Each team should bear these issues in mind as it plans its QFD endeavor and as it builds its matrix. The team should not make entries on a matrix because it has seen a model matrix with the entries or because the software has the capability. Each entry to the matrix should be reviewed and developed and entered into the matrix only if the team agrees that it represents value-added benefit.

# Reviewing the Matrix
# for Priority Items

*chapter six*

C hapters 4 and 5 discussed the development of the QFD product planning matrix. Chapter 4 covered the development of the customer portion of the matrix, and Chapter 5 discussed the technical portion of the matrix.

At this point, it is obvious that the development of one of these matrices involves a major commitment by an organization. The matrix concept forces an organization to examine each voice and each technical requirement in detail. All the necessary data and information, such as the voices, the competitive customer evaluations, and the competitive technical assessment data, must be available to complete the matrix.

Organizations are not willing to devote this level of time and commitment to a project unless there is obvious value received. The principal purpose of developing a QFD matrix is to put the organization in touch with its customers' wants and needs and to help determine the priority items for improved customer satisfaction. The determination of these priority items is the subject of this chapter.

The majority of organizations in the United States have no organized method to determine the customers' wants and needs. Many have programs for collection of field failure information and customer complaints. Few have organized efforts to periodically listen to customers express their wants and needs. Still fewer take advantage of the opportunity to observe customers using their products. When there is an absence of information about the real customers' wants and needs, an organization must fill the void with internal decisions. One common practice is to simply upgrade last year's product or service based on knowledge of its successes and failures. The decisions about overall direction are made by engineers and managers.

This practice can lead to declining customer satisfaction, fewer return purchases, and ultimate loss of business. Many items that make customers unhappy will never be disclosed through the normal practice of listening to complaints and examining service costs. If customers are unhappy about something that is inherent in the product design, they are seldom willing to take the time to write to the organization. They simply look for another product next time that does not have the design problem. It is only through one-on-one conversations with people that these built-in dissatisfiers become apparent. Once they are known, they can be remedied. Conditions that are not known will likely be repeated in the next product offering and will continue to create customer dissatisfaction. Even if the condition is a minor irritant, people are reminded of it each time they use the product. The level of dissatisfaction increases as the number of built-in dissatisfiers increases. Some examples are as follows:

- Household cleaning product that produces an allergic reaction
- Self-serve copy machine that is stocked with cheap paper
- A restaurant with slow service or poor food
- A coffee cup that is too hot to handle
- A shirt that does not fit properly
- Products that wear out too fast and do not meet the customer's expectation of a reasonable life expectancy
- An operating switch that is in an inconvenient position
- An operating effort that is too high
- No cup holder in the car

## Analysis of the Customer Information Portion of the Matrix

The analysis of the QFD matrix should begin with the customer portion of the matrix. This contains the customers' wants and needs, measures of their levels of importance, and their competitive evaluations of products. The objective is to review this data and to determine those customer requirements that should receive attention by the company as it plans its new product offerings. The selected high-priority items can be ranked by the team and balanced against the human resources and budget available for product modifications.

Any new product program has budget restraints. The analysis of the QFD matrix customer information is designed to help the organization balance its resources against its customers' requirements. The decisions about which items are priority items are then based on customer requirements rather than internal experience and intuition.

Figure 6.1 is the customer portion of the coffee matrix used as an example in Chapters 4 and 5. It can be used separately as shown and is an excellent tool for managing the selection of priority items at the start of a new project. A variety of columns

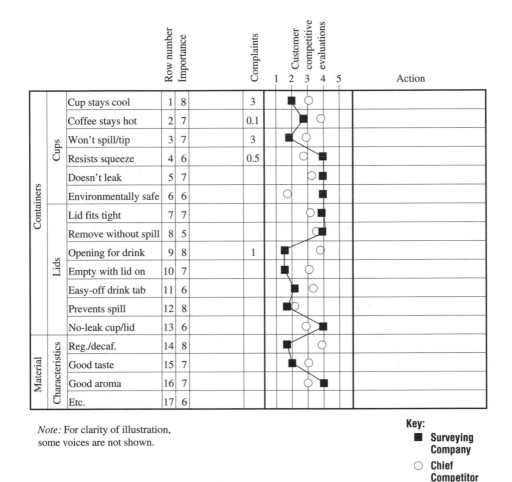

| | | | Row number | Importance | | Complaints | Customer competitive evaluations 1 2 3 4 5 | Action |
|---|---|---|---|---|---|---|---|---|
| Containers | Cups | Cup stays cool | 1 | 8 | | 3 | | |
| | | Coffee stays hot | 2 | 7 | | 0.1 | | |
| | | Won't spill/tip | 3 | 7 | | 3 | | |
| | | Resists squeeze | 4 | 6 | | 0.5 | | |
| | | Doesn't leak | 5 | 7 | | | | |
| | | Environmentally safe | 6 | 6 | | | | |
| | Lids | Lid fits tight | 7 | 7 | | | | |
| | | Remove without spill | 8 | 5 | | | | |
| | | Opening for drink | 9 | 8 | | 1 | | |
| | | Empty with lid on | 10 | 7 | | | | |
| | | Easy-off drink tab | 11 | 6 | | | | |
| | | Prevents spill | 12 | 8 | | | | |
| | | No-leak cup/lid | 13 | 6 | | | | |
| Material | Characteristics | Reg./decaf. | 14 | 8 | | | | |
| | | Good taste | 15 | 7 | | | | |
| | | Good aroma | 16 | 7 | | | | |
| | | Etc. | 17 | 6 | | | | |

*Note:* For clarity of illustration, some voices are not shown.

**Key:**
■ Surveying Company
○ Chief Competitor

**Figure 6.1**    Examining the customer portion of the planning matrix to determine priority items for action.

can be added on the right side of the matrix to help in the decision process. This example shows a column added to record the team's decisions about what action might be appropriate for selected items.

One of the most direct approaches to analysis of the customer information table is to discuss each of the items of high importance. Ideas stemming from the discussion can be noted in the action column. These notes do not represent a commitment to respond to each of the items. There may not be sufficient resources to permit this. Instead, at this point, the action is directed at a presorting of the items into those possibly deserving attention and those that currently appear satisfactory. The available resources should be balanced against this list of challenges as a second step in the process.

A logical approach is to examine the items based on the customers' level of importance, starting with levels of high importance and working in descending order. Thus, in Figure 6.1, the team would look for any items of importance levels 8 or 9. The discussion would involve those items first and then proceed to items of importance levels 7 and 8. The process would continue until the team decides it has reached a point of diminished return. For example, the team may decide that the list contains more items than resources could handle. It may decide to discontinue discussion when the level of importance is sufficiently low that it does not represent a wise investment to consider product changes (for example, a level of importance of 5 or lower).

Each customer requirement that is reviewed should be examined for the customer competitive evaluation and the presence of any complaints. The customer competitive evaluation is a key determinant in this examination process. The competitive evaluation data examination can be categorized into three key issues:

1. A catch-up position: The customer judges the competition to be better than the QFD company. The competitor is rated on the high end of the 1 to 5 scale and the QFD company is significantly lower. Row 9 (Figure 6.1) is an obvious example. The QFD company must take action to correct this situation; it must "catch up."

2. A position of current strength: This is the reverse of the above. The QFD company is the leader and the competitor is the follower. The QFD company must decide whether it needs to take action to maintain this lead. If the competing companies are also talking with their customers, they are aware of this situation and can be expected to act to correct it. This could indicate a need to increase the level of competitive strength for the QFD company. Row 6 is an example of an obvious lead by the QFD company.

3. An opportunity: If no company is judged to be superior, then there is an opportunity to develop or modify products (or services) to move the company to a position of superiority in the customers' eyes. Row 3 is an example. The QFD company is rated as a 2 (on a 1 to 5 scale) by customers, and its best competitor is rated as a 3. If the QFD company can determine a way to more effectively respond to the customers' requirement of "Won't spill or tip," it can gain a competitive advantage. This advantage can become an advertising point or a sales point.

If examination of a customer requirement indicates that there is a need for action, and there are complaints recorded in the complaint column, these reinforce the need for action. *It is important to remember that for most products, letters and calls registering complaints represent only a small portion of the customers who had the problem.*

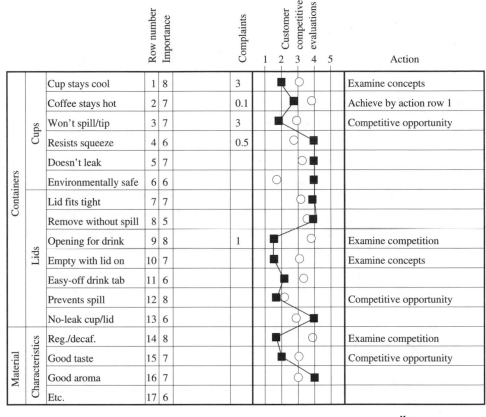

| | | | Row number | Importance | | Complaints | Customer competitive evaluations 1 2 3 4 5 | Action |
|---|---|---|---|---|---|---|---|---|
| Containers | Cups | Cup stays cool | 1 | 8 | | 3 | | Examine concepts |
| | | Coffee stays hot | 2 | 7 | | 0.1 | | Achieve by action row 1 |
| | | Won't spill/tip | 3 | 7 | | 3 | | Competitive opportunity |
| | | Resists squeeze | 4 | 6 | | 0.5 | | |
| | | Doesn't leak | 5 | 7 | | | | |
| | | Environmentally safe | 6 | 6 | | | | |
| | | Lid fits tight | 7 | 7 | | | | |
| | Lids | Remove without spill | 8 | 5 | | | | |
| | | Opening for drink | 9 | 8 | | 1 | | Examine competition |
| | | Empty with lid on | 10 | 7 | | | | Examine concepts |
| | | Easy-off drink tab | 11 | 6 | | | | |
| | | Prevents spill | 12 | 8 | | | | Competitive opportunity |
| | | No-leak cup/lid | 13 | 6 | | | | |
| Material | Characteristics | Reg./decaf. | 14 | 8 | | | | Examine competition |
| | | Good taste | 15 | 7 | | | | Competitive opportunity |
| | | Good aroma | 16 | 7 | | | | |
| | | Etc. | 17 | 6 | | | | |

*Note:* For clarity of illustration, some voices are not shown.

**Key:**
■ Surveying Company
○ Chief Competitor

**Figure 6.2**  Examining the customer portion of the planning matrix to determine priority items for action.

The team can record its determinations in the action column. Figure 6.2 shows an example of this for the coffee matrix. In this case, the team only examined items of importance levels 7 and higher. In some cases, such as rows 5, 7, and 16, the team determined that no action was necessary. In each of these cases, the team's company was the leader in terms of customer competitive evaluation, and there were no complaints. There are cases in which the overall customer competitive evaluation, is high but there are a few random complaints. In such situations, the team may make a note to investigate the complaint.

These investigations sometimes reveal problems that are related to a small segment of the population and to special circumstances. A door chime may not be loud enough for a hearing-impaired person. A lever may be too difficult to operate for certain elderly people. Sometimes the complainant has an idea about a product improvement that they would like to see. Therefore, it may be valuable to investigate any customer complaints on voices where the competitive evaluation is good. Insight may be gained about simple improvements to the product that could represent sales points.

Examination of Figure 6.2 shows the following determinations for rows 1 through 10. Items in rows 11 through 16 are similar.

- Row 1: The QFD company is in a catch-up position with three complaints. The best company is only judged as a 3 (of 5), so there is also an opportunity. The presence of complaints reinforces the need to respond to the customers' voice. The team believes new concepts should be explored.
- Row 2: The QFD company is in a catch-up position. Because of the close linkage between the customer requirements for a cool cup and coffee that stays hot, the team believes row 2 can be resolved through work on row 1.
- Row 3: There is a competitive advantage to be gained here. Neither company is good in the customers' view, and complaints have been received.
- Row 9: The competitor is doing well in the customers' eyes, and the QFD company is doing very poorly. There have been complaints. The solution may be as simple as examining the competitor's cup/lid combination for ideas.
- Row 10: This appears to represent another competitive opportunity. Different concepts should be explored.

## Establishing Priorities

Some organizations add information to the customer portion of the matrix to help them in their analysis and in setting priorities. Figure 6.3 illustrates a typical approach.

The first column on the right is entitled "Goal." It is used to record the results of the team's judgment concerning the customer satisfaction goals for the new product. For example, in row 1, the goal of 4.5 means that the team believes its company should strive to improve this requirement so that the customers' evaluation of the new product would average 4.5 on the 1 to 5 scale. The current product is rated as a 2 by customers. Some companies use the term "planned quality" to describe this process of establishing goals.

In many organizations, there is inherent danger in using a column for goals. Some managers still have a mindset that to establish a target less than maximum represents some form of weakness for the organization. If the organization's personality is such

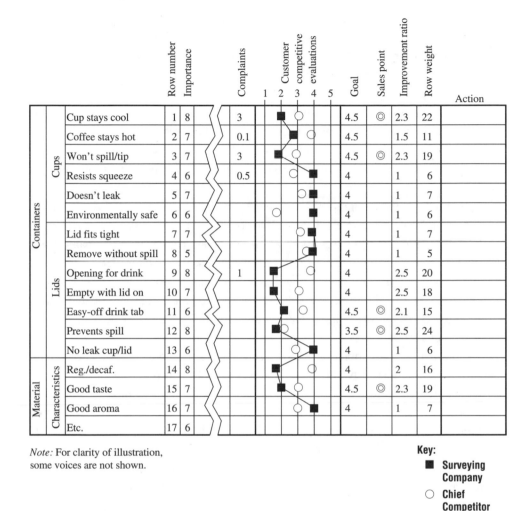

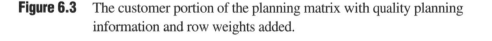

*Note:* For clarity of illustration, some voices are not shown.

**Key:**
- ■ Surveying Company
- ○ Chief Competitor

**Figure 6.3**   The customer portion of the planning matrix with quality planning information and row weights added.

that establishing any goal less than 5 would be judged as improper, then there is no value in using this column. If the organization is tolerant of realistic goal setting, then goals such as those shown in the illustration can be established.

The next column is for "sales points." This should be used to highlight those rows in which action to improve the product can provide a competitive edge. In these cases, the company can advertise this competitive edge. The advertising should have a significant effect because these items had high levels of importance coupled with current low to moderate customer competitive evaluations. An arbitrary weight can be assigned to the presence of a sales point and used in calculation of the final column, row weight.

The next column, "Improvement ratio," is a calculated measure representing the scope of the improvement required to achieve the goal shown in the first column. A number of approaches can be taken to calculate this factor. One common approach is represented in Figure 6.3. For example, in row 1, a goal of 4.5 was established. With a current customer evaluation level of 2, the improvement ratio is 4.5 divided by 2, or 2.25. In several cases, such as rows 4 through 8, the goal represents the current level of customer evaluation and the ratio is shown as 1, meaning that no further improvement action is required.

This method produces ratios that indicate that it is harder to improve from low levels of rating than from higher levels. This tends to conflict with the inherent sense of logic of most teams. For example, if the current customer evaluation places your company at level 2 and the team wishes to move this to a level 4, the ratio is 4 divided by 2, or 2. If the customer evaluation is a 3 and the team wishes to move the company to a 5, the ratio is 5 divided by 3, or 1.67. Most people believe it would be harder for a company to move from a 3 to a 5 in customer opinion than to move from a 2 to a 4. The calculations do not agree with this sense of logic.

A number of other approaches have been tried to compensate for this condition. One approach is to simply subtract the current level from the goal. This treats all changes equally regardless of where they occur on customer evaluation scale. The problem with this approach is that when no change is necessary, the difference becomes zero. If this ratio (or value) is to be used to help calculate a row weight, the presence of a zero creates major problems.

Other approaches have met with similar problems. It is suggested that teams recognize that this approach will introduce some distortion. *This is not of major significance if the team continues to recognize that these calculations of goals, ratios, and row weights are simply to help in the decision process. They are not a substitute for common sense. They are not algorithms that replace judgment. They are simply aids in the decision process.*

The final column, "Row weight," is the product of three columns: the customer level of importance, sales points, and the improvement ratio. In this case, the presence of a sales point was assigned 1.2 as an arbitrary weight. Thus, in row 1, the row weight was determined to be 8 times 1.2 times 2.3, or 22.08, which was rounded off to 22.

These row weights can help an organization evaluate the relative significance of rows. They can assist a team by lending some quantitative value to use in conjunction with judgments about competitive evaluations, complaints, and other data, such as marketing and sales trends, and changing societal issues and demographics.

Figure 6.4 shows the coffee customer matrix with row weights and a completed action column. In this case, the actions were coded as shown in the lower portion of the matrix. Three categories were chosen:

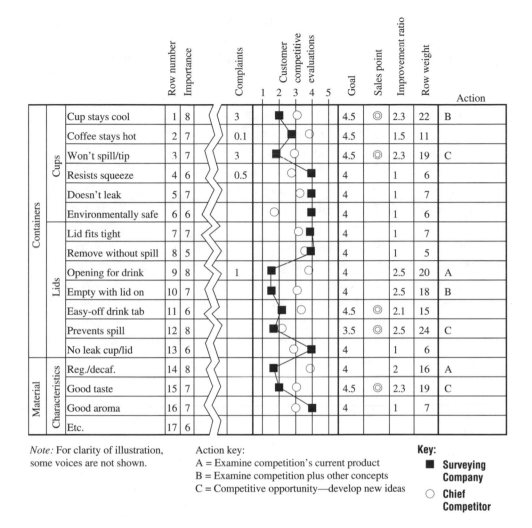

| | | | Row number | Importance | | Complaints | Customer competitive evaluations 1 2 3 4 5 | | | | Goal | Sales point | Improvement ratio | Row weight | Action |
|---|---|---|---|---|---|---|---|---|---|---|---|---|---|---|---|
| Containers | Cups | Cup stays cool | 1 | 8 | | 3 | | | | | 4.5 | ◎ | 2.3 | 22 | B |
| | | Coffee stays hot | 2 | 7 | | 0.1 | | | | | 4.5 | | 1.5 | 11 | |
| | | Won't spill/tip | 3 | 7 | | 3 | | | | | 4.5 | ◎ | 2.3 | 19 | C |
| | | Resists squeeze | 4 | 6 | | 0.5 | | | | | 4 | | 1 | 6 | |
| | | Doesn't leak | 5 | 7 | | | | | | | 4 | | 1 | 7 | |
| | | Environmentally safe | 6 | 6 | | | | | | | 4 | | 1 | 6 | |
| | Lids | Lid fits tight | 7 | 7 | | | | | | | 4 | | 1 | 7 | |
| | | Remove without spill | 8 | 5 | | | | | | | 4 | | 1 | 5 | |
| | | Opening for drink | 9 | 8 | | 1 | | | | | 4 | | 2.5 | 20 | A |
| | | Empty with lid on | 10 | 7 | | | | | | | 4 | | 2.5 | 18 | B |
| | | Easy-off drink tab | 11 | 6 | | | | | | | 4.5 | ◎ | 2.1 | 15 | |
| | | Prevents spill | 12 | 8 | | | | | | | 3.5 | ◎ | 2.5 | 24 | C |
| | | No leak cup/lid | 13 | 6 | | | | | | | 4 | | 1 | 6 | |
| Material | Characteristics | Reg./decaf. | 14 | 8 | | | | | | | 4 | | 2 | 16 | A |
| | | Good taste | 15 | 7 | | | | | | | 4.5 | ◎ | 2.3 | 19 | C |
| | | Good aroma | 16 | 7 | | | | | | | 4 | | 1 | 7 | |
| | | Etc. | 17 | 6 | | | | | | | | | | | |

*Note:* For clarity of illustration, some voices are not shown.

Action key:
A = Examine competition's current product
B = Examine competition plus other concepts
C = Competitive opportunity—develop new ideas

Key:
■ **Surveying Company**
○ **Chief Competitor**

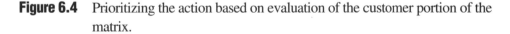

**Figure 6.4**   Prioritizing the action based on evaluation of the customer portion of the matrix.

- Category A designates an item for which the first step would be to examine the competitor's product for ideas because the competitor has a significant current lead in the customers' eyes.
- Category B designates those items for which the competition has a minor lead. The competitor's product should be examined first. This should be followed by development of a number of concepts for evaluation and synthesis to develop the best idea.
- Category C is for items for which there is a competitive opportunity. No company has a significant lead, and new ideas and concepts should be explored.

These categories are in order of increasing difficulty. Category A would be the easiest, and category C the hardest. All of the designated items in the action column represent priorities for increasing customer satisfaction with the next generation of product.

This coding approach can help an organization when it is forced to balance proposed product improvements against resources. Items in category A may be easy to change by using the competitor's current product as a starting point. Category B items involve more resources. To properly work on a category B item, the organization should develop a number of concept proposals and use some concept evaluation method to synthesize a "best concept." The competitor's product can be used as a source of reference because the competitor has some superiority in the customers' eyes. Category C items are the most difficult. They are similar to category B items, but no advantage can be gained by examining competition.

Figure 6.5 shows both the customer and the technical portions of the coffee matrix. A decision column has been added that ranks the items to show the suggested order of action, with item 1 representing the first action item. These decisions must represent a team balance of issues such as the estimated time, cost, and human resources involved in working on the priority item. For example, items that simply involve examining the competitive product to determine a course of action take little time and few resources and can have major payback.

## Balancing Resources: Establishing Action Plans

All of the preceding determinations are made with the customer portion of the matrix. *Organizations do not usually work on customer voices. They work on technical requirements that represent the translations of the voices.* The next step, therefore, is to determine which technical requirements should be selected for action.

This is most easily represented by example. In the "Decision" column, the item chosen as a first priority is row 9 concerning the presence of a drink opening in the cup lid. This is a category A item and should be easily resolved by examining the competition's ideas and generating any obvious improvements. Examination of row 9 shows strong and moderate relationship symbols. The strong symbol is related to the technical requirement in column 13, "Drink opening area." The moderate symbol is related to the requirement in column 12, "Depth of the drink well to the rim." Both have targets that were based on a review of both the customers' competitive evaluations and the competitive technical assessments, as discussed in Chapter 5.

These two technical requirements should form the basis for the engineering examination of the action required to respond to the customers' voice. There is no additional information in columns 12 and 13 related to warranty, field expense, technical difficulty,

**Co-relationships**

**Direction of improvement**

**Technical requirements**

**Key:**
- ■ **Surveying Company**
- ○ **Chief Competitor**

**Customer requirements**

| Containers | | Customer requirement | Importance | | Temperature at hand | Fluid temp. loss over time | Tip force at top | Fluid loss vertical impact | Fluid loss horizontal impact | Indent/force relation | Puncture resistance | Porosity | Material life cycle impact | Cup/lid interference | Retention force | Depth drink well to rim | Drink opening area | Evacuate angle | Tab remove force | Complaints | Customer competitive evaluations 1 2 3 4 5 | Sales point | Row weight | Action | Decision |
|---|---|---|---|---|---|---|---|---|---|---|---|---|---|---|---|---|---|---|---|---|---|---|---|---|
| Containers | Cups | Cup stays cool | 1 | 8 | ◎ | ○ | | | | | | | | | | | | | | 3 | | ◎ | 22 | B | 3 |
| | | Coffee stays hot | 2 | 7 | ○ | ◎ | | | | | | | | | | | | | | 0.1 | | | 11 | | |
| | | Won't spill/tip | 3 | 7 | | | ◎ | ◎ | ◎ | ○ | | | | | | | | | | 3 | | ◎ | 19 | C | 4 |
| | | Resists squeeze | 4 | 6 | | | | | ◎ | ○ | | | | | | | | | | 0.5 | | | 6 | | |
| | | Doesn't leak | 5 | 7 | | △ | | | ○ | ◎ | ◎ | | | | | | | | | | | | 7 | | |
| | | Environmentally safe | 6 | 6 | | | | | | | | ◎ | | | | | | | | | | | 6 | | |
| | Lids | Lid fits tight | 7 | 7 | | | | △ | | | | ◎ | | | | | | | | | | 7 | | |
| | | Remove without spill | 8 | 5 | | | | ◎ | | | | ◎ | ◎ | | | | | | | | | 5 | | |
| | | Opening for drink | 9 | 8 | | | | | | | | ○ | ◎ | | | | | 1 | | | 20 | A | 1 |
| | | Empty with lid on | 10 | 7 | | | | | | | | ○ | ○ | ◎ | | | | | | | 18 | B | 5 |
| | | Easy-off drink tab | 11 | 6 | | | | | | | | | | | ◎ | | | | ◎ | | 15 | | |
| | | Prevents spill | 12 | 8 | | | | | | | | ○ | ◎ | ○ | | | | | ◎ | | 24 | C | 4 |
| | | No-leak cup/lid | 13 | 6 | | | | | | | ◎ | ◎ | | | | | | | | | 6 | | |
| Material | Characteristics | Reg./decaf. | 14 | 8 | | | | | | | | | | | | | | | | | 16 | A | 2 |
| | | Good taste | 15 | 7 | | | | | | | | | | | | | | | | ◎ | 19 | C | 6 |
| | | Good aroma | 16 | 7 | | | | | | | | | | | | | | | | | 7 | | |
| | | Etc. | 17 | 6 | | | | | | | | | | | | | | | | | | | |

**Competitive technical assessment**   5 4 3 2 1

**Operational goals/targets**

| | Temperature at hand | Fluid temp. loss over time | Tip force at top | Fluid loss vertical impact | Fluid loss horizontal impact | Indent/force relation | Puncture resistance | Porosity | Material life cycle impact | Cup/lid interference | Retention force | Depth drink well to rim | Drink opening area | Evacuate angle | Tab remove force |
|---|---|---|---|---|---|---|---|---|---|---|---|---|---|---|---|
| Operational goals/targets | 110° max. | 3 deg/min. | 0.5 pounds | zero | zero | 0.42 ratio | 0.8 pounds | meet test req. | to be determine | 0.020 inches | 7 ounces | 0.40 inches | 0.35 sq inches | 100°F | 3 oz. max. |
| Organization concerns | 2 | | | | | | | | 4 | | | | | | |
| Field experience — Freq | | | | | | | | | | | .3 | | | | |
| — $/case | | | | | | | | | | | .6 | | | | |
| Regulatory technical company issues — Environmentally OK | | | | | | | | ◎ | | | | | | | |
| — More cups/box | | | | | | | | | | | | | | | |
| Column weights | 93 | 87 | 70 | 63 | 63 | 134 | 118 | 63 | 54 | 162 | 123 | 117 | 117 | 53 | 54 |
| Column number | 1 | 2 | 3 | 4 | 5 | 6 | 7 | 8 | 9 | 10 | 11 | 12 | 13 | 14 | 15 |

**Action Key:**

**A =** Examine competitor's current product

**B =** Examine competition plus other concepts

**C =** Competitive opportunity— develop new ideas

*Note:* For clarity of illustration, some voices, technical requirements, and relationships are not shown.

**Figure 6.5**   Analyzing the matrix.

or other requirements. Examination of the co-relationship matrix shows that action to improve the lid for these technical requirements will not have an adverse effect on any other technical requirement. The basic task will be to investigate the leading competitor and to exercise some engineering creativity to create a drink opening in the lid that has the best area and the depth of well. If the QFD company is the manufacturer, these requirements will lead the way to lid design revisions. If the QFD company is a restaurant or fast-food organization, the technical requirements and targets become the issues for investigation of current product offerings by cup and lid manufacturers.

Row 1 is an example of a category B item in the "Decision" column. Two technical requirements are related to this customer voice: column 1, "Temperature at the hand," and column 2, "Fluid temperature loss over time." There is an organizational difficulty of level 2 for the temperature at the hand. Both items are negatively related to the technical requirement in column 9, "Material life cycle impact." The challenge to the organization is to work on these three technical requirements. The first obvious step is to examine the leading competitor's product for ideas on how it has achieved a higher vote of customer confidence. Other concepts should then be developed. All concepts should be evaluated in a systematic manner to narrow the investigation to an ultimate "best concept." One approach to this challenge will be examined in Chapter 7. If there is field service experience and expense for any of the selected technical requirements, this provides an additional impetus for the improved performance of the requirement(s).

Priority items should be determined with the customer matrix, as described above. The determination of which technical requirements to work on follows the selection of the priority items. It requires an examination of the relationships and co-relationships shown in the technical portion of the matrix. Bear in mind that the matrix is being examined to determine those items for which action will provide a significant increase in customer satisfaction. It is not necessary to work on a large number of items. Balance the resources available for product improvement against the team's judgment of the customer priorities. In some cases, it may make sense to concentrate on only a single high-priority item. As an illustration, the Kao Corporation in Japan decided that a key customer priority was a more highly-concentrated laundry detergent. Japanese apartments are small, and space is at a premium. The storage of large boxes of laundry detergent presented a major challenge. So Kao Corporation worked to develop a concentrated product that could be packaged in smaller, lighter containers. As reported in the *Wall Street Journal*, "Kao introduced a powerful detergent called Attack which quickly won a 30% stake in the Japanese markets....When Attack hit the shelves in 1987, P&G's share of the Japanese market fell to about 8% from more than 20%" (Swasy 1989: B6).

The column weights that are calculated during development of the QFD matrix *should not* be used to determine priority items. They represent an artificial number and do not consider key issues, such as customer competitive evaluations, complaints, sales points, or goals. If the column weight supports the selection of a technical requirement based on row-wise determinations, then that is a plus. As an example, note that the weight of 162 for column 10 (Figure 6.5) is the highest for all columns. However, when column 10 is examined vertically, the three strong symbols are related to rows that were not chosen based on the current level of customer evaluation and complaints. Thus, the choice of the technical requirement in column 10 as a priority item would not produce a significant impact on customer satisfaction. Column weights can have significant value in helping prioritize technical requirements that were chosen as a result of the selection of priority voices.

## Technical Specifications

The foregoing discussion has centered on the idea of using the matrix as a basis for selecting those customer requirements that should be given priority attention to improve the level of customer satisfaction. That should be the principal intent for the QFD product planning matrix. It gives the organization an opportunity to balance its product planning priorities against the resources available for the new product planning. Generally, the bottom line for most companies is that a number of customer requirements do not receive special attention due to resource constraints. Because the QFD matrix is such a valuable source of customer-related knowledge, good business practice would dictate that its use go beyond the priority determination stages.

One way to expand the impact of the QFD product planning matrix is to use it as a driver for the development of technical specifications. Through experience and analysis, most organizations have developed technical standards (specifications) for their products. Often, these standards do not effectively reflect the inputs of the ultimate customer because this information has been lacking in so many organizations.

The QFD matrix provides companies an opportunity to combine the inputs from their customer research with the normal inputs used in product (or service) planning. These can be used to generate a set of technical specifications and targets that reflect both the voice of the customer and the voice of the experienced organization.

Figure 6.6 illustrates this process. An abbreviated QFD matrix for a portable hand-held screwdriver is shown on the left. The customer requirements have been translated into technical requirements, and target values have been determined. In this case, they are labeled "Ideal target values." Some typical internal standards are shown on the far right of the illustration. These represent inputs from such areas as established design standards, internal manufacturing and company experience, and any regulatory concerns.

The ideal set of technical specifications for any organization is one that combines existing internal standards with those that are customer driven based on the QFD study. Inputs from both sources can be combined and evaluated as indicated. This is an excellent opportunity for team action. The inputs can be discussed and weighed, and a composite technical specification can be developed that reflects the interests of both the

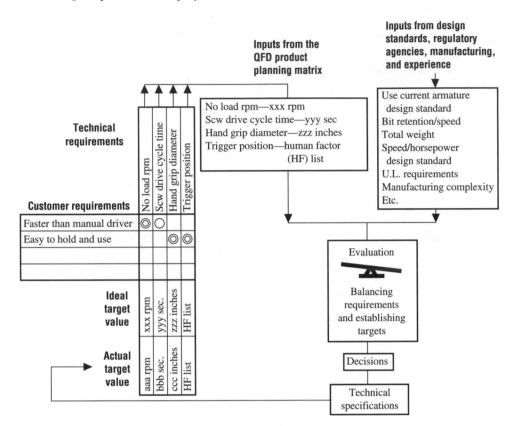

**Figure 6.6** Using the QFD technical requirements as inputs for the development of technical specifications.

customer and the organization. The targets should also be a part of this discussion. In many cases, when the target determination is based on this broader set of standards, experience, and knowledge, it becomes apparent that the QFD targets are not achievable in the short term. The targets that are established for the technical specifications, therefore, may not agree with those in the QFD matrix.

If this is the case, the QFD matrix can be altered to add rows so that the ideal (long-range) and the actual (short-term) targets can both be recorded. As the organization works on the priority items selected from the QFD matrix, its effort should lead to product changes that achieve the ideal target values. In this way, as priority items are chosen and product changes are made in response, the number of differences between ideal and short-term targets will decrease.

The above approach *ensures that all of the customer requirements developed during the QFD study have their impact on the technical specifications that the organization uses as a basis for its products.* Priority items selected from the QFD matrix receive special attention. Other items that are not chosen for priority attention have their impact on the organization's technical specifications. In this way, a company uses the QFD process to become customer driven.

In summary, the following key points are stressed relative to the analysis of the completed QFD matrix:

- The analysis to determine the priority items for improved customer satisfaction should be conducted using the customer portion of the matrix.
- The analysis should represent an integrated decision based on the customers' level of importance, their competitive evaluation, and any customer complaints. The decision process can be assisted by development of goals for improved customer satisfaction, determination of sales points, and improvement ratios.
- Once the priority items of customer concern are determined, the complete QFD matrix should be used to determine which technical requirements should be worked on to respond to the priority items.
- To ensure that all of the customer requirements affect the organization, some process or system should be considered that combines the customer and the company requirements. This can become the basis for the development of technical specifications for product development. Some of the target values that result from these discussions will differ from the ideal customer satisfying targets listed on the QFD matrix. This can be recorded through the addition of a set of rows for short-term targets. Disparities between short-term and ideal targets represent areas of challenge for product improvement.

# Deployment to Subsequent Levels: Part Deployment

*chapter seven*

For prime suppliers who sell their products directly to customers, the chief contribution of the QFD concept is in the product planning area. Every company needs to be in close contact with its customers. In today's world, technological developments coupled with the aggressive growth of many key countries on an international basis make competition extremely difficult. Knowledge of the customers' wants and needs is a prerequisite to effective competition. If the QFD concept is used only for product planning, it will measurably improve a company's opportunities for long-range survival and success. However, the QFD process can also be a valuable tool for planning at subsequent levels of the product's deployment: at the part, process, and manufacturing levels. This chapter and Chapters 8 and 9 will discuss the use of the QFD process as a planning tool that can be used in part, process, and manufacturing planning.

Anyone examining the QFD process for the first time will find that the development of a product planning matrix and the selection of priorities appear complex. The product planning matrix is the most complex matrix and requires considerably more information than the matrices used for part, process, and manufacturing planning. Completion of a product planning matrix requires the development of a number of pieces of information, such as the voice, the importance level, and engineering test data. By contrast, part and process matrices are simpler and easy to manage. Furthermore, everything that was learned relative to development of a product planning matrix is repeated for the part and process matrices. Thus, learning to use the matrix concept is much like learning to ride a bicycle. Once the product planning matrix is mastered, any remaining matrices follow the same pattern.

In the scenario for the coffee cup, assume that the company has a chain of take-out restaurants and also operates a manufacturing facility for the various paper products used by the chain of restaurants. The cups currently manufactured by the company are a paper product. Thus, the company is both a direct sales retailer and a first-tier supplier of materials. In this case, it is supplying cups to itself and others. Normally, a first-tier supplier does not have access to the customer who buys and drinks the coffee. Consequently, a typical first-tier supplier would not have the customer information that was used in the development of the matrix. The application of the QFD matrix to this supplier situation is discussed in Chapter 11.

## Determining the Inputs to the Matrix

The completed coffee cup matrix discussed in Chapter 6 is repeated here for illustration (Figure 7.1). In Chapter 6, one priority voice selected for discussion was "Cup stays cool." This voice will be used as an example in this chapter.

The technical requirements associated with this voice are "Temperature at hand" and "Fluid temperature loss over time." A negative co-relationship exists between these technical requirements and column 9, "Material life cycle impact."

After the priority items are determined, as described in Chapter 6, the organization must determine an action plan for these items. An organization can use a number of resource alternatives in planning its action. Most depend on the size of the organization, the complexity of the priority item, and existing organizational practices.

1. Responsible person: The responsibility can simply be delegated to the engineer or other person who is planning the product or service modification.
2. Special team: The responsibility can be delegated to a team for resolution. In large organizations, the team might consist of the persons responsible for the design, the testing, and the processing for manufacturing. In smaller organizations, it might simply be the product engineer and the test technician.
3. Problem solving team: The responsibility might be delegated to a cross-functional team that has experience in problem solving and normally processes concerns of this type.

Similarly, the organization may choose several process alternatives.

1. Brainstorming: A simple team approach of brainstorming and assignment of responsibilities may be elected.
2. Organizational process: Organizations that have a strongly ingrained process for design development or problem solving may elect to use it.

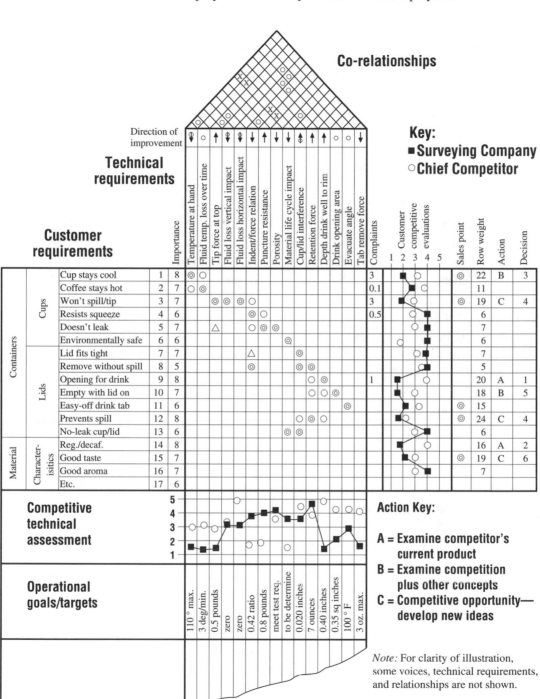

**Figure 7.1**    Determining priority items.

3. QFD process: Organizations that have used the QFD process for product planning and have developed an appreciation for the rigor it contributes to the planning process may elect to use it.

For purposes of illustration, it will be presumed that a cross-functional team has been selected to continue the deployment of the selected priority issues using the QFD process. Therefore, the next step is to transfer the selected technical requirements to a new matrix for part planning.

Figure 7.2 illustrates the idea of transferring the technical requirements to a new matrix. The three technical requirements selected during analysis of the product planning matrix are shown on the left side of the matrix. Note that these three items represented "hows" in the product planning matrix. In this matrix they become the input—the "whats." If the team decided to work on a second voice, its associated technical requirements would be transferred to a second new matrix.

A column for importance levels has been inserted into this matrix immediately to the right of these three "whats." The column weights were transferred from the product planning matrix. In this example, the three technical requirements being transferred had column weights of 93, 87, and 54 in the product planning matrix (Figure 7.1). To make these more manageable, they were divided by 10 and rounded to the closest whole number. For example, 93 became 9.3 when divided by 10, and 9 when rounded to the closest whole number.

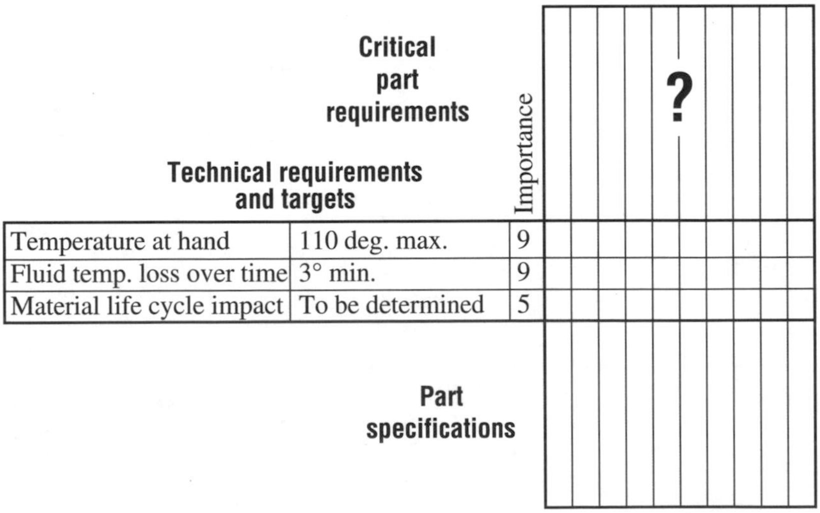
Critical part requirements
Technical requirements and targets
Importance
?
Temperature at hand
110 deg. max.
9
Fluid temp. loss over time
3° min.
9
Material life cycle impact
To be determined
5
Part specifications

**Figure 7.2** Technical requirements are transferred from the QFD planning matrix to a new matrix.

These column weights can be entered into the matrix and handled exactly like the importance numbers in the product planning matrix. In this manner, column weights can be determined for the part planning matrix and for the subsequent process planning matrix. There are differing schools of thought relative to this approach. Many companies believe that column weights are valuable in determining the priority issues. This can be especially true in the part and process planning matrices because there is no customer competitive evaluation or complaint data to examine. Thus the decisions about which "voice" or input needs the most attention cannot be made in the same way as in product planning. Column weights can be valuable in this respect. Other industries minimize the use of column weights for the product planning matrix and do not continue the practice beyond that matrix. It is their opinion that the transfer of these weights to successive matrices becomes an exercise in numbers and that the value of the numbers is diluted with each successive manipulation in each matrix. Furthermore, they believe that the determination of critical part and process requirements can be made more effectively by examining the density and type of relationship symbols in each column and combining this with their internal experience about the part and process.

Notice that this matrix format is much simpler than that of the product planning matrix. It contains only the four parts of a basic matrix: the whats, the hows, the relationships, and how much.

The figure shows a question mark in the area of the part requirements (hows). This illustrates the idea that *these requirements cannot be determined until the design concept is established*. For example, the part requirements for the coffee cup would be far different for a paper product with a handle than for a molded Styrofoam cup. Part requirements for the paper cup would involve material, blank size, and adhesives, while those for the Styrofoam cup would involve material, wall thickness, and molded density. Thus, the question mark in the illustration signifies that the next step in this process is to determine the best design concept for satisfying the customers' voice.

## The Need for a Concept Selection Process

Historically, many organizations have not utilized a specific process for concept evaluation and selection. The task was left to the product engineer, who may have worked out a couple of alternatives for the product, selected one, and begun the task of building prototypes and testing and revising the design. This process of building, testing, and correcting works until the clock runs out. At that point, the design usually still has flaws, but production must start. This is a costly process that does not lead to customer satisfaction.

Most companies can look back on their own experience and justify the need to use a more rigorous concept evaluation and selection process. Several studies have also shown the major impact that the design concept selection and planning has on an organization's costs and manufacturing difficulties. In his article "Quality by Design," Robert Chapman Wood reported

> Excellence in design—especially the first stages of design when engineers outline the essentials of a product—offers any business its most fundamental opportunity to achieve quality at low cost. One study by the U.K. firm British Aerospace suggests that decisions made in the first 5 percent of any design effort determine 85 percent of a product's quality, cost, and manufacturability. (Wood 1988: 22–27)

Daniel E. Whitney, in an article in the *Harvard Business Review,* reported

> According to General Motors executives, 70% of the cost of manufacturing truck transmissions is determined in the design stage. A study at Rolls-Royce reveals that design determines 80% of the final production costs of 2000 components. (Whitney 1988: 83–91)

A study of computer chip engineering practices established that designers invariably worked out an initial concept and developed a prototype. The concept was then tested, and changes were made to correct for test deficiencies. This action of building prototypes, testing them, and changing them to correct for deficiencies became an iterative process that continued into and through the start of production. Multiple concepts were not considered for evaluation in a concept selection process.

These examples are supported by other studies that emphasize the major impact that the design effort has on subsequent costs and operational difficulties. They reinforce the discussion in Chapter 1 about proactive organizations that plan carefully and reactive ones that tend to use the prototype, test, correct cycle. In light of these facts, it would seem wise to use the QFD planning concept in conjunction with engineering and analytical tools designed to promote more effective planning.

## A Concept Selection Process

The QFD process does not dictate use of a specific design concept selection process or even that a process be followed. Good business judgment, however, would dictate the use of some organized process.

Several techniques can be used effectively for concept evaluation. In all cases, the basic approach is to establish the criteria against which various product proposals are evaluated. This set of criteria should evolve from the knowledge of the customer (from

QFD) coupled with the knowledge and experience of the organization. A number of design alternatives are developed that are aimed at satisfying the criteria. The concepts are then compared with the criteria and evaluated. The discussion of these evaluations should lead to a synergy from which a best concept can be synthesized and developed.

In their book *The New Rational Manager,* Charles H. Kepner and Benjamin B. Tregoe describe one approach in the chapter "Decision Analysis." "We divide the objectives into two categories: MUSTS and WANTS. The MUST objectives are mandatory; they *must* be achieved to guarantee a successful decision....All other objectives are categorized as WANTS. The alternatives we generate will be judged on the *relative* performance against WANT objectives, not on whether they fulfill them" (Kepner, Tregoe 1981: 83–102).

Many companies use methods based on the precepts of the Kepner-Tregoe decision analysis approach. The product criteria are divided into two categories: musts and wants. Those criteria that are absolutes—*that must be present to satisfy the customer—* are listed as musts. Other criteria that are "nice but not necessary" are listed as wants. Each concept is compared against the musts and wants. The concept *must* satisfy every criteria listed as a must. If it does not, it is not an acceptable concept. Changes must be proposed to allow it to satisfy every must.

Wants are normally assigned weights to help in the decision process; a 1 to 10 scale is commonly used. When a concept is compared with the wants, judgments are made concerning the extent to which the concept satisfies the want. This "score" is assigned using a scale (such as from 1 to 10). The weight assigned to the want is then multiplied by the score assigned to the want to develop a weighted value. These weighted values can be added and used as a method to evaluate the ability of a concept to meet the wants. If a product appears to satisfy most of the want criteria, then its areas of weaknesses can be examined by exploring other concepts that may have performed well in these areas. This process of "synthesizing" usually leads to a concept that differs from the original ideas but contains the best of several concepts and emerges as a best concept.

Another approach is that recommended by Stuart Pugh of the University of Strathclyde, Scotland. The basic steps in this approach are described below:

1. Develop a set of criteria based on knowledge of the customers' wants and needs.
2. Enhance these customer-based criteria by including any items of a functional nature. Also include concerns from the organization based on experience and knowledge of similar products.
3. Develop a group of design concepts that are aimed at satisfying the criteria.
4. Using a matrix format, list the criteria on the left and the concepts across the top of the matrix. Use simple line sketches to illustrate each of the concepts.
5. Select one of the concepts as a datum against which all other concepts will be compared.

6. Evaluate each concept against the datum for each of the criteria. Determine whether it is better (+), worse (-), or the same (S).
7. Record the team decisions (+, -, S) on the matrix.
8. For each column, determine the total number of pluses, minuses, and sames.
9. Work to improve those concepts that scored best by incorporating strong ideas from other concepts.
10. Continue the process of synthesizing concepts. Rerun the analysis several times with the synthesized concepts.

The number of criteria should be limited: 20 is suggested as a maximum. Many concepts should be generated, not just a few. The idea is to get a number of ideas for evaluation and discussion because synthesis from a large pool of ideas will normally be more productive than from a small group.

Any one of the concepts can be selected as a "datum." Frequently, teams use the existing design for this purpose. Steps 6 through 8 involve the actual comparison process. Each concept is compared to the datum. The team should *work across each row,* comparing each of the concept proposals to the criteria in that row. Each concept is judged either better than the datum (+), worse than the datum (-), or the same as the datum (S). These are judgments based on experience, engineering, and manufacturing knowledge. *No weights are used.* The symbols (+, -, and S) are used to record the judgments. The symbol totals for each column are determined. The last two steps discuss the process of synthesis. The first usual action is to determine those columns (design concepts) that have the most pluses. The negatives for these concepts are then examined versus other concepts that were judged positive for the criteria. The team determines if there are aspects of the concept with the pluses that can be utilized to overcome negatives. The process is continued through many stages.

For example, if 20 concepts were examined, three might appear to be the best based on the number of pluses. Each of these three "best" concepts would be examined. Any minuses indicate that the concept was judged weak for certain criteria. Other concepts may have been judged positive for those same criteria. The team seeks to make changes to the "best" concepts by adopting ideas from other concepts that were judged better for a specific criteria. The end product of this examination might be three new concepts, similar to the originals but containing changes to overcome minuses. During the discussion, a new idea often emerges. The three concepts, plus any new ideas, would move to a new matrix and the process would be repeated. Through several iterations of this selection process, a best design is synthesized and determined.

Figure 7.3 shows a typical list of criteria that a team might consider for satisfying the customers' voice "Cup stays cool." *If the team decided to work on more than one voice, the concept selection process criteria should be designed to include consideration for all the voices.* Otherwise, the concept selected might satisfy some but not all of the

**Cup functional requirements**

Hold liquid (porosity) ✓
Fit hand
Restrict spill
Retain temperature (Temperature loss over time) * ✓

**Manufacturing requirements**

Minimum number of pieces (No. of pieces) ✓
Minimum number of operations (Manufacturing complexity) ✓
Recyclability of trim, scrap (Recycling of plant offal) ✓

**Restaurant concerns**

Ease of handling/use (Ease of use for customer) ✓
Safe to handle (Outside cup temperature) ✓
Logo capability
Storage space (No. of cups in standard stack) ✓
Cost
Impact on taste of coffee (Cup has taste impact) ✓

**Customer concerns from QFD**

Temperature at hand *  ✓
Material life cycle impact * ✓
Indentation force (Indent force) ✓
Set force ✓
Fluid integrity (Porosity) ✓
Temperature loss over time ✓

**Society**

Litter

**Key:**

\* Priority requirement from QFD matrix
✓ Selected item for concept analysis

**Figure 7.3**    Examining requirements for concept analysis.

selected priority items. These criteria have different origins: some are functional, some originate with manufacturing, and some represent other customers in the chain, such as a restaurant and its personnel. Using this list, the team can examine the items and judge which it believes should be used as criteria. The checkmarks indicate the criteria that would most likely be selected for the concept analysis. Some of these, such as "Litter," are valid concerns and should be part of the overall cup requirements. However, "Litter" has no apparent relationship to the temperature of the cup at the hand. Similarly, cost was not used as a criterion because it is impossible to develop quick estimates of the cost of the various concepts with any accuracy. Factors such as "Number of pieces" and "Number of operations" can be used to provide a cost estimate.

Figure 7.4 shows an example of a Pugh concept selection matrix. The selected criteria are listed at left, and six concepts are listed across the top. Simple sketches of each concept are shown. This is to avoid any misunderstanding about what the concept is. While doing the analysis, the team needs to avoid the distraction of having to constantly refer to some auxiliary notes to remind it of the concept it is examining. The Pugh concept selection process is not intended to be a micrometer. Teams frequently

| Concepts / Requirements | Current paper  | Styro-foam  | Rigid injection mold plastic  | Double-wall plastic 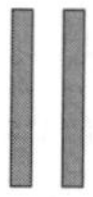 | Paper fold-out handle 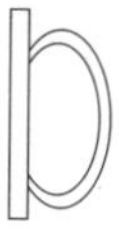 | Paper core stock 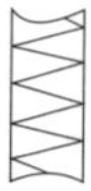 |
|---|---|---|---|---|---|---|
| 1. Temperature at hand | Datum | + | + | + | + | + |
| 2. Outside cup temperature | | + | – | + | S | + |
| 3. Material life cycle impact | | + | + | + | S | – |
| 4. Indent force | | + | + | S | S | + |
| 5. Set force | | + | + | + | S | + |
| 6. Porosity | | + | + | + | S | – |
| 7. Number of pieces | | + | + | S | – | S |
| 8. Manufacturing complexity | | + | + | S | – | – |
| 9. No. of cups in standard stack | | – | – | – | – | – |
| 10. Ease of use for customer | | S | – | S | – | S |
| 11. Cup has taste impact | | + | + | + | S | S |
| 12. Recycling of plant offal | | + | + | + | S | – |
| 13. Temperature loss over time | | + | – | + | S | + |
| **Totals** + | | 11 | 9 | 8 | 1 | 5 |
| – | | 1 | 4 | 1 | 4 | 5 |
| S | | 1 | 0 | 4 | 8 | 3 |

**Figure 7.4**    Using the Pugh concept selection process.

want to add weights or show double pluses to emphasize that one concept is better than another for a criterion. This is not recommended. The objective is simply to compare each concept to a datum. *In a thorough Pugh study, the datum should be changed several times to permit a more comprehensive examination of the concepts.*

In this study, the Styrofoam construction has 11 pluses and one minus. It is the "best" concept among these six ideas. The next closest concept is the rigid injection molded cup with handle with nine pluses and four minuses. The criteria "Number of cups in standard stack" was the only minus for the Styrofoam construction. The team's first action should be to examine this minus and to explore whether it can be changed to a plus. Examination of the row for this criteria quickly reveals that no cups have pluses in this row. No ideas can be generated by examining other cups. Thus, there is no other concept from which a good idea for solution can be extracted. This emphasizes the value of having a large number of concept proposals in the matrix. If there were 15 to 25 concept proposals, it is possible that some of these would have received pluses and could be used to generate ideas for improvement of the "best" concept. If no ideas for improvement emerge, this cup concept may be the best concept, and the one negative feature will have to be accepted. This is a simple example for illustration only. As mentioned, the datum should be switched several times, and the concepts should be reexamined. The differing datums may reveal some additional insights into the design concept. Similarly, there should be a much larger number of proposals for comparison.

Figure 7.5 shows a partial example of the "must/want" approach to concept selection. Seven criteria were chosen as musts. Another six were chosen as wants. Weights are assigned to the wants to indicate the team's judgment of their relative importance. Note that on a scale of 1 to 10, the team assigned a 9 to manufacturing complexity and a 5 to the number of cups in a stack. A judgment was made of the relative capability of each concept for each want, and a score was assigned. For example, for the Styrofoam concept and for "Number of pieces" (item 8), the team assigned a score of 10. In determining the total for the column, the row entry of 10 would be multiplied by the row weight of 8 for a value of 80. This is exactly the same process used to determine QFD matrix column weights where the customers' level of importance is multiplied by the weight assigned to the relationship symbol. Note that the Styrofoam cup has all yeses (Y) and has the highest numerical score of the three concepts shown, reflecting the same general pattern of the Pugh analysis.

For purposes of this illustration, the concept selection process will not be pursued beyond these simple examples. It will be assumed that the Styrofoam cup emerged from the analysis as the best concept.

The selected product concept involves the use of polystyrene beads that can expand two to 50 times their original size. Beads are preexpanded by exposing them to steam in a chamber. The expansion rate is controlled by the temperature, feed rate, or time in chamber and steam pressure. Expanded beads are conveyed to a storage

| Concepts<br><br><br><br><br>Requirements | Current paper | Styro-foam | Rigid injection mold plastic | Double-wall plastic | Paper fold-out handle | Paper core stock |
|---|---|---|---|---|---|---|
| **Musts** | | | | | | |
| 1. Temperature at hand | N | Y | Y | | | |
| 2. Indent force | Y | Y | Y | | | |
| 3. Set force | N | Y | Y | | | |
| 4. Porosity | N | Y | Y | | | |
| 5. Cup has taste impact | N | Y | Y | | | |
| 6. Recycling of plant offal | N | Y | Y | | | |
| 7. Outside cup temperature | N | Y | Y | | | |

| | Weight | Rating | Wt. x Ring | Rating | Wt. x Ring | Rating | Wt. x Ring | | | |
|---|---|---|---|---|---|---|---|---|---|---|
| **Musts** | | | | | | | | | | |
| 8. Number of pieces | 8 | 7 | 56 | 10 | 80 | 10 | 80 | | | |
| 9. Manufacturing complexity | 9 | 6 | 63 | 9 | 81 | 9 | 81 | | | |
| 10. No. of cups in standard stack | 5 | 10 | 50 | 6 | 30 | 1 | 5 | | | |
| 11. Ease of use for customer | 6 | 7 | 42 | 8 | 48 | 6 | 36 | | | |
| 12. Temperature loss over time | 7 | 5 | 35 | 10 | 70 | 6 | 42 | | | |
| 13. Material life cycle impact | 8 | 6 | 48 | 8 | 64 | 7 | 64 | | | |
| **Wants totals** | | | 294 | | 373 | | 308 | | | |

**Figure 7.5**    Using the must/want approach for concept selection.

area. They are retained there usually for 3 to 12 hours to help them reach equilibrium. They are then moved to the dies by air-conveying systems. The molds are filled with the desired amount of material. Steam is admitted through holes in the mold, forcing the beads to further expand and fill the mold cavity. The mold is cooled with water until the part stabilizes. The part is then ejected.

The issue of material life cycle impact is critical. The increasing emphasis on environmental impacts and recycling possibilities must be considered with any new product. The concern must be for total environmental impact. A model to examine impact should be determined for each of the promising concepts to provide documentation of the rationale for the decision. Figure 7.6 is a table from a study reported in the *Wall Street Journal* that considers the total impact on the environment throughout the life

### Paper vs. foam

• Environmental costs of producing and disposing of 10,000 cups

| | | Polystyrene | Wax-Coated Paper |
|---|---|---|---|
| **Energy** | Millions of BTUs | 5.50 | 8.78 |
| **Solid Waste** | Weight in pounds | 96.9 | 287.9 |
| | Volume in cubic yards | 0.54 | 0.36 |
| **Selected Air Pollutants (in pounds)** | Particulates | 0.8 | 4.0 |
| | Nitrogen Oxides | 1.6 | 4.6 |
| | Hydrocarbons | 5.7 | 2.4 |
| | Sulfur Oxides | 2.6 | 8.6 |
| | Carbon Monoxide | 0.8 | 1.8 |
| **Selected Air Pollutants (in pounds)** | Dissolved Solids | 1.4 | 1.7 |
| | Suspended Solids | 0.2 | 1.1 |
| | Acid | 0.2 | 0.9 |

Reprinted by permission of the *Wall Street Journal*, Thursday, February 28, 1991. Dow Jones & Company, Inc. All Rights Reserved Worldwide.

**Figure 7.6**   Life cycle impact.

cycle of the material and the product. This analysis indicates that Styrofoam is generally superior to the existing paper product (Stipp 1989: B1, B4).

Once the product concept has been determined, the next logical step is to generate a bill of materials (or recipe) depending on the industry terminology. In this example, there is a single product—the cup—and a single material—the polystyrene beads. A more typical product at this stage would have several parts, not all of which would be of the same material.

At this point, it is possible to move back to the matrix (Figure 7.2) and to begin to fill in the critical part requirements for the selected best-design concept. The collective experience of the team members and any specialists can be used to determine these critical requirements. Different organizations use terminology that is familiar to them rather than the term "critical part requirements." Terms such as "critical part characteristics," "key product characteristics," and "critical criteria requirements" are typical. In most companies, these are the requirements that are believed to be most likely to vary in production and whose variation may significantly impact customer satisfaction. While every dimension and specification on a product drawing is important, some require a greater level of attention; *these are the critical requirements.*

## Examining the Causes of Potential Failure

At this point, many organizations examine the proposed product from the viewpoint of its potential for failure. These failure analyses force the organization to think through the potential for failure and to plan for its control through the design requirements, the process controls, and product quality checks. There are two common approaches: failure mode and effects analysis (FMEA) and fault tree analysis (FTA). Either of these techniques can be used to examine the potential failures of the design and the process.

Both approaches follow the same basic concept. The functions of the product are expressed negatively. For example, one function of the cup is to "hold liquid." Expressed negatively, this would be "cup does not hold liquid." The team would then discuss the various ways that the cup might fail to hold liquid. The discussion should proceed from macroconcerns to more specific issues. The team may conduct a failure mode study, confining the potential failures to design concerns, a process failure mode study, or a combination of these two.

Figure 7.7 shows a generic *design* failure mode and effects analysis worksheet. Formats vary from organization to organization. A cup example is shown. The function of the part "to hold liquid" is examined to determine macrotypes of *design-oriented* failure modes. One such failure mode is "porosity." This mode is then examined to determine the possible ways the cup might develop porosity as a result of the design.

| Part | Function of part | Possible failure mode | Effect of failure | Cause of failure | Occurrence | Severity | Nondetect | Risk level | Action | Who | When |
|------|------------------|-----------------------|-------------------|------------------|------------|----------|-----------|------------|--------|-----|------|
| Cup | Hold liquid | Porosity | Leaks | Improper expansion of polystyrene beads | 1 | 5 | 2 | 10 | Specify expansion rate | K.J.S. | 9-12-92 |
| | | | | Inadequate amount of polystyrene material | 2 | 5 | 2 | 20 | Specify weight of material required for a cup Specify particle size | P.S. | 9-17-92 |

**Figure 7.7**    Design failure modes and effects analysis worksheet.

One probable failure mode would be improper expansion of the beads. Another could be inadequate amount of material. Both of these characteristics should be covered by appropriate design requirements. This is shown in the action column, along with the responsibility and the completion date.

The risk assessment columns are provided for assessment of the probable effect of the failures using a 1 to 5 scale (with 5 indicating high level). The column "Occurrence" is for evaluation of the likelihood that the condition will occur. Severity is a measure of the seriousness of the consequences of the failure. "Non-detect" refers to the level of detection associated with the condition. A high level means that the fault could occur and it would not be immediately obvious by visual examination of the part. The "Risk level" is the product of the other three columns. Use of the risk assessment approach helps an organization weigh the relative importance of the potential failures.

The fault tree analysis (FTA) approach appeals to many teams because it appears to be a more structured approach than the FMEA method. As shown in Figure 7.8, FTA

## Symbols

A fault in a box indicates that it is the result of subsequent faults

"Or" symbol. Connects a preceding fault with a subsequent fault that could cause the failure

"And" symbol. Connects two or more faults that must occur simultaneously to cause the preceding fault

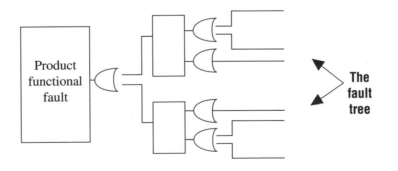

**Figure 7.8**    Fault tree analysis.

uses symbols to indicate faults and to indicate whether the failure is the result of either individual faults or the result of certain faults that occur simultaneously. The illustration at the bottom of the figure shows a typical format for an FTA.

Figure 7.9 shows an example of an FTA of the design-related failures for the coffee cup. It illustrates the process and the use of the symbols. The top branch of the top tree will be used as an example. The reverse function shown on the extreme left is "Cup doesn't hold liquid." This may be the result of two possible macrocauses: punctures or porosity. These are shown immediately to the right. The next step is to ask how these failures (punctures and porosity) could occur. If it were punctured, this might be the result of a high ratio between the deflection of the cup and the force applied. This could cause the cup to break or puncture under pressure from the hand or a cup holder.

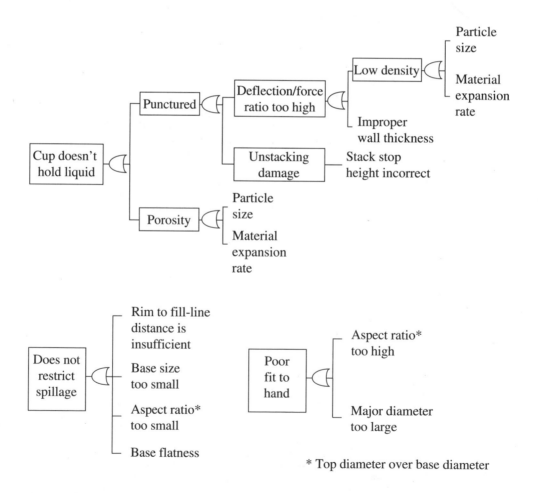

**Figure 7.9**    Using fault tree analysis to determine potential design concerns.

Another possible cause would be damage in the cup holder during the process of unstacking or pulling the cup from the holder. These two failure causes are listed to the right of the macrofailure "punctured." Each of these is then examined to question how they might occur. High deflection/force ratios could be the result of low density or a thin wall. These are listed, and the questioning process continues. Low density could be the result of improper particle size or material expansion rate. The items that are not in boxes and that are on the right side of the tree are the actual causes or mechanisms of failure. These items—particle size, expansion rate, and stack-stop height—must be properly specified on the part drawings to avoid these potential failures.

## Completing the Part Planning Matrix

Once the concept selection and failure analysis (FMEA or FTA) are complete, work can begin to complete the QFD part planning matrix. The part planning matrix shown in Figure 7.2 is repeated in Figure 7.10. "Material life cycle impact" was an entry in

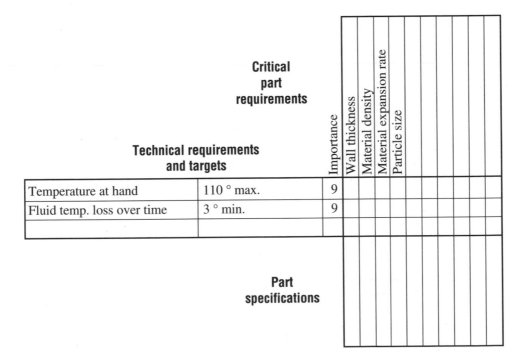

| Technical requirements and targets | | Importance | Wall thickness | Material density | Material expansion rate | Particle size | | | | |
|---|---|---|---|---|---|---|---|---|---|---|
| Temperature at hand | 110 ° max. | 9 | | | | | | | | |
| Fluid temp. loss over time | 3 ° min. | 9 | | | | | | | | |
| | | | | | | | | | | |

**Figure 7.10**   Part requirements are determined for the transferred technical
requirement(s).

the matrix (Figure 7.2) based on its co-relationship with the hand and coffee temperature issues. Note that this item no longer appears on the left side of the part planning matrix shown in Figure 7.10. It was eliminated from the matrix because the determination made during the Pugh analysis revealed Styrofoam to be superior to the current paper product.

The failure mechanisms determined in the FMEA or FTA can be used by a team in conjunction with its experience to determine the critical part requirements for the part planning matrix. From a design viewpoint, the issues of wall thickness, material density, material expansion rate, and particle size appear to be the major issues. These would be put in the matrix across the top, as shown in Figure 7.10. Each of the part requirements listed across the top of the matrix should answer the question "What are the elements we must control to ensure that the technical requirements (the inputs to this matrix) are met?"

When a new design concept is being examined by the team, its discussions will reveal a variety of issues. Ideas may emerge that could lead to exciting quality. Major concerns may arise. Opportunities may be present as a result of the change to a new material or new concept. Based on the team determinations, some of these issues could be added to the part matrix. In this case, the team was concerned that the polystyrene material needed control for the crush or squeeze resistance—something not historically considered as a variable in the paper cup. It also recognized that the process of applying logos to the cup was significantly different, and it was concerned about logo precision. Three new technical requirements were added to the part planning matrix to cover these concerns, as shown in Figure 7.11. This resulted in the addition of one new critical part requirement, "Logo definition."

In this part planning matrix, importance values were carried over from the previous matrix. When additional item are added as result of internal concerns, importance values must be determined for these. This is accomplished by comparing each of the internal issues against the technical requirements transferred from the previous matrix. In this example (Figure 7.11), the two transferred requirements each had weights of nine. An internal technical requirement such as "Indent/force relation" must be compared to these transferred items. The team must determine the weight it believes should be assigned to the indent/force relation by balancing its importance against the importance levels assigned to the transferred items. These are team judgments based on knowledge and experience. In the example shown, weights of 7, 4, and 6 were chosen for the three added items.

The QFD part planning matrix can be completed once the critical part requirements have been added across the top in response to the technical requirements on the left. The next step is to add the relationships and specifications, as shown in Figure 7.11. In the product planning matrix, the items "targets" or "goals" were used to described the team determinations for the levels of performance needed to satisfy the technical requirements. In the part and process planning matrices, these values no

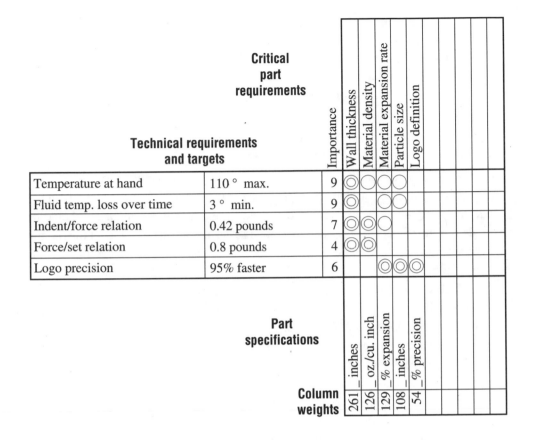

| Technical requirements and targets | | Importance | Wall thickness | Material density | Material expansion rate | Particle size | Logo definition | | | | |
|---|---|---|---|---|---|---|---|---|---|---|---|
| Temperature at hand | 110° max. | 9 | ◎ | ◎ | ○ | ○ | | | | | |
| Fluid temp. loss over time | 3° min. | 9 | ◎ | | ○ | ○ | | | | | |
| Indent/force relation | 0.42 pounds | 7 | ◎ | ◎ | ○ | | | | | | |
| Force/set relation | 0.8 pounds | 4 | ◎ | ○ | | | | | | | |
| Logo precision | 95% faster | 6 | | | ◎ | ◎ | ○ | | | | |
| Part specifications | | | _ inches | oz./cu. inch | _ % expansion | _ inches | _ % precision | | | | |
| Column weights | | | 261 | 126 | 129 | 108 | 54 | | | | |

**Figure 7.11**    Part requirements are determined for the transferred technical requirement(s).

longer represent "targets." Instead, they are specifications for the requirements listed in the top of the matrix. The four areas of the part matrix are as follows:

1. The "whats," which are the selected technical requirements from the part planning matrix that were transferred to this part planning matrix along with their targets. In addition, internal concerns may be added.
2. The "hows," the part requirements that are responses to the technical requirements. These are the characteristics that the part(s) must meet to satisfy the listed technical requirements. Customarily, only the "critical" requirements are listed. The objective is to list those requirements whose conformance is strongly related to the performance of the product.
3. "Relationships" between the technical requirements and the critical part requirements.

4. "How much," or the specifications for the "critical" part requirements. These are based on engineering knowledge and experience.

## Analyzing the Completed Matrix

The completed matrix should be evaluated by the team. During the product planning stage of the QFD process, the QFD team would have a typical membership of marketing, product planning, product engineering, and process and manufacturing personnel. The marketing or product planning representative will usually take a major role in the leadership. At least one member of the processing and manufacturing areas should be included. If the team decides to deploy certain selected items to a part level matrix, the constituency of the team will change. Product engineering will take on the role of leadership. The number of representatives from the marketing/product planning area will diminish. The number of people representing processing, manufacturing, and product assurance will increase.

Implicit in the selection of a best-design concept is concern for manufacturability. Issues such as the number of parts and operations are vital criteria in the concept selection process. Other criteria on operation complexity and variability can be added if sufficient knowledge exists for effective comparison. *The judgment concerning the best design concept must include concern for the best processing concept for part manufacture.* The team needs to be aware that its choice of a "best concept" must not be one that is unacceptable to the production organization. Thus, the team decision of the "best design concept" also includes a determination of the "best processing and manufacturing concept."

In an evaluation of the matrix, the concern is for how these critical requirements will be controlled in production. This is a judgment call by the team based largely on experience with similar products and knowledge of their variability. In the absence of internal experience, the team can obtain insight through discussion with other companies and specialists that are willing to share their knowledge.

If there are many requirements, the team may examine those that have the largest number of "strong" relationship symbols as a starting point. Factors such as experience and the likelihood of occurrence (risk) should be considered in the selection. The risk assessment area of the FMEA can be consulted as an aid. The column weights can be utilized to help in the decision process.

The final result is a determination of those requirements that should be given special attention during the processing of the part. In the example shown (Figure 7.11), the team might decide that wall thickness is die controlled and will be assured once the dies are inspected and approved. The four remaining requirements concern characteristics that can vary as a result of material or process variations. Because the company has never made Styrofoam cups, these would be logical selections for further study during examination of the processing.

In summary, the following are the key points presented in this chapter:

- A company can use a number of options for working on the product and the process for any selected priority voice.
- When the QFD process is selected as the method, the first step is to transfer the technical requirements associated with each selected priority voice to a new matrix, the part planning matrix. Generally, if more than one voice is selected, a new matrix will be used for each.
- The part planning matrix has four essential parts: the transferred requirements, the critical part requirements, the relationships, and the part specifications. Column weights can be added if desired.
- The critical part requirements cannot be determined until a design concept is chosen. It is strongly recommended that some organized concept selection process be used to determine the "best" design concept.
- Determination of "critical" part requirements is based on experience and knowledge. A organized approach such as FMEA or FTA is recommended to ensure that the issues of potential failure are fully explored.
- Once the best design concept has been selected and its potential failures have been listed, the part planning matrix can be completed.
- The completed matrix should be examined to determine those part requirements that are considered to be of concern in processing. These would be items that are liable to vary and, therefore, need process control. Generally, the best approach is to rely on the experience of the team members. Their judgment can be assisted by examination of the number of strong relationships in the columns, column weights, and the risk assessment in the FMEA.

# Deployment to Subsequent Levels: Process Deployment

*chapter eight*

At the completion of each matrix, the organization needs to determine the plan for the next level of deployment. Some of the most common options for this were reviewed in the introduction to Chapter 7. Priority items can be handled by special teams, by individuals, or by continuing the QFD team and process.

The primary objective of continuing the QFD process is to increase customer satisfaction. The principal aim of the product planning matrix is get the company in touch with its customers and to provide a framework for developing the information needed to make factual decisions about the priority issues of customer concern. The objective is not simply to continue the QFD process. Teams sometimes lose sight of this fact. They continue use of the QFD process when the situation might better be handled by another approach.

A second objective is to make sure that the responses to customer wants and needs flow down, or are deployed, through the organization. As they are deployed, they affect the product concept, the identification of critical part requirements, the process selection, the identification of critical process requirements, and the plans and instructions for manufacturing control. The result is that everyone in the organization is aware of the customers' wants and of the actions that the organization must take to ensure that those wants and needs are satisfied at every step of the product's development, manufacture, distribution, and service. The deployment or "flow down" does not have to be achieved using the QFD matrix concept. However, using the QFD methodology lends emphasis to the continuity of the process and helps link the customer and the organization.

In the example of the coffee cup, the critical part requirements identified from the part planning matrix will be deployed to a process planning matrix. The process planning matrix is like the part matrix. The selected requirements from the previous matrix become the input to the new process matrix. Other issues representing internal voices can be added. These would be processing concerns voiced by members of the organization based on their experience. The next step is to determine the critical process requirements. These are similar to the critical part requirements in the previous matrix. They are parameters that must be controlled to ensure that the part characteristics and the internal voices are satisfied. Relationships are then determined, and process specifications are established. The final step is to examine the process planning matrix to determine which items should be chosen as priority issues to be deployed to the next stage—manufacturing planning.

QFD part and process matrices can be valuable for suppliers. A first-tier supplier receives its requirements from a prime supplier that is its customer. The drawings and specifications furnished by the prime supplier are the customer's input to the first-tier supplier. In addition, a first-tier supplier can talk with the people who use and install its parts at the prime supplier's facility. This helps a supplier gain additional insight into the voice of its customer. A second-tier supplier has a somewhat similar relationship to the first-tier supplier to whom it supplies products or services. First-tier and second-tier suppliers are seldom involved in interviews with the final customer and will normally start their QFD process at either the part or the process deployment stages. For them, the QFD matrix is an orderly way to ensure that they have adequately responded to each input from their customers. It can serve as excellent documentation to share with their customers to indicate their intent to satisfy.

## Determining the Inputs to the Matrix

In Chapter 7, four critical part requirements were selected based on the organization's knowledge and experience with the proposed manufacturing process. These four characteristics would be transferred to a new matrix—the process planning matrix shown in Figure 8.1. The specifications would also be transferred. In this example, no numerical values are shown for the specifications; in actual practice, the organization would determine these during development of the part planning matrix.

The comparable matrix for part deployment had a question mark in the areas of the "hows." This was done to illustrate that the team could not proceed to determine critical characteristics until the design concept had been chosen. The process planning matrix is similar. The critical process requirements cannot be determined until the process is known.

| Critical part requirements & specifications | Critical process requirements | | | | | | | | | |
|---|---|---|---|---|---|---|---|---|---|---|
| Material density | oz./cu. inch | | | | | | | | | |
| Material expansion rate | % expansion | | | | | | | | | |
| Particle size | inches | | | | | | | | | |
| Logo definition | precision % | | | | | | | | | |

**Process specifications**

**Figure 8.1**    Selected part requirements are transferred to a process planning matrix.


## The Need for a Concept Selection Process

During development of the part planning matrix, the QFD team is involved in the discussion of both the design concept proposals and the processing associated with them. Methods such as the Pugh concept selection study force a team to consider both part and process concepts. Criteria such as the number of pieces and the number of operations force the organization to consider processing while examining design alternatives. Once the field narrows and the synthesis of several design proposals begins, the manufacturing people on the team have to examine the processes associated with the design concepts in greater detail. They may even use some form of Pugh or Trade Study format to compare the process concerns against processing proposals. The ultimate decision of the team must involve both the design concept and its processing. During the last decade, many U.S. industries have come to the realization that these two activities—design and processing—must work together rather than sequentially. They recognize that an excellent design concept created in isolation from processing considerations can be difficult or expensive to build and can have a number of variables that make manufacturing control difficult or impossible. For this reason, U.S. industry has changed the way the design and processing teams interact. Terms such as "simultaneous engineering" and "co-location of engineers" have become part of the language as companies move to change their processes to reduce functional rigidity and isolation.

The product of the "simultaneous engineering" concept is that the process should be well established at the point of design concept determination. Therefore, there should be no need for a separate study, at this point, to determine the best process for the product.

A first- or second-tier supplier developing a QFD matrix may *start with the process planning matrix*. In many cases, it will be using its existing process. In fact, its process ability may have caused the customer to select it in the first place. However, when the supplier may be considering revisions to the process, such as the use of increased automation, a Pugh comparison or similar approach should be considered for use.

Once the process has been determined, a process flow diagram should be developed. A typical example is shown in Figure 8.2. The symbols and level of detail vary among companies. Figure 8.2 shows use of three symbols for storage, operation, and inspection, as defined in the key in the lower right corner. The flow diagram lists the operation's steps, and the symbols indicate the nature of each step. This diagram delineates the verbal description of the polystyrene cup molding process summarized in Chapter 7. The flow diagram illustrated here is typical of that seen in many United States and Japanese factories, large and small.

## Determining the Critical Process Requirements

As in the part planning matrix, the critical requirements can be determined based on the experience within the organization. Typically, process engineers, problem-solving team members, and quality assurance people have experience with problems and complications associated with the process issues. Setup, maintenance, process variability, and up-time issues are typical areas of difficulty. The QFD team can use people from these areas as resources to help it determine the critical process requirements and specifications. The team should be strongly urged to include production operators who have had experience with the machines and processes on a daily basis.

The team should seriously consider documenting the results of these determinations. The documentation provides a history of the process. It can be used whenever the process is revisited. The results can be documented on the FMEA worksheet reviewed in Chapter 7. This is an excellent format for reporting the potential problems and listing the proposed solutions and responsibilities. It is also an excellent format for building a historical record and reporting the effects of ideas for continual improvement of the process.

For newer processes that represent more unknowns, the use of a failure analysis approach is even more valuable because it causes the organization to think about the

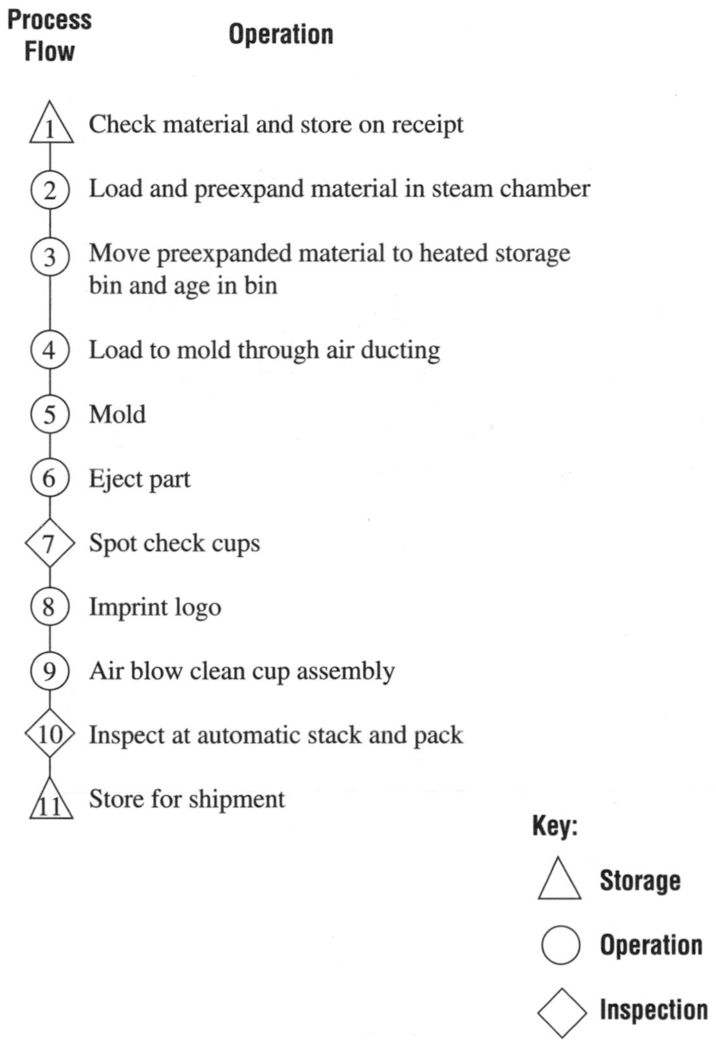

**Process
Flow**          **Operation**

1. Check material and store on receipt

2. Load and preexpand material in steam chamber

3. Move preexpanded material to heated storage
   bin and age in bin

4. Load to mold through air ducting

5. Mold

6. Eject part

7. Spot check cups

8. Imprint logo

9. Air blow clean cup assembly

10. Inspect at automatic stack and pack

11. Store for shipment

**Key:**

△ **Storage**

○ **Operation**

◇ **Inspection**

**Figure 8.2**    Process flow diagram for the molded polystyrene cup.

potential for failure. Either the FMEA or FTA approach discussed in Chapter 7 can be used effectively. In either case, the FMEA recording format is recommended. An example of this is shown in Figure 8.3. The examples shown in Chapter 7 were design-oriented failures; those shown here are process-oriented failures. Design failure modes were determined on the design FMEA discussed in Chapter 7. It is possible to use either FTA or FMEA to develop a listing of all possible failures for both design and processing. The failure mechanisms determined through this approach can be sorted

| Part | Function of part | Possible failure mode | Effect of failure | Cause of failure | Risk assessment | | | | Action | Responsibility | |
|------|------------------|----------------------|-------------------|------------------|-----------------|---|---|---|--------|----------------|---|
| | | | | | Occurrence | Severity | Not detect | Risk level | | Who | When |
| Cup | Hold liquid | Punctures | Leaks | Mechanical handling on cup line | 1 | 5 | 1 | 5 | Follow chute design standards. Leak test every 100th cup. Auto line shut down | G.H. | 2-12-93 |
| | | | | Carton damage in warehousing or transit | 1 | 5 | 2 | 10 | Investigate special forklift rack and package design | P.S. | 2-12-93 |
| | | | | Damage from cup dispenser | 1 | 5 | 1 | 5 | Initial sample approve check to include all commercial dispensers | B.L. | 3-15-93 |
| | | Squeezes too easily | Forces fluid out top or causes user to loosen grip on cup | Thin wall | 1 | 5 | 1 | 5 | Control through die approval | B.L. | 1-1-93 |
| | | | | Lack of density of material | 3 | 3 | 4 | 36 | Control material properties through supplier certification and receiving check | B.L. | 12-21-92 |
| | | | | Undersize particles | 2 | 2 | 3 | 12 | Put heat and time control on expanders | G.H. | 2-12-93 |

**Figure 8.3**    Process failure modes and effects analysis worksheet.

into those involving design and those involving processes and listed on separate worksheets. The worksheet in Figure 8.3 is a generic example. Worksheets should be tailored to fit an organization's needs.

The FMEA format lists the possible failure mechanisms and permits an assessment of their risk based on likelihood of occurrence, severity, and ease of detection. The QFD team can use this format to determine those failure mechanisms that it believes are a matter of serious concern—those that are critical. These critical failures can then be examined to determine the process elements that are responsible for their control. These can be listed in the action column of the worksheet. In Figure 8.3, for example, the second possible failure mode is "Squeezes too easily." Three failure causes (mechanisms) are shown: thin wall, lack of proper material density, and undersize particles. The team decided that the wall thickness would be determined by the die. The action would be to check out the die on its completion. Once approved, wall thickness would likely be ensured for the life of the die. By contrast, the lack of density and the possibility of undersize particles are things that can occur every time the process runs. The critical process requirements (actions) for these are shown in the action column. They involve supplier certification, receiving inspection of the material, and controls for heat and time in the expanding chamber. These critical process requirements can be transferred to the process planning matrix.

The process planning matrix is shown in Figure 8.4. Note that this differs from the part planning matrix across the top. A section has been added to show the process flow diagram and verbal description. This helps the team organize placement of the process requirements in the matrix by process step. It also helps the team talk through its experience in an organized manner, moving through the process step by step.

The critical process requirements are listed across the top of the matrix. In the product planning matrix, the design requirements responded to the question "What measurable items would we work on to satisfy this customer voice?" In the part planning matrix, the part requirements responded to the question "What are the elements we must control in the part to assure that the design requirements are met?" The process requirements respond to a similar question: "What are the elements we must control in manufacturing to assure that the part will meet its requirements?"

Not every process requirement is measurable in the sense that it can be evaluated with a measuring tool or gauge. Many process requirements involve conformance to a procedure. Some requirements simply involve inspections for conformance to an established standard. In the service industry, most process requirements involve conformance to some specified way of performing an operation, such as the steps involved in greeting and registering a guest at a hotel registration desk. Operations of this type are measured by monitoring or auditing the conformance to the procedure or the specification. In the coffee cup example, conformance to the process steps that represent inspections and

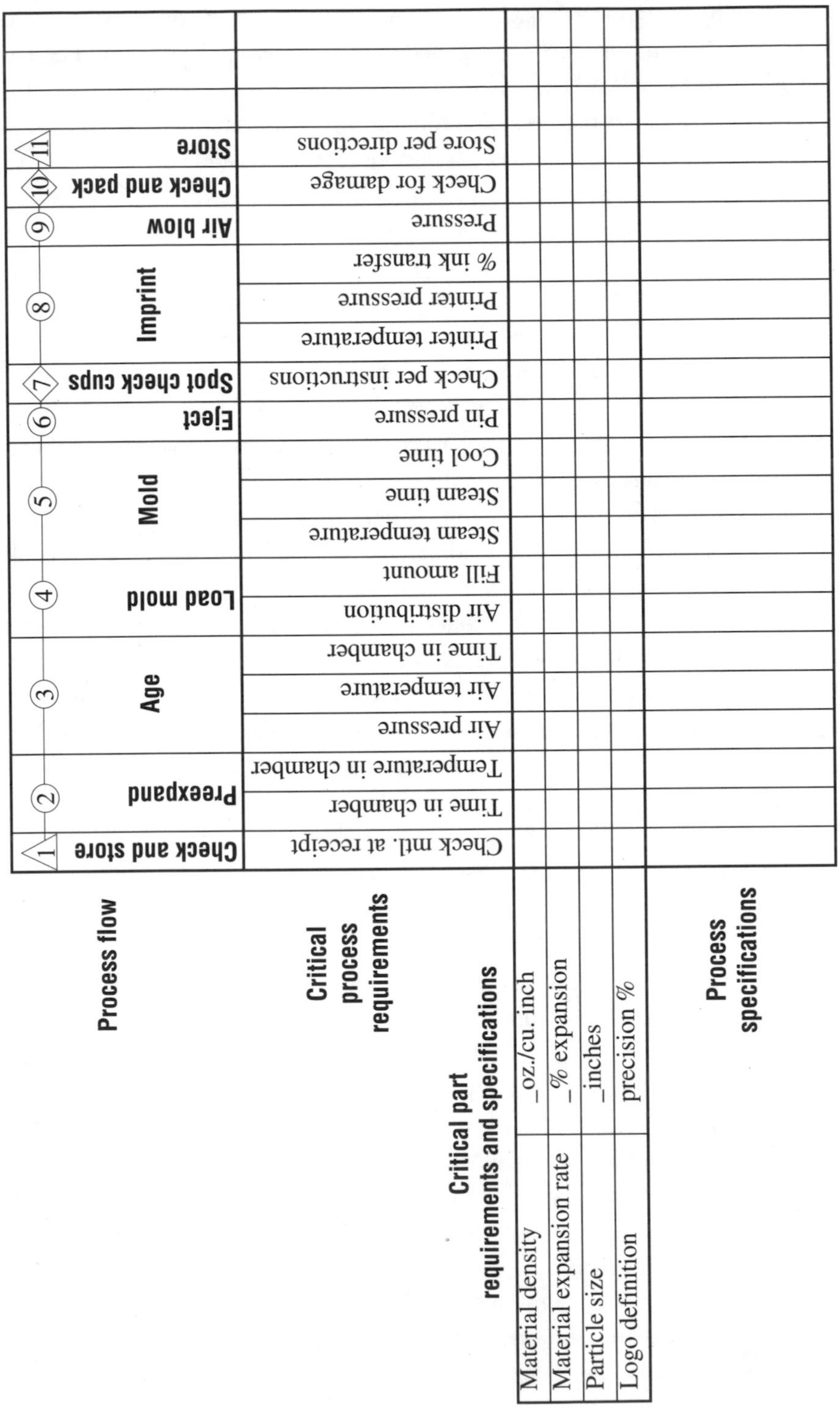

| Process flow | | Critical process requirements | Material density _oz./cu. inch | Material expansion rate _% expansion | Particle size _inches | Logo definition precision % | Process specifications |
|---|---|---|---|---|---|---|---|
| ① | Check and store | Check mtl. at receipt | | | | | |
| ② | Preexpand | Time in chamber | | | | | |
| | | Temperature in chamber | | | | | |
| ③ | Age | Air pressure | | | | | |
| | | Air temperature | | | | | |
| | | Time in chamber | | | | | |
| ④ | Load mold | Air distribution | | | | | |
| | | Fill amount | | | | | |
| ⑤ | Mold | Steam temperature | | | | | |
| | | Steam time | | | | | |
| | | Cool time | | | | | |
| ⑥ | Eject | Pin pressure | | | | | |
| ⑦ | Spot check cups | Check per instructions | | | | | |
| ⑧ | Imprint | Printer temperature | | | | | |
| | | Printer pressure | | | | | |
| | | % ink transfer | | | | | |
| ⑨ | Air blow | Pressure | | | | | |
| ⑩ | Check and pack | Check for damage | | | | | |
| ⑪ | Store | Store per directions | | | | | |

Critical part requirements and specifications

**Figure 8.4**   The process planning matrix with the process flow diagram and process requirements added.

storage require that the operation be checked in accordance with a specified procedure. In the product planning matrix, every item should be truly measurable. In the part planning matrix, the items represent part specifications that will appear on the engineering drawings and specifications. Some may be directly measurable, such as dimensions. Measurement of some may be more difficult, requiring tests of things such as durability and environmental exposure. In process planning, many of the requirements will take the form of attribute (yes/no) checks, audits, or procedural checks. The more the process is oriented toward service, the greater will be the number of procedural requirements.

## Completing the Matrix

Figure 8.5 shows the completed process planning matrix. The relationships have been determined and added, and specifications have been added. Again, these have been left generic; no values are shown. Note that for the inspection and storage items, as well as for one process item, "Percent of ink transfer," the measures involve a procedure to ensure conformance.

The process matrix can present a dilemma in terms of the extent of its development. From a strict QFD viewpoint, the matrix should probably contain only those process requirements that meet two tests: (1) they are critical to ensure that the part will meet its customer intent and (2) they respond only to the part requirements transferred from the prior matrix (part planning). On the other hand, it can be argued that once the team is immersed in the process of determining the process flow, the potential failures, and the critical process requirements, it ought not to limit its scope. Most processes can be examined for flow, potential failures, and critical requirements in a reasonable time frame. Concentrating on just those part requirements transferred from the prior matrix may reduce this time by 30 percent. In all likelihood, however, the organization will want a complete process study and determination of critical characteristics as it moves to determine its manufacturing planning. Therefore, the QFD team should seriously consider doing the whole process study for the part involved. This was done in the case shown. Note that some of the process steps do not have relationship symbols in their columns. These steps are part of the process but not measurably related to the four critical part requirements that were the inputs to the matrix.

No QFD matrix should conform to a recipe or cookie cutter approach. Each should have great flexibility, limited only by the team's imagination and needs. For example, a row could be added for process capability, as shown at the bottom of the matrix in Figure 8.5. Most industries recognize the value of statistical analysis of critical process requirements. Thus, for many of the requirements listed across the top of this matrix, there may be process or machine capability study information or

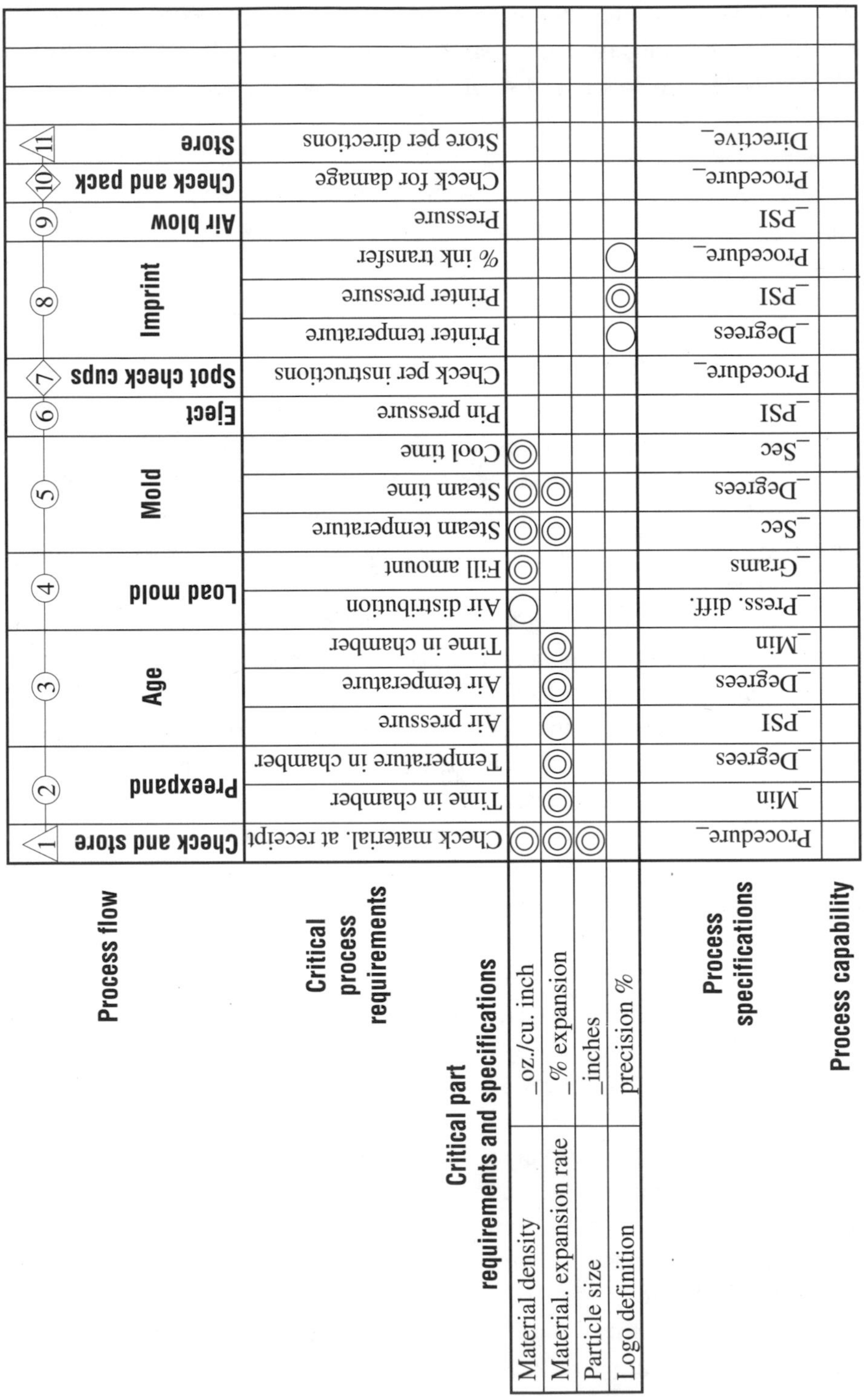

| Process flow | Critical process requirements | Material density _oz./cu. inch | Material. expansion rate _% expansion | Particle size _inches | Logo definition precision % | Process specifications |
|---|---|---|---|---|---|---|
| 1. Check and store | Check material at receipt | ◎ | ◎ | ◎ | | Procedure_ |
| 2. Preexpand | Time in chamber | | ◎ | | | Min_ |
| 2. Preexpand | Temperature in chamber | | ◎ | | | Degrees_ |
| 3. Age | Air pressure | | ○ | | | PSI_ |
| 3. Age | Air temperature | | ◎ | | | Degrees_ |
| 3. Age | Time in chamber | | ◎ | | | Min_ |
| 4. Load mold | Air distribution | ○ | | | | Press. diff._ |
| 4. Load mold | Fill amount | ◎ | | | | Grams_ |
| 5. Mold | Steam temperature | ◎ | ◎ | | | Sec_ |
| 5. Mold | Steam time | ◎ | ◎ | | | Degrees_ |
| 5. Mold | Cool time | ◎ | | | | Sec_ |
| 6. Eject | Pin pressure | | | | | PSI_ |
| 7. Spot check cups | Check per instructions | | | | | Procedure_ |
| 8. Imprint | Printer temperature | | | | ○ | Degrees_ |
| 8. Imprint | Printer pressure | | | | ◎ | PSI_ |
| 8. Imprint | % ink transfer | | | | ○ | Procedure_ |
| 9. Air blow | Pressure | | | | | PSI_ |
| 10. Check and pack | Check for damage | | | | | Procedure_ |
| 11. Store | Store per directions | | | | | Directive_ |

Critical part requirements and specifications

Process capability

**Figure 8.5**   The process planning matrix.

ongoing statistical process control charts. Similarly, teams often bring up experience with control of the process. Issues such as the type of gauges and fixtures required, qualification studies of first-run parts, correction of known conditions, the need for ongoing SPC, and need for operator involvement will surface. These should be documented as they develop and should be an integral part of the discussions in the next stage—manufacturing planning.

In addition, for more complex products and processes than shown in the coffee cup example, a number of valuable tools can be used effectively to increase the assurance of product success. Typical examples include design of experiments, design for assembly and manufacturability, variation simulation, and value engineering tools such as cost versus function and product simplification.

*Typically, QFD practices suggest that the process matrix be examined in a similar manner to the previous matrices. The critical items should be selected for deployment to the next stage—manufacturing planning. This selection would be based on a judgment of the significance of the columns. Those with weak and moderate relationship symbols would probably be disregarded. The remaining ones would normally be deployed to the next stage.*

For most processes, the number of steps and the number of critical process requirements are not major issues involving many items and pages of data. Therefore, it is not a major undertaking to deploy *all* of the critical process requirements to the next planning stage. Teams are encouraged to examine the scope of their process planning endeavor at the outset and to seriously consider including the whole process rather than just those items that respond to the matrix inputs. Similarly, they are encouraged to think about transferring all the critical requirements from the process planning matrix to the next stage. The rationale is that it involves very little additional time and it completes an essential task—the critical requirements are all identified and can all be transferred to manufacturing planning. *Manufacturing planning cannot be done selectively. Every process requirement represents an item that must be controlled during manufacturing to ensure that parts will meet their design requirements and their customer expectations. Thus, it seems logical at this point to deploy all the requirements to the next stage.*

In summary, the process planning matrix is almost identical to the part planning matrix. The essential pieces of the matrix are the same: "what," "how," "how much," and relationships. Columns and rows can be added to the matrix to tailor it to the team's needs. In the example shown, one row was added to show the process flow diagram, and a second row was added for process capability.

Many of the process specifications in a typical matrix are not as specific or measurable as their counterparts in the product or part planning matrices. Instead, they involve procedures or instructions that must be followed to ensure that the process conforms. The number of these procedurally oriented requirements increases as the process becomes more service oriented.

# Deployment to Subsequent Levels: Manufacturing Deployment

*chapter nine*

P revious chapters have discussed the application of the QFD matrix for examination of various inputs and the determination of appropriate responses. This works well in the deployment process as the project moves from the product planning stage to the part and process planning levels. During these deployments, the "hows" from one matrix are transferred to the subsequent matrix and become the "whats." Once the manufacturing stage is reached, a different situation arises. There is still a need to determine the actions necessary to respond to various product and process requirements. A matrix-like table works well for initial manufacturing planning and is substituted for the typical QFD matrix. Subsequent planning normally involves use of existing company processes for documenting the manufacturing plans.

## The Flow of Information Through the Organization

Typical product drawings contain a large number of dimensional and performance requirements to define the product. While each is necessary, not all are of equal concern when examining manufacturing concerns.

Many organizations have recognized this need to classify part and process requirements based on their degree of concern. They use terms such as "safety related," "key," and "critical" to identify requirements that need frequent attention. With work force downsizing, the identification of these critical characteristics becomes more important as a determinant for allocating scarce resources. Experience demonstrates that this identification is best done with a team representing product and process engineers and manufacturing personnel. Determining the critical requirements at the product engineering level without processing and manufacturing input leads to too many subsequent problems and changes. The value judgments involved in the selection of critical requirements involve the following principal issues:

- The part and process are examined to determine those requirements that the team believes are subject to potential significant variation.
- This variation, if uncontrolled, could cause product problems that would create customer dissatisfaction.
- The variation might also create internal problems, such as downtime, scrap, and rework.

In the coffee cup example, basic dimensions such as height, diameter, and wall thickness should be defined by the die cavities. Once the die cavities have been checked and determined to be correct, these dimensions will probably not change during the life of the product. On the other hand, issues such as material density, particle size, expansion rate, time, and temperature will vary during each process run. Some of these may be harder to control than others and will require more sophisticated control devices and/or more frequent examination.

Once such a process has been in effect for several years, the historical information can be consulted for new, similar products. The process becomes faster and more efficient. There is no need to reexamine each process completely. Because the information is documented, there is no longer a need for long memories relative to what is "critical."

First- and second-tier companies can benefit measurably by this approach. They can examine the product specifications and requirements supplied to them by their customer. Based on their experience, they can identify those requirements that they believe are critical. They can then request a meeting with their customer to review this listing of critical characteristics. Normally, some will be added and some will be deleted from the original list. It is an opportunity for shared communication and agreement on critical issues.

## Typical Manufacturing Planning

During the last decade, many organizations realized the need to stabilize their product development process. They examined typical industry practices, strengths, and weaknesses and determined a "best" process. Typically, these "best processes" describe the key steps from concept initiation through concept development and selection, design, prototype, process planning, pilot, launch, manufacturing, and service. Many have also developed flow charts to describe the process and responsibilities for developing product, process, and manufacturing requirements. Frequently, steps have been included to identify the critical product and process requirements. The overall process plan and the flowchart descriptions help in the development of a chain of documents that describe the part and its processing and identify the critical requirements. In such an organization, manufacturing's task is one of determining how to ensure conformity to these requirements. The general sequence of events is as follows:

- Critical part requirements are identified.
- The process steps that will affect variation of the critical part requirements are identified.
- The process variables that will influence part variation, such as time, speed, amount, and temperature, are determined.
- The operating windows for these process variables are then established. These are the windows within which the process must be operated to ensure that variation is under control.
- The last step is one of developing the manufacturing plans that define and describe the implementation of the necessary process controls to ensure operation within these windows.

Companies that do not have a process for developing this information make manufacturing's task more complex. The information about critical requirements must still be developed, and the responsibility generally falls on the manufacturing group. Companies that are using QFD will develop pieces of this information related to the items of customer concern. The FTA or FMEA documents developed in conjunction with the QFD planning will be of major value to the manufacturing organization as it develops its assurance program.

If an organization does not identify these critical requirements during the part and process development, the manufacturing group will do the job anyway, *by default*. One typical example involved a metal stamping plant that was planning the production of an automotive floor pan and rear compartment pan assembly. Critical requirements had not been identified in product or process engineering. Examination of the drawing requirements and the fixtures provided by the process engineering group revealed 265 checkpoints. If each of these was given equal value, an inordinate amount of time would be required to check a single assembly. The use of automated checking devices would have reduced the time but added significant cost. Based on experience, the plant chose 27 checkpoints which were believed to represent the critical items. It reasoned that the remaining points could be checked at various frequencies, such as at initial sample approval, once at each setup, or once every 8 hours. The

27 items, however, were variation-sensitive and critical to the customer. They obviously needed a far greater degree of attention. The plant subsequently conferred with its customers and agreed on 11 additional points. These 38 points became the selected critical concerns. The stamping plant started production of this new major component with less difficulty than it had experienced on similar assemblies in the past. The number of complaints received from customers was cut to approximately 15 percent of the normal start-up level on comparable products. As problems were revealed, the list of "critical" requirements was modified.

Organizations are sufficiently different that it is impossible to describe a universal system. The following discussion assumes that the manufacturing organization has accumulated all the necessary information relative to the critical product and process requirements and is ready to plan its manufacturing controls.

Figure 9.1 shows an initial planning document that is related to the QFD process planning matrix discussed in Chapter 8. A portion of the process flow and the critical process requirements have been transferred directly from the process planning matrix (Figure 8.5) to the first two columns of this planning document.

The example in Figure 9.1 is a generic document. Each organization must tailor its format to represent the company and its planning concerns. For example, a team might also include a column for the process specifications, the "windows of operation," for each of the process requirements. This sample document includes a risk assessment. The structure is similar to that shown in the FMEA documents, such as Figure 8.3. If an FMEA was developed during the part and process planning, many of these risk assessment figures may have been developed and can simply be transferred.

The next columns are for consideration of the planning required. In the example, tooling, manufacturing, and quality assurance are shown as functions or departments that will have responsibility for action. A number of categories are shown under each of these functions. These categories represent a checklist of possible actions required by each of the functions. For the tooling group, categories such as "Mistake proofing," "Maintenance instructions," and "Gauge design" are shown. Under the heading "Manufacturing," the categories capture such ideas as "Work analyses" for the operation, and the development of "Operator instructions" and "Operator training." Figure 9.2 illustrates a similar planning document for a more complex process—spot welding for inner and outer stamped metal panels.

For each process step, decisions can be made and responsibilities can be denoted for the actions necessary to ensure effective manufacturing control. The format of the document can be altered to provide room for notes on specific actions to be taken, persons responsible, and completion dates. This is an overall planning document. *It should be a team-developed document. In line with the QFD concept, this document suggests that an overall approach be developed by a cross-functional team so that the whole challenge is addressed.* Often, this is not the case. The various functional activities such

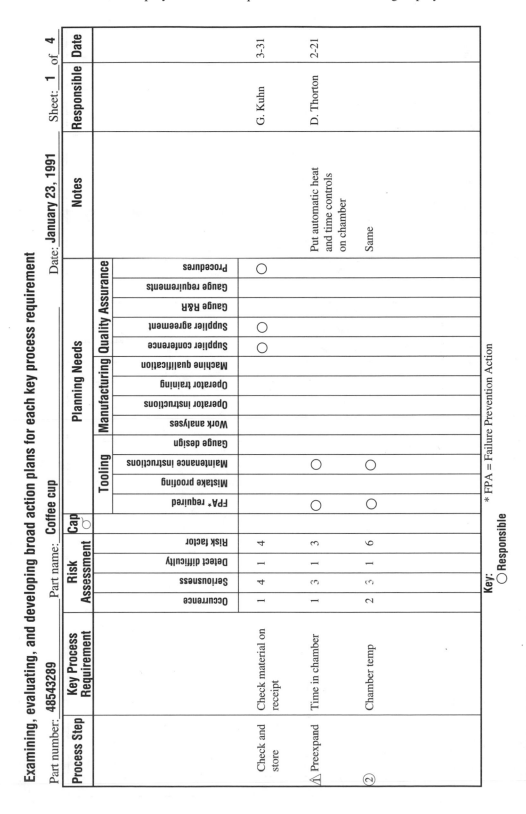

Examining, evaluating, and developing broad action plans for each key process requirement

Part number: 48543289     Part name: Coffee cup     Date: January 23, 1991     Sheet: 1 of 4

| Process Step | Key Process Requirement | Risk Assessment | | | | Cap | FPA* required | Mistake proofing | Maintenance instructions | Gauge design | Work analyses | Operator instructions | Operator training | Machine qualification | Supplier conference | Supplier agreement | Gauge R&R | Gauge requirements | Procedures | Notes | Responsible | Date |
| | | Occurrence | Seriousness | Detect difficulty | Risk factor | | | | | | | | | | | | | | | | | |
| | | | | | | ○ | | | | | | | | | | | | | | | | |
| Check and store | Check material on receipt | 1 | 4 | 1 | 4 | | | | | | | | | | | ○ | | | ○ | | G. Kuhn | 3-31 |
| △ Preexpand | Time in chamber | 1 | 3 | 1 | 3 | | ○ | ○ | | | | | | | ○ | | | | | Put automatic heat and time controls on chamber | D. Thorton | 2-21 |
| ② | Chamber temp | 2 | 3 | 1 | 6 | | ○ | ○ | | | | | | | | | | | | Same | | |

Planning Needs — Tooling / Manufacturing Quality Assurance

* FPA = Failure Prevention Action

Key:
○ Responsible

**Figure 9.1**    Initial planning document.

**Examining, evaluating, and developing broad action plans for each key process requirement**

Part number: __7925978__      Part name: __Rear lock pillar__      Date: **January 10, 1992**      Sheet: **1** of **6**

| Process Step | Key Process Requirement | Risk Assessment | | | | Cap ○ | Planning Needs | | | | | | | | | | | | | Notes | Responsible | Date |
|---|---|---|---|---|---|---|---|---|---|---|---|---|---|---|---|---|---|---|---|---|---|---|
| | | | | | | | | Tooling | | | Manufacturing | | | | | | Quality Assurance | | | | | |
| | | Occurrence | Seriousness | Detect difficulty | Risk factor | | FPA* required | Mistake proofing | Maintenance instructions | Gauge design | Work analyses | Operator instructions | Operator training | Machine qualification | Supplier conference | Supplier agreement | Gauge R&R | Gauge requirements | Procedures | | | |
| △ Load pillar | Position gauge hole on gauge pin | 3 | 5 | 1 | 15 | | | ○ | ○ | | ○ | | ○ | | | | | | | Install part presence detector and automatic shutdown | J. Grace | 3-20 |
| ② Load inner panel | Position on magnetic holder | 3 | 5 | 1 | 15 | | | ○ | ○ | | ○ | | ○ | | | | | | | | | |
| ③ Spot weld | Time | 1 | 3 | 1 | 3 | | ○ | ○ | | | | | | | | | | | | Try out new automatic controllers with steppers | J. Grace | 3-28 |
| | Pressure | 1 | 4 | 5 | 20 | | ○ | ○ | | | | | | | | | | | | | | |
| | Amperage | 1 | 4 | 1 | 4 | | ○ | ○ | | | | | | | | | | | | | | |
| | Weld tip condition | 4 | 3 | 1 | 12 | | | ○ | ○ | | | ○ | | | | | | | | | | |
| ④ Check part | Weld strength | 3 | 3 | 4 | 36 | 96% | | | | | | ○ | ○ | | | | | | | | G. Simms | 6-1 |
| | Part outline and shape | 1 | 2 | 1 | 2 | 6.2 | | | | ○ | | ○ | ○ | | | | ○ | ○ | ○ | | | |

* FPA = Failure Prevention Action

**Key:**
○ Responsible

**Figure 9.2**   Initial planning document.

as tooling and quality assurance do their planning separately. Things fall through the cracks with this approach.

Once an initial planning document is completed as an overall team project, individual functions can then develop their plans. Typically, these take the form of "bedsheets," documents that show items such as the various process steps and related instructions, data sheets and documentation required, equipment needs, frequencies, and acceptance criteria. An example of a typical document for the quality assurance function is shown in Figure 9.3. The tooling, manufacturing, and material handling groups would develop similar documents based on their assignments from the initial planning document. Note that this quality assurance worksheet (Figure 9.3) identifies the numbers associated with the instructional documents, data sheets, and fixtures. Figure 9.4 shows a typical instruction sheet generated by the maintenance department for setup and maintenance of a spot welder for a metal stamped rear lock pillar. Figure 9.5 shows an instruction sheet for preparation of coffee.

In summary, manufacturing planning has always existed in plants out of necessity. Manufacturing operations require a major level of planning to ensure such things as proper plant layout, conformance to engineering requirements, development and maintenance of necessary documentation, and generation of measures of performance. The presence of the QFD concept in a plant can help workers understand the

| Part number: 7925978 | | Part name: Rear lock pillar | | | Date: January 10, 1992 | | Sheet 1 of 6 | |
|---|---|---|---|---|---|---|---|---|
| **Process Step** | **Key Part Requirements** | **Instructions Procedure** | **Data Sheet** | **Sample Size and Frequency** | **Tools and Fixtures** | **Acceptance Criteria** | **Calibration Requirements** |
| ◇4◇ Check part | Weld strength | WS-211 | WS-211A | 4 every 2 hours | Ultra sound-U.S.-4572 | Meet STD. | Each usage |
|  |  |  |  | 1 every 2 hours | Chisel check | Pull nugget |  |
|  | Part outline and shape | PM-34 | PM-34A | 1 at start-up 1 at midday 1 at last piece | Fixture U.S. 5692 | Outline— 1 mm max Contour— 2 mm max | Annually |

**Figure 9.3**    Quality assurance planning table.

Weld press number(s):____**45342**____          Sheet____**1**__ of **6**__

Part number:_**7925978**_____          Date:_**01-18-92**____

Part name:__**Rear lock pillar**_____

**Before start-up**

1. Replace all tips. Use tip number CU 46.

2. Check all hoses visually for wear and abrasion. Replace as necessary.

3. Check weld pressure with gauge WP22 at each tip. Must be within green area. Check calibration before use of gauge. Re-adjust when pressure is not in green range.

4. Reset all controllers to zero setting.

**At midmorning and afternoon breaks**

1. Dress all weld tips with blue file (Number 3). Dress per standard.

**At lunchtime**

1. Replace all tips. Use tip number CU 46.

2. Visually recheck hoses for any obvious wear.

3. Reset controllers to zero.

**Figure 9.4**    Maintenance, setup instructions.

value of using matrices and tables for planning and the strength involved in team reviews. The concept of an initial planning document, as illustrated in Figures 9.1 and 9.2, demonstrates the use of a team approach to overall planning coupled with a table to record the determinations.

Process name:  **Preparation of coffee**

| When | What | How |
|---|---|---|
| **Before starting equipment** | 1. Check for cleanliness of equipment | 1. Hold glass container against the light. Examine for cleanliness. Reclean if required. Use one package of A60 cleaner in one gallon of warm water. Rinse thoroughly. |
| | 2. Check inventory | 2. Check regular and decaf coffee cartons and filter cartons. When supply of either type of coffee is down to last two cartons, reorder. When supply of filters is down to last carton, reorder. See reorder instructions on inside surface of coffee/filter storage cabinet. Stock coffee and filter drawers as necessary. |
| **Performing the operation** | 1. Remove coffee and filter holder and clean | 1. Grasp by handle. Pull directly toward you. Empty used filter and coffee into brown waste container under coffee unit counter. Rinse holder under hot water in sink next to coffee unit. |
| | 2. Place new filter in holder and add coffee | 2. Remove single filter from filters in filter drawer under coffee unit. Place in holder. Press against sides of holder. Remove coffee package from coffee drawer. Tear at tear line. Put contents in holder on filter and place empty package in waste container. |
| | 3. Brew coffee | 3. Push switch marked "Brew" to start brewing of coffee. |
| | 4. Place brewed coffee on auxiliary heater. | 4. When coffee is brewed, buzzer will sound. Remove container and place on auxiliary heater. Turn on heat for auxiliary heater. Numbers on switch panel correspond to numbers on heaters. |

**Figure 9.5**    Developing operator instructions: an example.

# Putting It All Together

*chapter ten*

**C**hapters 4 through 9 outlined the pertinent details of constructing a product planning matrix, determining the priority items, and deploying them through subsequent stages. Each step in the process for the coffee cup was illustrated. The accompanying text detailed the most common problems and concerns that teams will face during the QFD process. The use of ancillary tools such as FTA, FMEA and concept analysis were reviewed. This chapter is intended to serve as an overview of the process covered in these previous chapters. A simple example based on a customer survey of expectations for theater seats will be used. The text will be kept to a minimum. The purpose of the chapter is to illustrate each of the steps from the customer information matrix to the manufacturing plan using this brief example. This will help tie the process together in a few pages and will serve as an overview of the principal documents.

## The Customer Information Matrix

Figure 10.1 shows a portion of the customer information relative to theater seats. Four typical customers' voices are shown with their average levels of importance. Complaints are listed on the right side along with the customers' competitive evaluation between the theater in question and a leading competitor which uses another type of seat.

To simplify the example, only patrons' wants and needs are shown. Owners' wants and needs would also be included in the full matrix. The matrix in Figure 10.1 represents

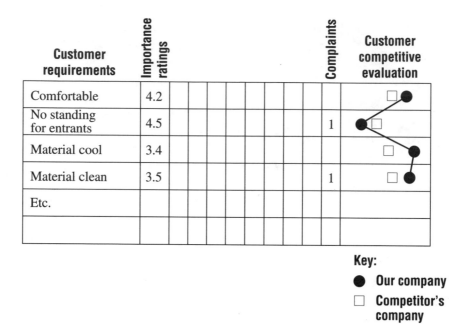

**Figure 10.1** Determine the customers' voices, their importance ratings, complaints, and competitive evaluations.

the customer information portion of the QFD matrix. As discussed previously, it could be used to determine the priority customer concerns at this point.

## Adding the Technical Matrix Information

Figure 10.2 shows the technical information portion of the matrix added to the customer information matrix. The team might easily have decided to use customary measures for the technical requirements. For example, the "verbatims" for the customer voice "Comfortable" involved such things as "Wide enough to hold a big person like my mother-in-law," "Doesn't feel like I'm sitting on a hard steel pan," and "Comfortable armrests—soft and big enough to share with next person." In traditional terms, these could have been translated into requirements such as seat width, seat height, cushion load/deflection, and armrest width; however, they fall into the general category of design-specific items. *They represent a repetition of the usual language employed to define seat comfort.* They represent a thought process following *standard patterns—a paradigm.* One of the chief cautions of the QFD product planning matrix is to avoid

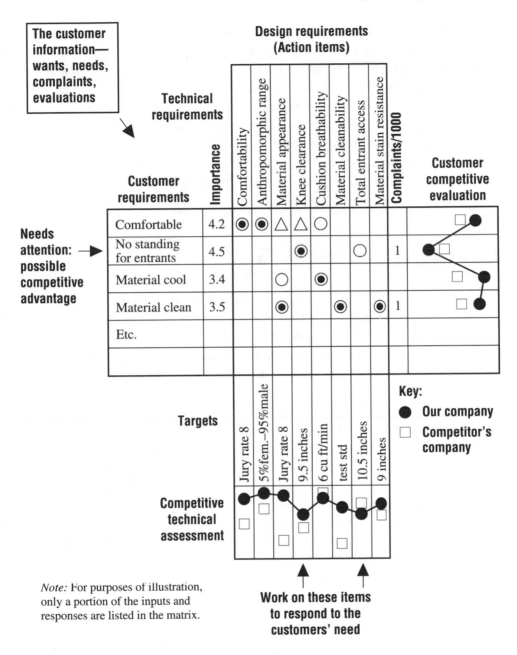

**Figure 10.2**   The product planning matrix.

these paradigms—to allow for some imaginative shift of the existing patterns of response. This is why the words *non–design specific* and *Global* were emphasized in an earlier chapter. In this example, terms such as *comfort jury* and *anthropomorphic range* were used to help break the usual design patterns. Broad global terms such as these tend to make the team think through other approaches and to brainstorm new ideas that may create competitive advantages for the company. Ultimately, the company should develop test methods to quantify issues like comfort rather than rely on jury ratings.

This illustration also shows the selection of the voice "No standing for entrants" as the priority item among those shown. The accompanying technical requirements are "Knee clearance" and "Total entrant access."

## A Research and Development Matrix

In Figure 10.3, a research and development matrix is shown in the lower right corner. The steps previously discussed are shown in block format proceeding from the upper left corner. The research and development matrix is optional. Its use has not been discussed in previous chapters, but previous chapters did mention that good imaginative ideas often emerge from the team discussions during development of the "hows." Some of these are excellent embryos for creative ideas related to new products and processes. For example, in a customer survey about small kitchen appliances, the voice "It [toaster] shouldn't take up much counter space" could lead to the idea of an under-the-counter model. The voices "Coffee shouldn't taste burned" and "It should never start a fire" might lead to the idea of using a thermos as a coffee pot to avoid the need for continued heating.

As such ideas emerge from team discussions, they should be captured and used as concepts for development of new products. A research-and-development–type matrix can be used for this purpose. The ideas that emerge from discussion are listed across the top of the matrix. The voices to which they respond are listed at the left. Relationship symbols help show which columns have the most potential for satisfying a number of voices. In this case, the ideas of an articulated seat and maximum-soil-shedding fabrics appear as the primary candidates.

## Determining the Best Concept

The organization should not move directly from the product planning matrix to a part planning matrix (Figure 10.4). The temptation is too strong to simply examine and modify the current product. Great opportunities for cost reduction, improved product performance, and enhanced competitiveness can be sacrificed by this approach. This is

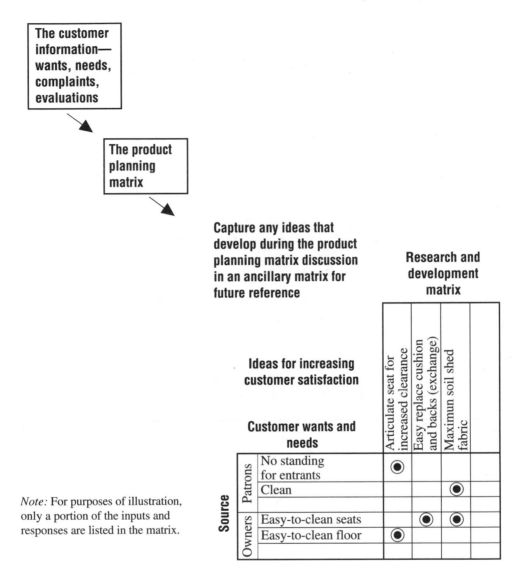

*Note:* For purposes of illustration, only a portion of the inputs and responses are listed in the matrix.

**Figure 10.3**   A research and development matrix.

the point of opportunity for design breakthrough and for doing some effective comparative planning and avoiding the desire to start building prototypes. The customers' needs are known; internal needs are known. This presents an ideal opportunity to develop many approaches (concepts) and to synthesize a best concept from among them. This is the place for a trade study or Pugh-type analysis. This concept is illustrated in the matrix in the lower right corner of Figure 10.4.

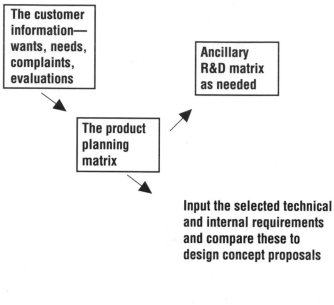

Input the selected technical
and internal requirements
and compare these to
design concept proposals

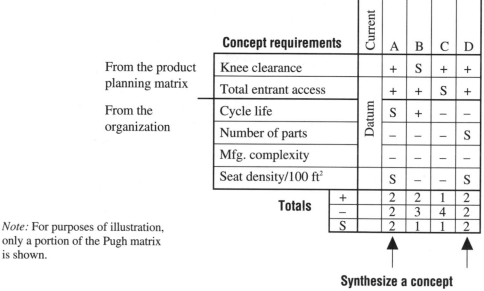

**Design concepts**

| Concept requirements | Current | A | B | C | D |
|---|---|---|---|---|---|
| Knee clearance | | + | S | + | + |
| Total entrant access | | + | + | S | + |
| Cycle life | Datum | S | + | − | − |
| Number of parts | | − | − | − | S |
| Mfg. complexity | | − | − | − | − |
| Seat density/100 ft$^2$ | | S | − | − | S |

From the product
planning matrix

From the
organization

| Totals | | A | B | C | D |
|---|---|---|---|---|---|
| + | | 2 | 2 | 1 | 2 |
| − | | 2 | 3 | 4 | 2 |
| S | | 2 | 1 | 1 | 2 |

*Note:* For purposes of illustration,
only a portion of the Pugh matrix
is shown.

Synthesize a concept
from examination of
these two ideas

**Figure 10.4**   Select a "best" design concept.

## The Part Planning Matrix

Figure 10.5 shows the sequence of prior events starting in the upper left corner; the part planning matrix is shown in the lower right corner. The two technical requirements—

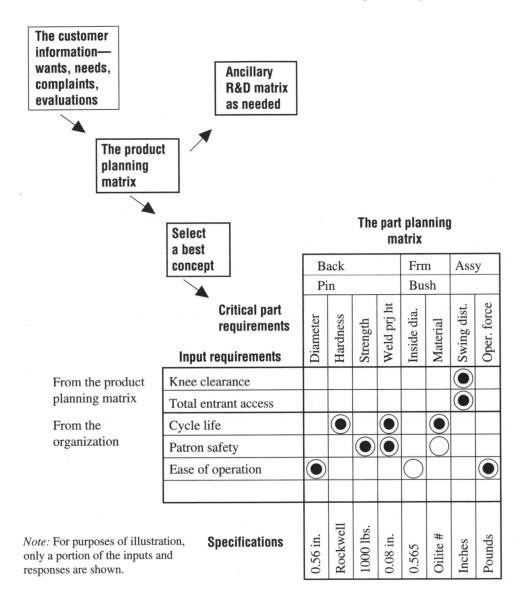

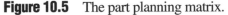

*Note:* For purposes of illustration, only a portion of the inputs and responses are shown.

**Figure 10.5**    The part planning matrix.

"Knee clearance" and "Total entrant access"—were associated with the priority voice "No standing for entrants." They are entered on the left side of the matrix. Three internal voices based on the organization's experience are also entered. For the selected new synthesized concept, the three main parts involved—the seat back, seat frame, and assembly of back and frame—are shown across the top of the matrix. The parts that are of concern, such as the pivot pin that is a part of the seat back assembly and the bushing that is part of the seat frame assembly, are shown in the row below.

A concept of a seat that swings back to allow entry without the need for the seated person to rise was developed from the Pugh analysis. Certain pins and linkages are involved in the concept. A parts list would be developed following selection of the best concept. Some form of failure analysis should be conducted to alert the organization to any potential design and process problems associated with this new design. Using the failure analysis and experience as a base, the team can then enter the critical part requirements across the top of the part planning matrix. Issues such as the back pin diameter, hardness, and strength represent critical part concerns. Relationships and specifications are shown.

The next challenge for the QFD team would be the selection of any of these critical part requirements that it believes should be examined at the process level. Some of these may be deployed using the QFD approach; others may be deployed using conventional systems and processes familiar to and effectively used by the organization. In this example, the back pin strength was selected for additional QFD deployment. It involves projection welding, which is relatively new to the organization and is of major concern. The design is "fail-safe." The pin goes through a pierced hole prior to welding so that if the weld fails, the seat will not fall. However, the customer would sense the failure, and the seat would need replacement. Obviously, the company does not want this to happen.

## The Process Planning Matrix

The next step in the QFD process is the process planning matrix shown in the lower right corner of Figure 10.6. Back pin strength has been entered as the item of concern from the prior matrix.

One effective approach is to conduct a failure analysis for the process at this point using those members of the organization who are most familiar with the welding process. Serious consideration should be given to including welder maintenance personnel who service the equipment every day. Not only is their knowledge beneficial, but their approach to problem solving can be most revealing when planning the process flow for this operation.

The critical process requirements are listed across the top of the matrix based on the team's inputs. In this case, a process flow diagram is not shown at the top of the matrix. In most cases, this is advisable both as a visual communication device and to provide assurance that all the process steps have been considered.

The first two critical process requirements concern checks of the pin to ensure its material and the height of the projections for welding. The remaining items, such as current, time, pressure, and cleaning of the seat back frame weld surface, represent processing concerns that must be controlled to ensure that the pin and back assembly meets strength requirements.

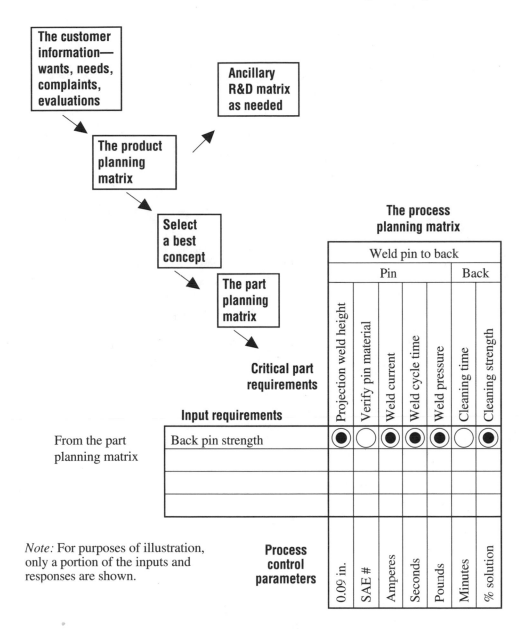

**Figure 10.6**   The process planning matrix.

## Manufacturing Planning

Figure 10.7 shows the overall flow of information to the manufacturing area. Selected
items from the product planning, part planning, and process planning matrices flow to

• **The following are typical tools that should be considered to assist analysis of key issues in the matrix**

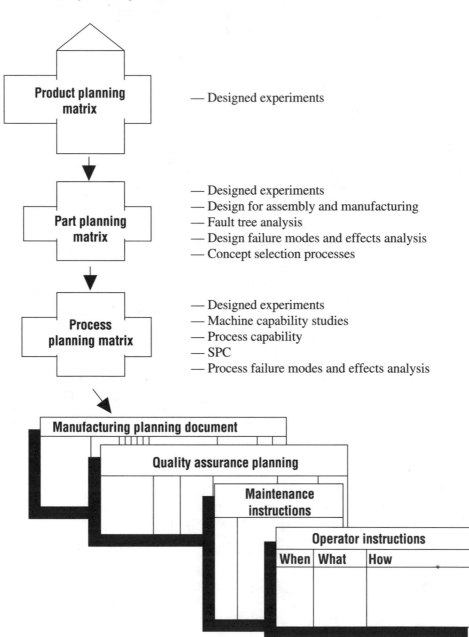

— Designed experiments

— Designed experiments
— Design for assembly and manufacturing
— Fault tree analysis
— Design failure modes and effects analysis
— Concept selection processes

— Designed experiments
— Machine capability studies
— Process capability
— SPC
— Process failure modes and effects analysis

**Figure 10.7**    Manufacturing planning.

the manufacturing area. Tools such as FTA, Pugh analysis, and designed experiments may be used in conjunction with the matrices as shown.

In the manufacturing area, an overall planning document is an effective starting point. This lists the key concerns from a design and process viewpoint and allows for a risk assessment and an orderly determination of what is needed for such key areas as maintenance, quality assurance, instructions, and training.

*The end result is that the information in the manufacturing area stems from knowledge of the customer. People producing products can be told that if they follow the job instructions, the resulting product should satisfy the customers' wants and needs. This is much more meaningful than the concept that following the instructions will produce a part that meets the print requirements.*

# Differing Levels of
# Customer Voices
*chapter eleven*

## Using Matrices for First- and Second-Tier Suppliers

Previous chapters have addressed the basic concepts of listening to customers, developing the customer matrix, and using the QFD process for selection and deployment of priority voices. This approach has application principally with "prime supplier" companies that market their products for end-user customer purchase and consumption. Companies that market kitchen appliances, cameras, automobiles, cosmetics, soap products, and packaged foods, for example, fall into this category. Similarly, in the service sector, airlines, telephone companies, cable TV companies, hotels, restaurants, and package delivery services are included in this category. For purposes of this text, these companies will be referred to as prime suppliers. Prime suppliers depend on customers who purchase and repurchase their products. If they offer products or services that are not competitive, that do not meet customer expectations, or that do not provide the long-term service expected, their reputation, sales, and profits will suffer. Every prime supplier should have some mechanisms for constantly listening to the voices of its customers. This has to go beyond asking a buyer to send in a card after the purchase of a product or service. Most of these cards tend to focus on marketing demographics, not on customer wants, needs, and motives for purchase. Prime suppliers need to find ways to constantly survey customers' wants and needs separate from the return of purchase cards, letters of complaint, or service records of defective and inoperative products.

Prime suppliers usually purchase some of their components from other suppliers. For purposes of this text, these other supplies will be called first-tier suppliers. Similarly, first-tier suppliers buy parts and raw materials from second-tier suppliers. Additional tiers of suppliers can be involved in more complex products. This text discussion will be limited to first- and second-tier suppliers. The issues that apply to them also apply to suppliers who are lower in the chain.

The product planning matrix (house of quality) has application for prime suppliers, the companies who need to survey their buying customers to determine their expectations and who need to plan their products to meet these expectations. In a similar way, first- and second-tier suppliers need to survey their customers and plan their products to match customer expectations. The prime supplier is the customer of the first-tier supplier. It is the prime supplier that provides the first-tier supplier with the drawings and specifications for the product or service to be delivered. A typical first-tier supplier starts its task with the drawings and specifications furnished by its prime supplier customer. These come from a number of sources, such as product engineering, purchasing, and the quality assurance departments of the organization.

In addition, there are a number of people in every prime supplier organization whose wants and needs are important in the whole scheme of customer satisfaction. These include the people who receive and transport the shipping containers in the customer plant, the operators who use or install the service or product, and sometimes repair people who service or correct malfunctions in the prime supplier's plants or in the field. *It is important that a first-tier supplier be aware of all of these customer expectations.* This knowledge of the customer puts the first-tier supplier in a position to provide better service to the prime supplier. This responsiveness to the needs of the customer can help distinguish the first-tier supplier as an extraordinary company—one that is deserving of continued business.

Figure 11.1 illustrates this concept of the supplier chain. The primary supplier is responsible for listening to its direct purchase customers and for producing products that respond imaginatively to the customers' voices. When this information is deployed at the prime supplier organization, the resulting technical requirements reflect the voice of the customer. These requirements are subsequently furnished to the first-tier supplier.

The first-tier supplier has the obligation to develop appropriate responses to the requirements furnished by the prime supplier. An aggressive first-tier supplier will also talk with the people in the prime supplier company who handle, use, and service the first-tier company's products or services. In this way, the first-tier supplier can respond to all the voices within the prime supplier. The situation is the same for a second-tier supplier. In addition to responding to the requirements furnished by the first-tier supplier, it can also determine the internal needs of the supplier and develop ways to respond to them. It is this extra measure of interest and service that will help distinguish these suppliers and ensure them of continued business.

First- and second-tier suppliers must depend on their prime suppliers for knowledge of the wants and needs of the ultimate purchaser of the product or service. Thus, they will not usually be involved in the development of a product planning matrix. This

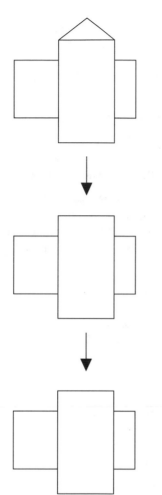

**Primary supplier**

The primary supplier translates customer and product needs into a set of requirements that are furnished to the first-tier suppliers.

**First-tier supplier**

A first-tier supplier listens to its customers— the users of the product at the prime supplier and adds these to its matrix. In addition, knowledge of field performance, customer concerns, and internal voices may be added.

**Second-tier supplier**

A second-tier supplier listens to its customers at the first-tier supplier company and couples these with internal voices and any specialized knowledge of the product or material.

**Figure 11.1**    Application of the QFD matrix in the supplier chain.

is the domain of the prime supplier. It will benefit a prime supplier to ask some of its major first-tier suppliers to accompany it on customer interviews and surveys. This gives the first-tier supplier insight into and involvement in customer expectations that cannot be achieved in any other way. Similarly, first-tier suppliers that are aware of pending surveys can ask their prime supplier for permission to join them in listening and observing.

First-tier suppliers can use a form of the part planning matrix to list anything they learn from their conversations with people in the prime supplier organization. In effect, these are the voices of their customers, and they need effective response. The matrix is an excellent tool for listing these inputs and responses. This is best illustrated by the example shown in Figure 11.2, which involves a first-tier supplier relationship with a prime supplier. It could apply equally to a first- and second-tier supplier relationship.

Figure 11.2 shows a plastic clip that an automotive prime supplier is purchasing from a first-tier supplier. This clip is designed to be pushed into a punched opening in a metal panel. The molding is then pushed (snapped) over the clip to hold it in position. The clips have two small fins on either side to provide a slight separation of the clip and the panels for drainage and for anticorrosion concerns.

The prime supplier has furnished the first-tier supplier with a drawing showing the dimensional characteristics of the clip. The push-in force, retention force, and

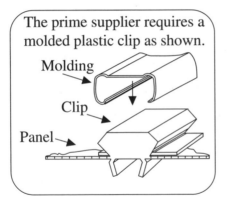

The prime supplier requires a molded plastic clip as shown.

Molding

Clip

Panel

**Critical product characteristics furnished to first-tier supplier by prime supplier:**

- Push-in force
- Retention force
- Dimension integrity

**Additional concerns determined by first-tier supplier from prime supplier's work force:**

- Clips sometimes tangle
- Other clips are very similar and get mixed up
- Takes time to position clip at installation

**Additional concerns determined by first-tier supplier based on field examination and knowledge within own work force:**

- Material stability due to moisture loss
- Degradation in field

**Figure 11.2**   Determining the customer requirements in a prime supplier–first-tier supplier situation.

dimensional integrity of the clip have been identified by the prime supplier as the "critical" requirements. The first-tier supplier can use these critical part requirements as the input to a QFD process planning matrix. The critical process requirements and their specifications can then be listed on the process planning matrix.

In addition, the first-tier supplier has talked with the operators in the prime supplier's plants. These conversations have generated some additional customer voices, as shown in Figure 11.2. These involve clips that sometimes tangle and mixups with similar clips. In addition, operators have complained about the time required to position the clips for installation.

Also, the first-tier supplier is aware that the clip material specified by the prime supplier is subject to become brittle under certain temperature and humidity conditions. In addition, teardown of junked older cars by the first-tier supplier has demonstrated that brittleness and cracking occur as a result of continued environmental exposure.

These issues of operator concern and clip longevity can be entered into a part planning matrix by the first-tier supplier. Using it as the planning tool, the first-tier supplier can develop recommendations for material changes, design changes to restrict tangling, color coding for part identification, and methods of orienting the clips for ease of positioning during installation.

Once the product design discussion has been completed, the first-tier supplier should begin to develop a process planning matrix. This matrix will describe the supplier's process flow and identify the critical process characteristics. This QFD process planning chart can be used as a part of the review process with the prime supplier. It provides an opportunity for the organizations to jointly verify that the critical product requirements have associated critical process requirements and specifications. *Discussions of both the part and process planning matrices reflect an interest on the part of the first-tier supplier and are evidence of a thorough and orderly approach to supplier responsibility.*

Experience has shown that suppliers that use the process planning matrix to show the critical process parameters related to the prime supplier's requirements find it valuable as (1) an internal communication tool and (2) a method of communicating with their prime supplier to demonstrate a planned response to its requirements.

## Using the Concept for Innovations: Unknown Customers

Most aggressive companies are constantly working to improve existing products or to develop new and exciting products that "go beyond satisfaction." The QFD process can be used to help in the planning process for such products.

The QFD process applications that have been discussed have involved cases in which there was an existing product that the company wanted to improve to increase customer satisfaction. When a current product exists, the company can interview or survey present owners to determine their wants, needs, and levels of satisfaction. If there are competitors, surveys can also determine the level of satisfaction with their products or services.

In other situations, however, when a product or service concept is in the embryonic stages of planning, it represents something revolutionary. There is no current product or service against which it can be compared. For example, assume that the toaster company mentioned in Chapter 10 decided to investigate to respond to the customer voice "Should not take up much counter space." The under-the-counter model proposal was judged to have some potential marketability. Assume that no other under-the-counter model is available in the marketplace, so no competitive customer evaluation data can be obtained. Because there are no similar products in the market, customers have no experience with the idea. A survey either by questionnaire or interview is of little value because there is no customer knowledge or experience to form a basis for responses.

In such a situation, the QFD customer matrix can serve as an excellent planning document. However, it needs to be approached in a different manner. The first step would be to examine ways to develop the customers' voice using products or services that the organization believes are similar to the proposed concept. For example, under-the-counter can openers or coffee makers can be used to generate conversation about the owner's/customer's likes and dislikes. All the "verbatims" collected in interviews of existing similar products should be examined for comments and clues about the customer. This can increase knowledge of what the customer might expect and accept as an alternative to the current toaster to save space. Literature should be consulted to determine if similar products available in other countries represent novel approaches to the space concern for kitchen appliances.

With this knowledge as background, the organization should then develop a series of concepts that might satisfy the customer voice. A set of criteria should be developed against which to compare these concepts. Using some form of concept selection process, the concepts should be narrowed down to some manageable number (for example, four ideas). Prototypes should then be constructed and used in small market clinics to permit customer observation and evaluation of these concepts. Information can be obtained about what customers like and dislike in this type of product. Customer importance levels and customer competitive ratings of the proposed concepts can be determined.

The information developed from the clinic can be used by the organization to develop a QFD product planning matrix. The customer portion of the matrix would consist of (1) customers' voices, (2) customers' importance levels, and (3) customers' competitive evaluations of the concept proposals. Technical requirements can then be established based on the customers' voices. Relationships can be determined. This partial QFD product planning matrix can then be used to prioritize the customers' needs and to generate a revised list of concept criteria.

The new criteria can be used as the basis for an additional review and synthesis of concept proposals. The company can then proceed to repeat the clinic experience using either a single "best" concept or multiple concepts. Based on the clinic results, a finalized product concept can be developed and test marketed.

# Controlling Inputs
# to the Matrix

*chapter twelve*

Chapters 3 and 4 addressed actions that could be taken to examine and consolidate and/or reassign customers' voices. The intent of both of these actions was to reduce the number of voices that are used in the QFD product planning matrix.

Concern for the number of voices is especially significant for the QFD product planning matrix. Generally, the number of "hows" transferred to any subsequent matrix for part or process planning is not large and poses no problem. In the product planning matrix, the inputs are the customers' voices. Depending on the complexity of the product, a large number of voices can be generated in the interview process. As the number of voices increases, the difficulty involved in developing and completing the matrix increases measurably.

A product planning matrix that is based on 25 or fewer voices is a very manageable matrix. Matrices containing between 25 and 50 voices can be managed, but the task becomes more onerous as the number of inputs grows. The reasons are obvious. A matrix with 25 voices will be used for illustration. If a team manages to control the number of responses (hows) to an average of 1.5 per voice, then there would be 25 x 1.5 or 38 technical requirements. This means that a minimum of 38 test requests need to be written. In addition, there is the time and cost involved in obtaining the parts and conducting the tests. In this example, the relationship matrix contains 25 x 38 or 950 opportunities to examine relationships. The number of co-relationship decisions is approximately 650.

All of these decisions and actions grow significantly as the number of voices increases. There is no way to predict the point at which the size of the matrix creates a feeling of diminished returns or outright fatigue and desperation for a team. It will vary with product and team. As a guideline, matrices with 25 or fewer voices are easy to develop and enable teams to keep their enthusiasm. Consensus is achieved with moderate discussion, and team members generally feel comfortable with the consensus decision. As the matrix grows, some team members will show signs of fatigue and loss of interest. The consensus decision process will suffer, and the overall value of the matrix will be diminished. However, if meeting time is controlled to reduce fatigue and if the team recognizes and agrees to the overall time commitments, matrices with 25 to 50 entries can be well managed. As a guideline, *and only as a guideline,* teams should consider 50 voices as a maximum.

In dealing with complex products, the number of voices can be very large. For example, the number of voices for the design of an automobile or a new building will easily exceed 100. To control the time involved in the construction and analysis of the product planning matrix, action has to be taken to condense this number in a manner that ensures that the impact of the customers' input is not lost. Following are some guidelines.

## Presorting and Combining Voices

A first step is to make sure the voices have been consolidated as much as possible, as mentioned in Chapter 3. Customers frequently say the same thing in slightly different words. When the "verbatims" are similar, they should be combined into a single statement that conveys the multiple meanings voiced by the customer. For example, shoppers commenting on the carts used in the store will say such things as "Shouldn't stick together," "Should be easy to separate," "Don't want carts that jam with each other when they're in a row," "I can't get them apart," and "Don't want carts that don't come apart—get hung up." These voices all refer to the same basic concern. They can be combined into a single voice, such as "Stacked carts should pull apart easily."

A second basic step is to review the voices to make sure that they are all the same level and that there are no styling or attribute (yes/no) voices included, as covered in Chapter 4. When the customer information portion of the QFD matrix is examined at the preplanning chart stage, styling and attribute items should be placed on separate lists for action by the responsible groups. Some items will refer to a lower-level concern, such as a system or part. These should be set aside for use when that system or part is examined. In the shopping cart example, some typical voices might be "Make it out of plastic," "Put a safety belt in for children," or "Make the wheels bigger so the cart moves more easily." The plastic issue represents a customer's suggestion for the design of the basket. During the interview, inquiry should have continued by repeatedly asking the customer "Why?" until the root want was established. Perhaps it was suggested for weight reduction or to reduce corrosion or for cleanliness. *The root want must be established during the interview.* Once the interview is over, the opportunity to learn the customers' wants and needs has disappeared. The plastic basket issue should be set aside for possible use and discussion when the basket is discussed as a system or part; it is a *lower-level* item. The belt issue is an attribute item. It should be put on a separate list for company decisions. Does the company want to add this feature? Is it good public relations? Does it have legal or liability concerns? These issues should be investigated and decided outside the domain of the QFD matrix. The issue of wheel size is twofold. The root want was the customer's concern for the effort required to push the cart. This should be a voice entry in the cart QFD matrix. The idea of wheel diameter is a design suggestion that should be set aside for use at a lower level, similar to the plastic basket concept.

## Use of the Preplanning Chart

Chapter 4 also discussed the idea of using the preplanning chart as a screening device to identify priority items. An organization can use the preplanning chart as a "short-form" approach if it has major time constraints and cannot undertake the whole chart. Based on review of the information in the preplanning matrix, high-priority items can be selected. These are normally items for which the company is at a competitive disadvantage or sees the opportunity to gain a competitive advantage. A product planning matrix can then be constructed using only the selected high-priority voices.

There are concerns when this approach is followed. As explained in Chapter 4, teams have to exercise an added degree of caution as they develop their product planning matrix. The technical requirements which are developed will be only those associated with the selected "priority" voices. As a result, some technical requirements necessary for the product will not show in the matrix. Thus some key tradeoff decisions may be missed when examining the co-relationship matrix. Also, there may be some cases where the customer competitive evaluation and the technical competitive assessment data differ. If these involve "nonpriority" voices, the opportunity to discover and correct these anomalies will be missed.

## Using the Affinity Diagram Process

Perhaps the best approach to this issue of limiting matrix size is to use the affinity diagram concept discussed in Chapter 3. An example will best illustrate how this process can be used to limit the inputs to a matrix when the total number of voices exceeds a manageable number.

A survey of a company to determine customers' wants and needs for onsite training produced a large number of voices. After elimination of attributes and duplicates, there were a total of 64 voices in the sampling. Some typical examples of verbatims are shown below:

"Want to be able to work on a bachelor's degree and advanced degree onsite after working hours."

"Would like to see some specialized courses in marketing offered."

"After the training in specialized techniques (like value engineering) is completed, I want access to some resident expert for help when I try to use the technique."

"Instructors should be of good quality....Observe them and certify them before we use them."

"Classes need a good balance between practical application and theory....Want to see how the ideas can be used in the company."

"The pages in the manuals should be numbered so we can find things quickly."

"All the visuals, chart pad illustrations, overheads, and so on must be readable from the back of the room!"

"Want a speed-reading class."

"Instructors should have some experience with our business and how we design and build products."

"Room should have good climate control—no radical changes in temperature."

A standard affinity diagram process was followed. The 64 voices were put on cards and arranged into natural groupings. Similar groups were combined, and secondary headings were developed. Primary headings were developed for similar secondary groups. Figure 12.1 shows this affinity diagram. For readability purposes, the figure does not show all 64 voices at the third level. Two actual groups of third-level voices are shown as a sample.

This is a typical example of the affinity diagram process. *All of the voices are at the third level because they were the content of the cards that were sorted into natural groups at this level.* This happens on the first arrangement of the voices. When each of

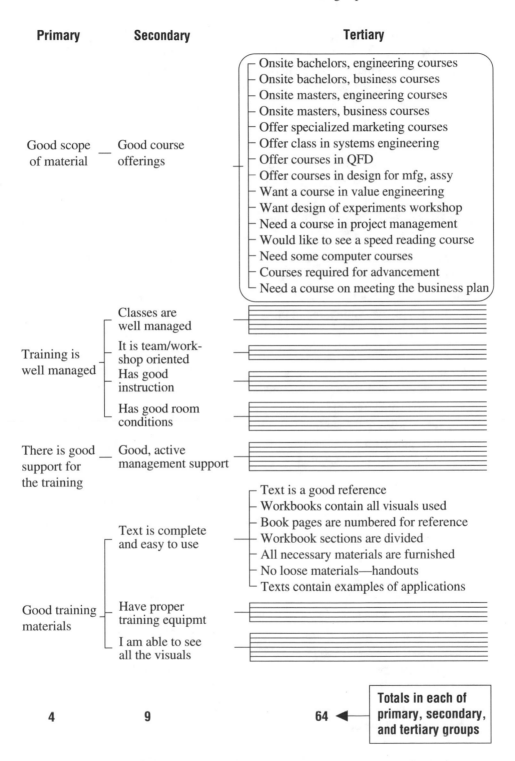

| Primary | Secondary | Tertiary |
|---|---|---|
| Good scope of material | Good course offerings | Onsite bachelors, engineering courses<br>Onsite bachelors, business courses<br>Onsite masters, engineering courses<br>Onsite masters, business courses<br>Offer specialized marketing courses<br>Offer class in systems engineering<br>Offer courses in QFD<br>Offer courses in design for mfg, assy<br>Want a course in value engineering<br>Want design of experiments workshop<br>Need a course in project management<br>Would like to see a speed reading course<br>Need some computer courses<br>Courses required for advancement<br>Need a course on meeting the business plan |
| Training is well managed | Classes are well managed<br><br>It is team/workshop oriented<br>Has good instruction<br><br>Has good room conditions | |
| There is good support for the training | Good, active management support | |
| Good training materials | Text is complete and easy to use | Text is a good reference<br>Workbooks contain all visuals used<br>Book pages are numbered for reference<br>Workbook sections are divided<br>All necessary materials are furnished<br>No loose materials—handouts<br>Texts contain examples of applications |
| | Have proper training equipmt | |
| | I am able to see all the visuals | |
| 4 | 9 | 64 |

Totals in each of primary, secondary, and tertiary groups

**Figure 12.1**    An affinity diagram for onsite education and training.

the third-level groups is reexamined, it is apparent that not all the voices in a group are at the same level. Some will appear to modify or further define another voice. Some will appear to be very similar and have the potential for grouping under another title card. *Therefore, a second arrangement of the affinity diagram may be valuable.* The objective is to reexamine the voices that are in each third-level natural group to determine if they can be logically redistributed. The idea is that certain of these voices may be moved to the right in the diagram—to other levels, such as the fourth or fifth level. This is not a scientific process or one for which specific rules can be prescribed. However, like the affinity diagram process itself, the redistribution process seems quite natural to groups.

Figure 12.2 illustrates this process for a portion of the affinity diagram illustrated in Figure 12.1. In Figure 12.1, 15 voices are shown in the top right group at the tertiary level. These 15 voices fall under the secondary heading of "Good course offerings" and the primary heading of "Good scope of material." In Figure 12.2, the same 15 voices are shown redistributed. Many of them have been abbreviated to help keep the illustration uncluttered. Each of the original 15 voices is italicized and underlined.

To illustrate some of the thought processes of the team, note the five entries at the fifth level that are enclosed by a box. These entries are "Systems engineering," "Design for assembly/manufacturing," "Project management," "Design of experiments," and "Value engineering." Each of these five voices was one of the original 15 third-level voices. The team felt that they represented a group of specialized engineering-related courses. Therefore, the team created a fourth-level heading, "Engineering," for this group of five voices. This heading was grouped with four other items: "Marketing," "QFD," "Computer," and "Speed reading." These five fourth-level items were then placed under the third-level heading "Specialized courses."

Many of the voices have been abbreviated. For example, "Marketing" as a fourth-level entry under "Specialized courses" was shown in Figure 12.1 as "Offer specialized marketing courses." Similarly, the fourth-level entry "Meeting the business plan" represents the voice "Need a course on meeting the business plan."

This "second arrangement" diagram also illustrates another condition. Note that under the third-level heading "Specialized courses" and the associated fourth-level heading "Computer," there are four entries: "WordPerfect," "Microsoft Word," "Excel," and "CAD." These were not part of the original 15 voices. During the preplanning examination of voices, these had been set aside as pertinent to a lower level of detail. The team felt that the real issue was to offer some computer software learning programs and that these issues should be consolidated into one voice: "Need computer courses." Because of the greater levels of detail in the second arrangement, these individual voices can be brought back into the diagram, if desired. There are shown here reentered on the diagram.

The numbers at the bottom of Figure 12.2 show the results of this second arrangement of the affinity diagram. The 15 voices that were originally grouped at the third level are now rearranged into three third-level, nine fourth-level, and 13 fifth-level items.

**The 15 third-level voices for good course offerings have been
divided into third-, fourth-, and fifth-level items as shown**

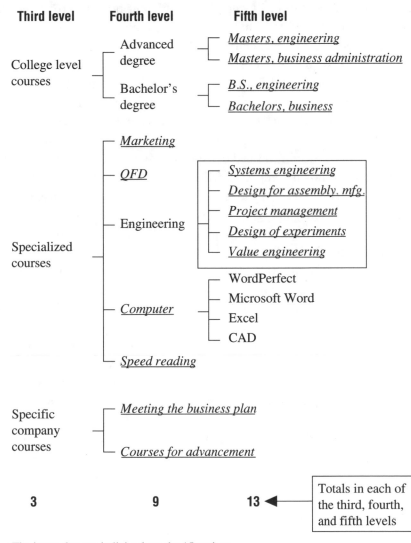

**Third level**  **Fourth level**  **Fifth level**

College level courses
- Advanced degree
  - *Masters, engineering*
  - *Masters, business administration*
- Bachelor's degree
  - *B.S., engineering*
  - *Bachelors, business*

Specialized courses
- *Marketing*
- *QFD*
- Engineering
  - *Systems engineering*
  - *Design for assembly. mfg.*
  - *Project management*
  - *Design of experiments*
  - *Value engineering*
- *Computer*
  - WordPerfect
  - Microsoft Word
  - Excel
  - CAD
- *Speed reading*

Specific company courses
- *Meeting the business plan*
- *Courses for advancement*

3          9          13 ◀── Totals in each of the third, fourth, and fifth levels

*Note:* The items that are italicized are the 15 tertiary
items shown in the box on Figure 12.1.

**Figure 12.2**  Using the affinity diagram process to resort the voices at the third level
into additional levels.

This action of making a second arrangement of the affinity diagram was accomplished for each of the tertiary groups shown in Figure 12.1. Figure 12.3 provides a partial picture of the rearrangement. Neither the four primary groups nor the nine secondary groups have been changed. There are now 21 third-level entries, 46 fourth-level, and 35 fifth-level entries. To keep the figure readable, the fourth- and fifth-level entries are not shown. However, Figure 12.2 represents a typical illustration of how these fourth- and fifth-level items were generated.

The value of a second arrangement of the voices is obvious. Instead of 64 voices at the third level, there are now 21 items. These items are not as specific as the original voices. It is necessary to continue to read the diagram, moving to the right, to gain understanding of the details. Instead of using the full 64 voices, a team could use the third-level entries shown here for its QFD product planning matrix. Thus, it would enter only 21 voices. *The affinity diagram would be used for reference.* For example, the first third-level entry in Figure 12.3 is "College level courses." When the team examines this voice to determine how to respond to it and what target to establish, it must examine the affinity diagram. Examination of the diagram will show that the entry "College level courses" must include consideration of both bachelor's and advanced degrees in engineering and business administration (Figure 12.2). Based on this, the "hows" for the entry might be "Number of bachelor's degree courses" and "Number of advanced degree courses."

Discussions in the 1990 American Supplier Institute study mission courses offered by the Japan Quality Control Society indicated that the Toyota Company had collected more than 900 customer voices related to its vehicles. Its affinity diagram had eight levels. At the first three levels, there were four items in the primary, 13 in the secondary, and 42 in the tertiary levels.

In summary, the first step in limiting the voices is to examine them carefully. Voices should be combined where possible. Those that involve attributes or styling or apply to lower levels should be placed on separate lists. A three-level affinity diagram should be developed. If the number of voices at the third level is too large for effective management, then a second arrangement of the diagram is recommended. In this arrangement, the third-level voices are examined and regrouped. Similar items can be grouped under a new heading. Voices that are obvious modifiers can be moved to the right of the voices they modify. The result will be an affinity diagram that extends to the fourth level and beyond. *In this expanded diagram, there will be a level of items that will be considered to be manageable, and this should be chosen for entry to the QFD matrix.* All of the items to the right of the level selected should be consulted during the process of determining the "hows" to make certain all the customer concerns are addressed.

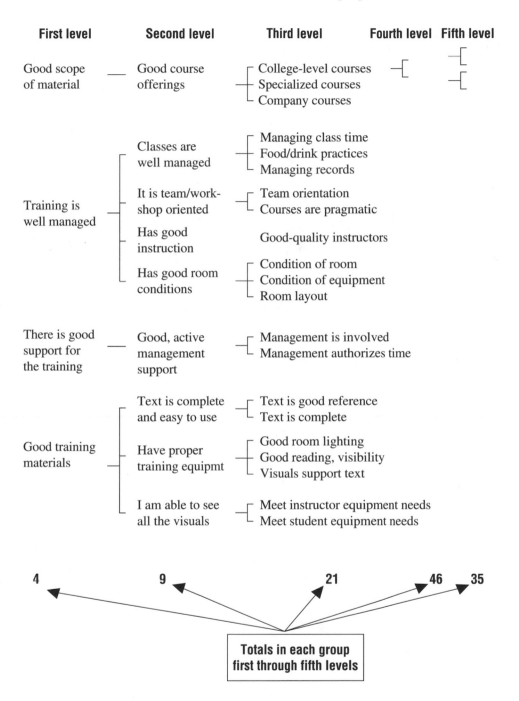

**Figure 12.3**  Affinity diagram for onsite education and training showing effect of developing a separate affinity diagram for the third-level voices.

# Ancillary Matrices with Potential Value

*chapter thirteen*

The matrix concept can be used in a variety of ways. Once people become familiar with the QFD matrix, they frequently find it useful for other projects and applications. This chapter will address some ancillary uses of the matrix that are closely allied with the QFD product planning concept. Other examples of this extended use will be covered in subsequent chapters.

## A Matrix of Voices Versus Functions

The Kano model was discussed in Chapter 3. The lower curve in this model represents basic or functional items. These are basic items that the customer has learned to expect in a product. They are taken for granted; they are not normally mentioned during the interview process. A basic function of a cup is "hold liquid." When people purchase a drink, they do not expect the cup to leak. In surveys of expectations for take-out food and drink, the issue of cups leaking is seldom expressed. If a customer does bring it up, further questioning invariably reveals that he or she had a cup that leaked, oozed, or dribbled within the last 24 hours or so. It was irritating, and it is fresh in their minds.

On established products, companies develop an awareness of the expected product functions through experience and/or value engineering examinations. Manufacturers of hand soap know it must meet functional requirements, such as to remove dirt, allow gripping, and develop suds. Manufacturers of rubbish containers know they must meet functional requirements, such as resist corrosion, hold material, resist puncture, resist abuse, and enclose contents.

In these established products, the functional requirements have been translated into some form of product requirement and measure of performance. These requirements and measures become a part of the company's established product requirements or standards. Companies that have defined their functional requirements in this manner should be able to satisfy their customers' basic expectations.

There are some areas where this level of confidence about functional requirements may not be as strong. On newer products, all of the basic customer functional expectations may not yet be fully identified and understood. Products such as electronics are in highly competitive fields. Constant changes are almost expected of these products as manufacturers try to capture new sales through innovation. These innovations may be constantly redefining the basic functional expectations of a product.

Whenever there is some doubt whether all the functional requirements have been identified or whether the range of customers' voices includes all the necessary functions, a matrix can be employed to cross-check the voices versus the functions.

An example is shown in Figure 13.1. The voices for the coffee cup are shown on the left side of this matrix. Some typical functions of the cup are shown across the top of the matrix. Each voice is examined against the functions to determine if the functional need is captured by the customers' voice. As an example, the two symbols of strong importance in the upper right portion of the matrix indicate that the customers' concerns for "Temperature at the hand" and "Fluid temperature loss over time" do address the functional requirement of "Control temperature." Examination of the completed relationship section shows that the functions of "Restrict spill" and "Control temperature" appear to be well addressed. When the design requirements are developed for the voices related to these functions, there is every indication that the function will be well covered by the requirements.

On the other hand, there is no voice related to the function of "Fit hand." This is an important function that cannot be overlooked. Because there is no customer voice for the function, the team may choose to add it to the list of voices to ensure recognition of this function. Similarly, there is no function for the voice "Material life cycle impact." This could be because the issue was not considered to be a functional need in the past. With the growing environmental concern in today's world, this must be added to the list of product functions.

This example illustrates the advantage of using the matrix format for this type of cross check. It can help disclose functions that are not captured by the customers' voices. It can help discover missing functions. It can reveal emerging customer interests that should be considered as additions to the list of basic product functions.

If a company plans to do any additional value analysis work, such as comparing function versus cost or making a functional analysis of competitors or concepts, it may wish to have an indication of the relative weight of the functions. This can be accomplished in the matrix by entering the customers' levels of importance and calculating column weights, as discussed earlier. This is illustrated in Figure 13.1.

**Cup functions**

| Design requirements from product planning matrix | Importance | Hold liquid | Fit hand** | Restrict spill | Control temp. |
|---|---|---|---|---|---|
| Temperature at hand | 9 | | | | ◎ |
| Fluid temp. loss over time | 9 | | | | ◎ |
| Tip force at top | 7 | | | ○ | |
| Fluid loss vertical impact | 6 | | | ◎ | |
| Fluid loss horizontal impact | 6 | | | ◎ | |
| Indent/force relation | 15 | | | △ | |
| Force/set relation | 15 | | | △ | |
| Porosity | 6 | ◎ | | | |
| Material life cycle impact | 5 | | | | |
| Cup/lid interference | 16 | | | ◎ | |
| Retention force | 12 | | | ◎ | |
| Depth drink well to rim | 12 | | | ◎ | |
| Drink opening area | 12 | | | ◎ | |
| Evacuate angle | 6 | | | ◎ | |
| Tab remove force | 5 | | | ◎ | |
| Function weights | | 54 | 0 | 726 | 162 |

**

*Note:* ** indicates that a function has no related design requirement or that a requirement has no related function.

**Figure 13.1**   Using the matrix to compare the product's functions against the product's design requirements.

## A Research and Development Matrix

During team discussions of customers' voices, ideas frequently emerge about possible responses to the customers. These represent ideas about "how to do it." Chapter 5 pointed out that technical requirements represent a "how to measure" issue rather than a "how to do it" issue. Most people in U.S. organizations have a hands-on, how-to-do-it mindset. *One of the hardest parts of any QFD matrix development is getting people to think in global terms of measures instead of specific how-to mechanisms.* We seem to be so problem/solution oriented that our attention is focused on how to solve the problem rather than on how to measure customers' expectations. It is common, therefore, for many "how-to" suggestions to arise as a team wrestles with the issue of developing technical requirement measures for the voices. Some of these ideas are highly innovative and represent concepts that might be excellent responses to the customer on a longer-term basis. It is suggested that teams capture these ideas and store them for later consideration. A research and development matrix works well for this purpose.

Figure 13.2 shows an example related to the coffee cup system. One voice was "Easy to add cream." The actual verbatim disclosed that the person wanted to be able to add the cream to the coffee in the car without stopping to remove the lid. During team discussion of the voice, several ideas were suggested, such as "Develop a one-handed cream adding device" or "Offer to add it for the customer." The voice and these ideas were entered on a research and development matrix, as shown. The idea of "freshly brewed" generated discussion about a procedure requiring that any coffee remaining in a container be dumped within a specified time after brewing. This led to a discussion of waste and the difficulty of ensuring that people would remember to

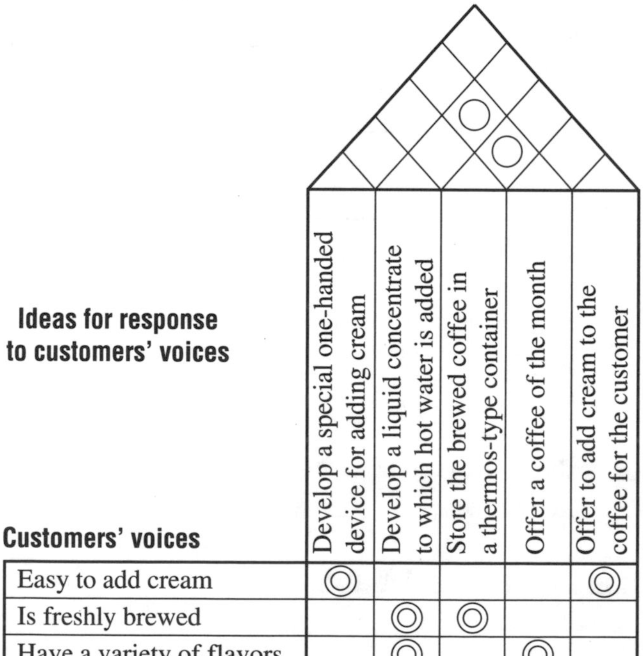

| Customers' voices | Develop a special one-handed device for adding cream | Develop a liquid concentrate to which hot water is added | Store the brewed coffee in a thermos-type container | Offer a coffee of the month | Offer to add cream to the coffee for the customer |
|---|---|---|---|---|---|
| Easy to add cream | ◎ | | | | ◎ |
| Is freshly brewed | | ◎ | ◎ | | |
| Have a variety of flavors | | ◎ | | ◎ | |

Ideas for response to customers' voices

**Figure 13.2**    Using a matrix format to record ideas that were generated during team discussions of "how to meet the customers' voices."

adhere to the procedure. This led to ideas involving a liquid concentrate or the use of thermos containers. The voice related to flavored coffee led to the idea of a coffee of the month. Further discussion might have led to the concept of flavor additives to regularly brewed coffee.

The basic idea behind this matrix is simply to use it to capture the ideas that grow out of team discussion and synergy. The number and weight of relationship symbols in any column gives some indication of the potential value of that idea. If numerical values are desired, the importance values for each voice can be entered, and column weights can be calculated.

## Continuous Processing Applications

The QFD process that has been outlined in the text has been used principally by companies involved in the development and manufacture of products that can be classified under the general heading of hardware. The QFD application is slightly different for industries involved in continuous processes, such as glass making, food preparation, steel making, and many chemicals. In these industries, the part planning matrix and the process planning matrix usually merge naturally into a single matrix.

In continuous processes, the final product is usually some form of a compound. A recipe is used to define the types and amounts of materials required for the compound along with any mixing and curing parameters, such as time and temperature. In a sense, the recipe defines the process steps. It resembles a process flow diagram. The principal purpose of process planning, then, becomes one of ensuring that the recipe amounts, times, and temperatures are assured.

This is best explained by an example. Figure 13.3 shows a product planning matrix for a chocolate cake mix. The example was prepared by Kurt Hofmeister of the American Supplier Institute.

The product planning matrix illustrated in Figure 13.3 is similar to previous examples in the text. The customers' voices are listed as third-level entries. The secondary headings show concern for the general categories of "Tastes good," "Easy to make," "Good packaging," and "Cost." Customer importance (using an 1 to 5 scale), complaints, and competitive evaluations are shown in the customer portion of the matrix.

The technical portion of the matrix is also similar. The technical requirements for the cake include items such as moisture, density, taste evaluation, color, number of utensils, and time to prepare. These are "measureables" that allow competitive technical assessments. Analysis of the customer evaluations versus the technical assessments allows development of operational goals or targets.

The matrix can be evaluated in the usual way to determine the priority items. A quick survey of the matrix indicates that "Moist flavor" (row 1), "Rises well, light" (row 4), and "Always turns out" (row 6) appear to be the principal priority voices.

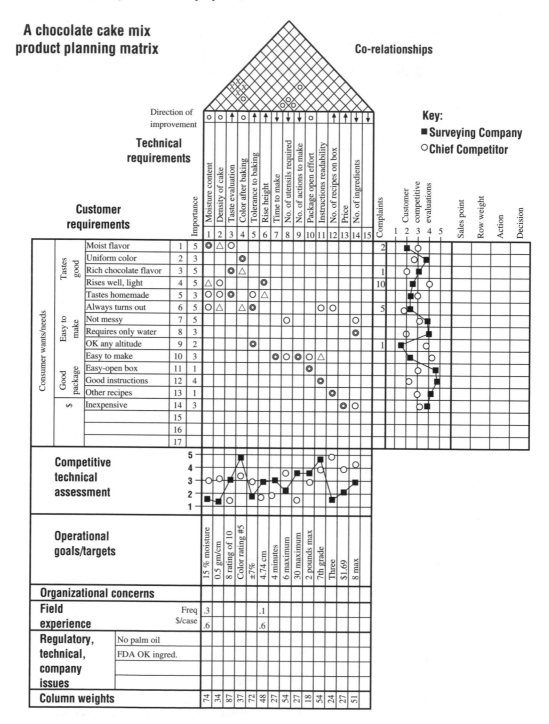

**Figure 13.3**   Continuous process industries.

An examination of the strong relationship symbols for these rows indicates the following technical requirements of concern: "Moisture content," "Tolerance to variation," and "Rise height." An examination of the negative co-relationships indicates that the "Density of cake" should also be included because it will be negatively affected by changes to improve "Rise height" and "Tolerance to variation."

The next step in the typical QFD process is to determine the concept that best satisfies these technical requirements and any internal criteria of concern. Typically, some form of concept selection process would be used to help the team determine which concept best satisfies the overall criteria. The illustration in the upper left corner of Figure 13.4 illustrates how this process would work. Several alternative recipes

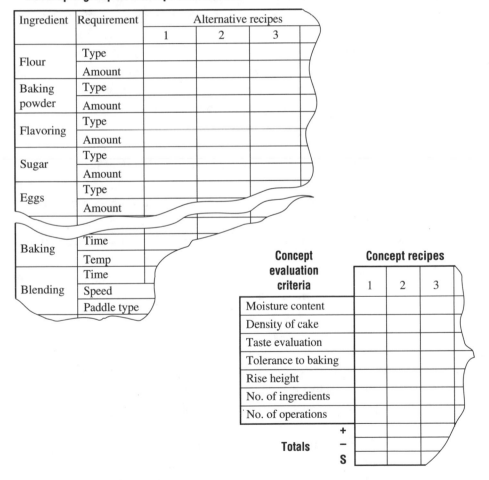

**Figure 13.4**   Design concepts (recipes) can be developed, and a concept selection process can be utilized.

(concepts) would be developed. The types and amounts of principal ingredients would vary for each. These recipes would also include the sequence of addition of the ingredients and processing parameters, such as mix time, container type, oven time, and temperature. These recipes would then be evaluated by some comparative approach, as shown in the lower right corner of Figure 13.4. Certain of the criteria can be evaluated by examining issues such as the number of ingredients and the number of operations. Others must be evaluated by processing each recipe and evaluating the end product. This process would lead to the selection of a recipe that best satisfies the priority customer concerns.

Once this is complete, there is no real need to create a part planning matrix; the determinations have already been made. Each of the ingredients, such as flour, baking powder, and flavoring, is similar to the parts which would normally be listed across the top of the part planning matrix. The material amounts and types, the blending time, and packaging issues that were determined during recipe development are similar to the critical part requirements. The part specifications are the specifics of the recipe for items such as the amounts, material types, and times. Thus, the determinations have been made; they are simply not listed in a matrix format. There is no value in rearranging them simply to put them in the format of a product planning matrix.

The process planning matrix represents a combination of both part and process considerations. The process flow is shown as a flow diagram across the top of the matrix. In the hardware examples previously discussed, the next entry would be the key processing steps. In this example, however, the processing steps involve the addition of the ingredients, their blending, and their packaging (Figure 13.5). These are the same issues of concern as the recipe considerations. Thus, the process steps become a repetition of the recipe. The row entitled "Process ingredients" represents both the part (recipe) and the processing concerns. The critical process requirements also stem from the recipe. They are the types and amounts of materials that must be controlled to ensure that the final compound is correct. The process specifications are shown in the lower part of the matrix. They are similar to typical hardware process planning matrices and involve the procedures and equipment characteristics that must be ensured to guarantee that the recipe requirements are met.

Once the mixture is complete, the operation turns to concerns such as packing and boxing, as shown on the right side of the matrix. These are typical process concerns. However, many of these, such as blending time, speed, and amount of total mix, originated with the recipe. Others, such as packing seals and box gluing, are more typical process issues.

The purpose of this illustration is to indicate the flexibility of the QFD process. No formula states that an exact sequence of matrices must be followed or that any one matrix, such as the part matrix, must follow an exact format. In the case of the

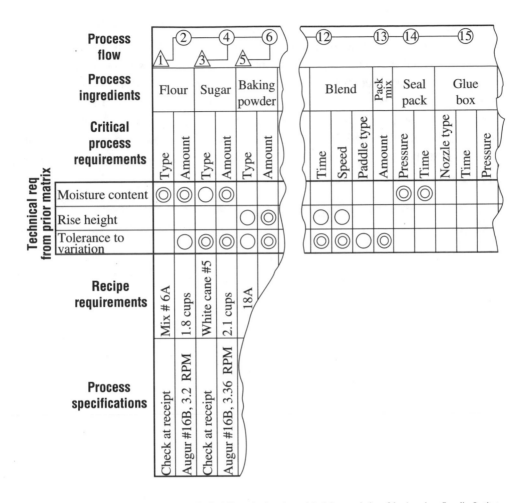

**Figure 13.5**  Continuous process industries: combined part and process flow diagram for the chocolate cake mix.

continuous process industry, a combination of the part and process matrices matches the need very effectively.

The intent in using any of these matrices is to help the organization in its planning process. They provide an orderly, structured approach to determining the responses (hows) for any set of inputs (whats). A team should use whatever format helps it determine the best concepts and the critical requirements for the product or service with which it is concerned.

In summary, people who have used the QFD matrix for product or service planning find it to be an extremely useful tool. The rigor of the matrix format helps an organization in the planning process. It is natural, therefore, that people will find other uses for the matrix approach. The matrix concept can be adapted to fit various needs. Matrices may be combined, their content can be altered, and they can be adapted to a variety of different situations. This chapter has examined three such possibilities: (1) voices versus functions, (2) research and development ideas that respond to customers' wants and needs, and (3) continuous process applications. Future chapters will examine other applications.

# Using the QFD Concept in Business Planning: An Overview

*chapter fourteen*

Organizations that have used the QFD matrix for product planning see its value as an organized approach to comparing and analyzing inputs against outputs, and they also recognize the value of listening to customers and using the matrix to evaluate how the organization should respond to the customers' inputs.

For many organizations, it is a simple extension of this thought process to recognize the potential for QFD in nonproduct applications. They realize that customers can be internal as well as external and that the matrix can be used to help organize and evaluate almost any issue.

This chapter will examine the use of the QFD matrix concept in a business planning application. It will provide an overview of the process. The following chapter will provide a more detailed examination.

Obviously, much of the information normally collected and used in a product planning application cannot be developed for many applications. It is often impossible to collect customers' competitive evaluations and importance ratings for many nonproduct applications. Competitive technical assessments can also be difficult to obtain; most companies have no source for comparison to another company for a specific process or procedural issue. Some insight may be gained if the company can engage in benchmarking with a recognized leader.

Despite this, the basic QFD matrix concept can be of real value to an organization:

1. Because the product planning matrix is so strongly customer centered, it raises an organization's consciousness about the importance of listening to

its customers. Thus, when the matrix is used in nonproduct applications, an organization starts to question who its customers really are and to make the effort to garner and listen to the voices of these customers.

2. There is a primary benefit simply in the organizational value of the matrix. It provides a clear, easily understood format for comparing inputs against outputs. Their relationships can be questioned and examined. Each input and output can be reviewed to make sure it is at the same level of operational detail.

3. A series of matrices can be used to help track the normal flow of a planning process. For example, in a business process, the first matrix may compare basic vision statements against basic objectives. A second matrix will use the output of the first matrix (the objectives) as inputs and compare these to the strategies to be employed to accomplish the objectives.

4. The relationship symbols help an organization visualize whether each input has a sufficiently strong response to ensure its achievement.

5. The matrix can be adapted to show targets or goals where applicable or to show responsibility. If appropriate, importance levels can be assigned and column weights can be calculated to help establish priorities.

## The Deployment of a Business Plan

The left side of Figure 14.1 shows an outline of the flow of a typical business plan. Different organizations use different terminology to describe this flow. The terminology shown here will be used in the following discussion.

As shown on the left side of Figure 14.1, a typical plan starts with a vision of where the company wishes to be in some period, such as 5 or 10 years. The vision is broad and is not in specific operational language (much like the customers' voice in product planning). The vision is normally translated into a set of objectives that represent broad translations of the vision. They are usually not at an actionable level. At subsequent levels, the organization can develop strategies and action plans. Measures can be established to evaluate performance. A review mechanism can be established to provide for periodic review of progress.

The matrix in Figure 14.1 is a generic example of the first step in this process. It involves the development and examination of objectives to translate the vision statement into more specific actionable issues. The conceptual diagram on the left shows the vision and objective boxes darkened to indicate that these are the subject of this matrix. *In each case, as the plan moves through a series of matrices, each subsequent matrix will add an additional level of detail to the overall plan.*

The vision statements are inputs on the left side of the matrix. They represent the "voice of the organization." Objectives developed to respond to the vision statements are shown across the top of the matrix. These describe how the organization intends to

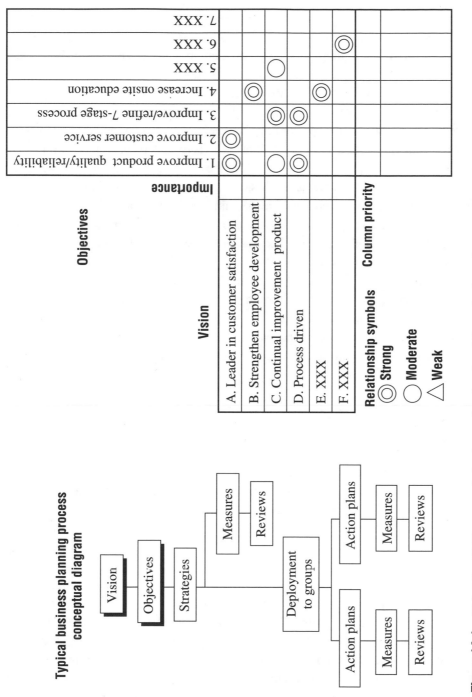

| Objectives | Importance | A. Leader in customer satisfaction | B. Strengthen employee development | C. Continual improvement product | D. Process driven | E. XXX | F. XXX |
|---|---|---|---|---|---|---|---|
| 1. Improve product quality/reliability | | ◎ | | ○ | ◎ | | |
| 2. Improve customer service | | ◎ | | | | | |
| 3. Improve/refine 7-stage process | | | | ◎ | ◎ | | |
| 4. Increase onsite education | | | ◎ | | | ◎ | |
| 5. XXX | | | | ○ | | | |
| 6. XXX | | | | | | | ◎ |
| 7. XXX | | | | | | | |
| Column priority | | | | | | | |

**Vision**

Relationship symbols
◎ Strong
○ Moderate
△ Weak

**Typical business planning process conceptual diagram**

Vision — Objectives — Strategies — Measures — Reviews — Deployment to groups — Action plans — Measures — Reviews — Action plans — Measures — Reviews

**Figure 14.1**   Using the QFD process in business planning (partial matrix shown).

accomplish its vision. The relationships between the vision statements and the objectives are shown in the center portion of the matrix. Only a few vision statements and objectives are shown for illustration purposes. Certain of these, such as the vision statements E and F and the objectives 5 and 6, are intentionally lined out and unreadable to illustrate that more items would be involved.

The relationship symbols represent a judgment by the planning team. They show the presence and strength of relationships between the objectives and the vision statements. Examination of each row shows that each vision statement is strongly related to at least one of the objectives. Examination of the columns shows that each objective has a strong relationship to at least one vision statement, except for column 5, in which only one moderate symbol appears. This should raise a question and lead to reexamination of the objective in column 5. Perhaps it needs broadening and strengthening. Perhaps it is not the right objective. Perhaps it is more typical of a strategy or an action plan and belongs at some lower level.

Importance levels can be established and placed in the matrix. Normally, at this level of the planning process, most companies are reluctant to indicate levels of priority for issues as broad as the vision statements.

Targets can also be shown in the matrix. Usually, objectives are so broad that there is no suitable measurement. Thus, no targets or measures are shown.

## Objectives Versus Strategies

When the organization is satisfied that there is a good and strong set of objectives to match its vision statements, it can move to the next lower matrix level.

This is shown in Figure 14.2. The conceptual diagram is repeated at left. The steps in the planning process that are addressed by this illustration are darkened, as in Figure 14.1. The objectives (hows), which were the output in the previous matrix, become the input (whats) to a new matrix. All of the "hows" are transferred to the new matrix. No priority selection process is used as in hardware applications. Strategies answer the question of how the objectives will be accomplished. They are the next lower level of response and are placed across the top of the matrix.

Again, the relationship symbols provide an easy cross-check of the inputs and outputs. Each objective can be examined to make certain there is a strong strategy or set of strategies for its accomplishment. Examination of the objective in row E, for example, shows that there is only a moderately related strategy, and row F has only a weak strategy response; these bear additional examination. Similarly, the team might reexamine column 7 to see if the strategy can be strengthened.

At this point, an organization may feel comfortable with assigning importance values. These can be placed in the column shown. Column weights can be calculated by using these importance values in conjunction with weights assigned to the relationship symbols.

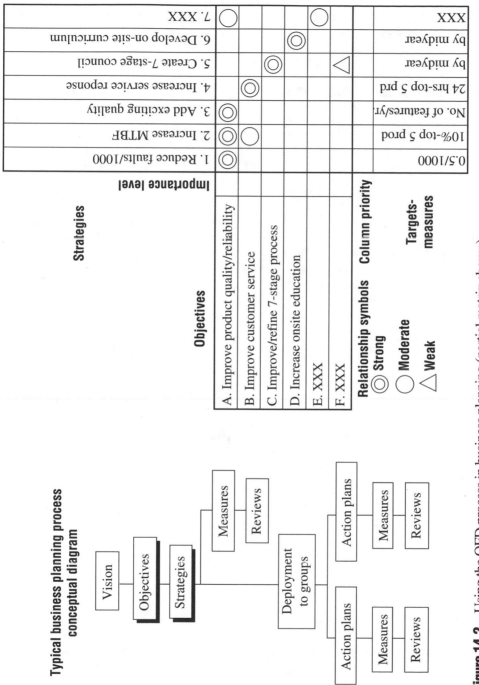

**Typical business planning process conceptual diagram**

Vision — Objectives — Strategies — Measures — Reviews

Deployment to groups — Action plans — Measures — Reviews

Action plans — Measures — Reviews

**Strategies**

**Objectives**

| | Importance level | | | | | | | Targets-measures |
|---|---|---|---|---|---|---|---|---|
| A. Improve product quality/reliability | | | | | | | | |
| B. Improve customer service | | | | | | | | |
| C. Improve/refine 7-stage process | | | | | | | | |
| D. Increase onsite education | | | | | | | | |
| E. XXX | | | | | | | | |
| F. XXX | | | | | | | | |

| Objective | 1. Reduce faults/1000 | 2. Increase MTBF | 3. Add exciting quality | 4. Increase service reponse | 5. Create 7-stage council | 6. Develop on-site curriculum | 7. XXX |
|---|---|---|---|---|---|---|---|
| Targets-measures | 0.5/1000 | 10%-top 5 prod | No. of features/yr | 24 hrs-top 5 prd | by midyear | by midyear | XXX |

**Relationship symbols**
◎ **Strong**
○ **Moderate**
△ **Weak**

**Column priority**

**Figure 14.2**   Using the QFD process in business planning (partial matrix shown).

Most strategies are at a level where measurement is possible. The lower portion of the columns can be used as shown to record these measures or targets.

## Strategies Versus Action Plans

In similar fashion, the plan can be deployed through other steps and evaluated at each point. The strategies and their targets from the objective/strategy matrix can be transferred to a subsequent matrix, as illustrated in Figure 14.3. The action plans across the

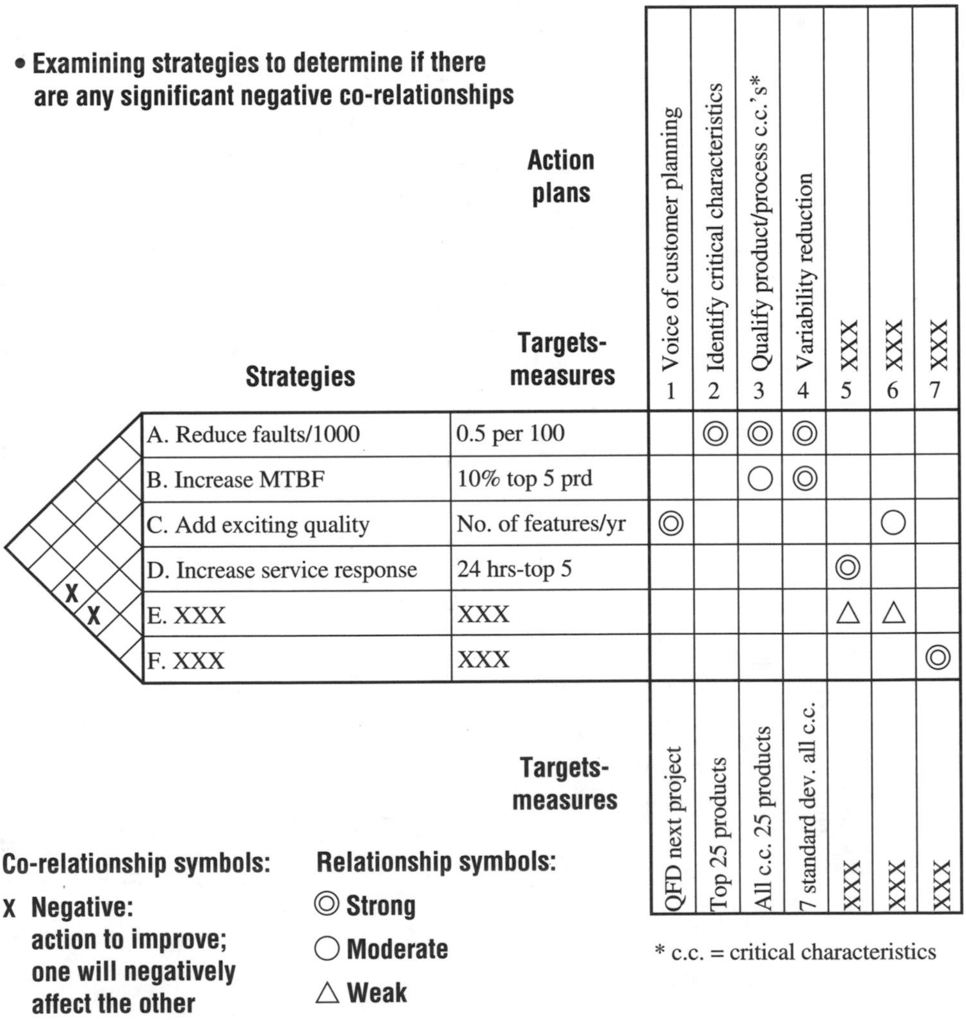

**Figure 14.3**    Using the QFD process in business planning (partial matrix shown).

top of the matrix represent the next lower level of detail and identify how the strategies will be accomplished. Again, relationships are entered and should be examined. Targets are entered, representing the measures and their goals for each strategy.

During this series of deployments, it may be advisable to question the interrelationship of inputs or outputs. Figure 14.3 shows the use of a co-relationship matrix to examine the strategy inputs. Using the co-relationship matrix concept, each strategy can be compared to the others. The basic questions asked are "If the company works on this strategy and accomplishes it, what is the effect on this other strategy? Will it benefit from the action or will the effect be detrimental?" As shown in the illustration, a negative co-relationship exists between strategies in rows C and F. A similar concern exists between the strategies in rows D and F. These need to be investigated to determine some alternate strategy that will negate or compensate for the negative interaction.

## Action Plan Reviews

Figure 14.4 shows how the matrix format can be used to define responsibility. The principal organizational groups are shown across the top of the matrix. The action plans are entered on the left side. Space is provided adjacent to the action plans for a review frequency for each of the entries. The familiar strong and moderate relationship symbols have been altered, as noted in the key. The double circle symbol is used to denote the responsible group. The single circle symbol denotes groups that will support the responsible group. The lower portion of the matrix can be used to record any ancillary information, such as review dates, responsible persons, and special actions planned.

Sometimes, large organizations develop an internal fiefdom atmosphere. Each section of the organization feels a need to develop plans that distinguish it from other sections and give it an aura of importance and independence.

This generates confusion and its attendant waste within the organization. People end up following diverse strategies, many of which conflict with other sections and are at odds with the basic operating strategy of the company.

Because the QFD matrix permits examination of the relationship of many details in an easily understood "outline" form, it has a potential application in these cases. One company that was plagued with this problem listed the basic company strategies as inputs on the left side of the matrix. The action plans from each major organizational group were then listed across the top of the matrix. Each of these sectional action plans was examined to determine its relationship and relevant strength to the basic company strategies. Appropriate symbols denoting the relationship strength were placed in the matrix. A co-relationship matrix across the top permitted examination of individual section strategies that interacted negatively.

| Action plans | Reviews | Marketing 1 | Product planning 2 | Product engineering 3 | Product assurance 4 | QFD team 5 | Critical char. team 6 | Manufacturing 7 |
|---|---|---|---|---|---|---|---|---|
| A. Voice of customer planning | Proj. A in 6 months | ◎ | ○ | △ | | ○ | | |
| B. Identify critical characteristics | Proj. W in 7 months | | | ○ | ○ | | ◎ | |
| C. Qualify c.c. mfg./prod. | Proj. W monthly | | | | ○ | | ○ | ○ |
| D. Variability reduce all c.c. | Proj. W quarterly | | | | ○ | | ○ | ◎ |
| E. | | | | | | | | ◎ |
| F. | | | | | | | | |

**Responsibility**

**Responsibility symbols:**

◎ **Responsible Group**

○ **Support Group**

**Figure 14.4**   Using the QFD process in business planning (partial matrix shown).

The result was a clear picture showing that many of the sectional action plans lacked relevance to the company's strategies. Furthermore, the overall number of action plans was too large to be managed by any organization. As a result, the whole business plan was blurred and its effectiveness was impaired. Thus, the matrix focused attention on an obvious problem that had to be resolved within the company to enable it to move ahead effectively.

In summary, this chapter has provided an overview of the concept of using the QFD matrix in business planning applications. At each stage of the business planning process, the input to the matrix is translated into a greater level of actionable detail. When used for business planning, the matrix is not examined for priority items. All items are transferred to the next matrix. In each case, the "hows" from a matrix become the "whats" for the following matrix. Chapter 15 will provide additional detail and insight into this application.

# Using the QFD Process in Business Planning: A Detailed Examination

*chapter fifteen*

This chapter extends the discussion of the last chapter and provides a detailed examination of the use of the QFD process in business planning. The issues involved will be reviewed and ideas suggested on how these can be handled. A generic example will be used to illustrate.

As described in Chapter 14, the business planning process usually starts with a vision statement. Figure 15.1 shows a typical vision statement. The statement addresses issues typically involved in a company's vision for the next 5 or 10 years. It includes the idea of satisfying customers, increasing the size of the business, and using the latest technologies. It addresses the issue of being process driven, the issue of continual improvement of capability, and several people oriented issues.

## Determining the Key Points of the Vision Statement

The first step in developing a business plan is to condense the vision statement into a set of key points. These simply restate the vision statement in abbreviated language. Following are the key points extracted from the vision statement:

- Satisfy our customers
- Provide innovative products and services

---

**ACME Products**

Vision statement

ACME products is dedicated to building products that satisfy our customers. We will grow our business through innovative products and services, building on our base of satisfied customers and using latest technologies. We seek to be an orderly, process driven company continually improving our overall capability. We are dedicated to the development and involvement of our people through education, communication, and teamwork.

---

**Figure 15.1**   Sample vision statement.

- Become process driven
- Encourage people development
- Continuously improve

Vision statements are not actionable issues; they are too broad. No uniform action will result from telling the organization "We are committed to continual improvement." The statement becomes a slogan because it is too broad for effective, focused action. As discussed in Chapter 14, the organization needs to translate this vision into actionable issues. These are developed in a series of steps as the planning moves through the detail of developing objectives, strategies, and action plans. The usual next step is to determine objectives for the organization to further define the vision's key points.

## Vision Statements and Their Associated Objectives

Most organizations have discovered that responses to challenges, such as problem solving and business planning, are most effectively developed through "team action." A single person could develop objectives for a business plan. However, team action provides the benefit of multiple brainpower and the synergy that occurs as people flesh out ideas through discussion.

The following are typical of ideas generated during brainstorming to develop objectives for the vision statements:

- Improve product quality/reliability
- Identify the critical product requirements so the organization knows where to concentrate resources
- Enlarge the scope of existing SPC applications
- Examine our educational needs to keep people knowledgeable of all new methods and technologies
- Develop a curriculum to match the educational needs
- Improve and refine the seven-stage process we are working on to define the details of product development from concept generation through manufacture and service
- Define our processes using simple flowcharts
- Improve our customer service
- Provide a 24-hour response time on customer service

Once the list of brainstorming ideas has been developed, it needs to be reexamined. In any brainstorming session, there will be some repetition of items; these should be identified and consolidated. There will be a mixture of items, some of which will be true objectives. They represent the next step to put the vision statements into action. However, there will also be items of greater detail that describe how an objective or even a strategy might be accomplished.

Often, it is wise to allow a 24-hour break in the process. Team members will return to the second meeting refreshed and can examine the list more objectively. The team should first address any items that appear to be duplicates or that need clarification. Then, as illustrated in Figure 15.2, the team should get consensus on the level of each brainstorming item. Is it an objective? Does it address a vision statement? Is it a strategy for accomplishing an objective? Is it an action plan aimed at accomplishment of a strategy?

Following this, the first matrix can be constructed. The vision statements are listed as inputs on the left side. The objectives are listed across the top of the matrix. Relationship strengths can be entered in the middle section using the three symbols.

The team should then examine the matrix to see if there is a good match between the vision statements and the objectives. Figure 15.3 shows this initial matrix. Note that there is no strong objective for the vision statement in the second row concerning "Innovative products/services." Similarly, there is no strong symbol in the column "Refine/improve communications." While there are two moderate relationships in this column, the team should examine and strengthen the objective.

- **Which of these ideas are objectives?**
- **Which are strategies? Action plans?**

| Ideas | Level |
|---|---|
| • *Improve product quality/reliability* | *Objective* |
| • Identify the critical product requirements | Strategy |
| • Enlarge the scope of SPC applications | Action plan |
| • Examine education needs | Strategy |
| • Develop curriculum to match education needs | Action plan |
| • *Improve/refine the seven-stage process* | *Objective* |
| • Use simple flowcharts for process descriptions | Action plan |
| • *Improve customer service* | *Objective* |
| • Provide 24-hour response on customer service | Action plan |
| • Etc. | Etc. |
| • Etc. | Etc. |
| • Etc. | Etc. |

**Figure 15.2**   Analyzing the brainstorming ideas.

| Vision \\ Objectives | Improve product quality/reliablity | Improve customer service | Increase onsite education | Refine/improve communications | Improve/refine 7-stage process | Estimate of level of achievement possible |
|---|---|---|---|---|---|---|
| Satisfy our customers | ◉ | ◉ | | ○ | | |
| Innovative products/services | | | | | ○ | |
| Process driven | | | | | ◉ | |
| People development | | | ◉ | ○ | | |
| Continuous improvement | | | | | ◉ | |

*Notes:*

**Figure 15.3**   Develop a matrix for the vision versus objectives.

- **Add any necessary objectives**
- **Evaluate the probable effectiveness**
- **Record points of discussion/definition**

| Vision / **Objectives** | Improve product quality/reliability | Improve customer service | Increase onsite education | Refine/improve communications | Improve/refine 7-stage process | Establish technology group | **Estimate of level of achievement possible** |
|---|---|---|---|---|---|---|---|
| Satisfy our customers | ◉ | ◉ | | ○ | | | |
| Innovative products/services | | | | | ○ | ◉ | |
| Process driven | | | | | ◉ | | |
| People development | | | ◉ | ○ | | | |
| Continuous improvement | | | | | ◉ | ○ | |

*Notes:*
- Onsite education to include differing assignments to broaden experience and knowledge.
- Technology group responsibility and process to be woven in with the 7-stage process.

**Figure 15.4**   Cross-check the vision versus objectives.

As a result of this cross-checking process, the team will find objectives that need strengthening or broadening and may add new objectives. Figure 15.4 shows the result of this process. The team left the objective "Refine/improve communications" unchanged but added a new objective, "Establish technology group," to broaden the scope of response to the vision statement.

## Conducting a Sanity Check

This vision/objectives matrix lays the foundation for the more detailed planning that follows. Therefore, it is wise for the team to stop and run a "sanity check" of the developing matrix. One way to do this is to examine each vision statement and the objectives that are strongly and moderately related to it. The following question can be asked: *If our company fully met its goals for these objectives, how well would the vision statement be accomplished?*

For example, if aggressive goals are set and met for each of the objectives (for example, improve product quality/reliability), how far would the company progress in meeting the vision statement? Would the vision be accomplished 100 percent, 90 percent, or 20 percent? The team's determinations relative to these issues are obviously qualitative. However, the questioning process makes the team come to grips with whether the objectives adequately address the vision.

As discussion about this matrix develops, some ancillary issues will arise. These may involve definitions of the team's understanding of a vision or objective statement or some thoughts about subsequent action relative to an objective. It is important to record such team comments and decisions so they do not get lost as the detail of the planning process increases. All QFD documents should be accompanied by documentation of the team's key ideas, definitions, and discussion points. This is illustrated in the "Notes" section of Figure 15.4.

Note that no levels of importance are shown in this matrix. As discussed in Chapter 14, organizations are normally hesitant to define levels of importance at the early stages of a business plan. Usually, there are only a few vision statements. Assigning weights is very difficult because the choices are so few and so difficult. Is satisfying our customers more important than developing our people or becoming process driven? This can be handled more easily later when the intensity of the items has been reduced by the presence of more detailed "hows."

Similarly, it may not be practical to develop targets for the stated objectives. Typically, objectives are broad issues and frequently cannot be measured with any accuracy. Measurement can be more effective at the next level of detail (strategies).

A co-relationship matrix can also be added as part of the sanity check. The objectives can be examined for any negative co-relationships. If any negatives are apparent, the team should determine how to resolve them before moving on to the next stage.

Some organizations conduct another form of sanity check at this point. They discuss who their customers are and check the relevance of the plan to these customers (Figure 15.5). In this example, the company used a matrix format to compare its objectives against its customers. The relationship symbols used in this instance are in a different context, as shown in the key in the lower left corner of the figure. The completed matrix shows that the company, its people, and its customers expect action on several listed objectives. In other cases, while there is no apparent expectation, customers will benefit from accomplishment of the objective.

Examination of this matrix shows a *strong internal (want it, need it) symbol for each objective*. This lends support to the selection of these objectives. However, the ultimate consumers and the distributors have only moderate symbols shown in their columns. This should encourage discussion about whether the objectives are too narrowly focused. Perhaps there should be an objective related to these external customers.

- **What do they expect?**
- **Is there a match to the objectives?**

### Objectives

| | Our people | Our company | Our consumers | Our customers | Our distributors |
|---|---|---|---|---|---|
| Establish technology group | | ◉ | | ○ | |
| Improve/refine 7-stage process | ○ | ◉ | | | |
| Refine/improve communications | ◉ | ○ | | | |
| Increase onsite education | ○ | ○ | | | |
| Improve customer service | ○ | ○ | ○ | ◉ | ○ |
| Improve product quality/reliability | ○ | ○ | ○ | ◉ | ○ |

**Key:**

◉  I want it, need it, expect it to be done

○  I can use/profit from the results of the action

**Customers**

**Figure 15.5**   Matching customers' wants and needs against the business plan objectives.

The discussion might lead to addition of an objective such as "Determine our customers' wants and needs."

This initial matrix comparing vision statements and objectives is a key document and should be examined carefully. Obviously, misinterpreted visions or misdirected objectives can be the source of a weak final plan. The sanity checks described above are typical of the thought processes that a team should use to examine, discuss, and reexamine the initial matrix.

## Developing Strategies

Once the initial matrix is satisfactory, the team can move to the next step: determining what strategies are needed. Strategies provide an additional level of detail. They permit the organization to start discussion about real day-to-day issues of "How do we really do this?"

Brainstorming is an effective tool. Any strategies developed in the first brainstorming session (Figure 15.2) should be used as starting points. Others will be developed as the team reviews the objectives, discusses them, and generates possible responses. Following the brainstorming session, the team should reexamine the list to sort out redundancies, consolidate items, and determine the level of items. Some items will truly be strategies; others will be at a lower level of detail addressing the action required to accomplish the strategy. Figure 15.6 shows results of a typical brainstorming session along with determination of the level for each idea.

• **Brainstorm ideas**
• **Sort for level: strategy? action plan?**

| Ideas | Strategy? | Action plan? |
|-------|-----------|--------------|
| Reduce faults/1000 products | X | |
| Increase MTBF | X | |
| Add exciting quality | X | |
| Open 800 lines | | X |
| Develop onsite education plan | X | |
| Establish annual education minimum hours | X | |
| Develop customer communication plan | X | |
| Develop internal communication plan | X | |
| Define 7-stage process | X | |
| Create 7-stage council | X | |
| Institute team training | | X |
| Survey the organization satisfaction | | X |
| Survey our customer satisfaction | | X |
| Increase service response time | X | |
| Increase customer contact opportunity | X | |
| Establish 7-stage implementation team | X | |
| Etc | X | |
| Etc | | X |
| Etc | | X |

**Figure 15.6**   What strategies do we need?

• **Group similar strategies**

| Group | Strategy |
|---|---|
| Product quality/rel. | Reduce process faults/1000<br>Increase MTBF<br>Add exciting quality<br>Determine critical characteristics |
| Service | Increase service response time<br>Increase service contacts |
| Process | Define 7-stage process<br>Establish 7-stage implementation team |
| Education | Determine education needs<br>Onsite curriculum plan<br>Establish minimum hours annual education |
| Communication | Develop internal communication plan<br>Develop external communication plan |

**Figure 15.7**   Use the affinity diagram process.

At this point in the process, the number of items grows measurably. There may be value in grouping the items. The affinity diagram process is a logical tool. Figure 15.7 shows the result of this process. The strategies were divided into five natural groups. Descriptive titles were developed for each of the groups.

## Developing Strategy Weights

At this level of detail, most organizations begin to feel comfortable with the idea of assigning levels of importance. When the items have been grouped, the process can be done in two logical steps. In the example shown, the team first determined group weights (Figure 15.8). In this case, with only five categories involved, the team ranked the items. Team members reached consensus on the weights to be assigned to the highest and lowest

- **For the groups**
- **For the individual strategies**

| Group weight | Group | Strategy | Strategy weight | Product of group and strategy |
|---|---|---|---|---|
| (5) | Product quality/rel. | Reduce process faults/1000<br>Increase MTBF<br>Add exciting quality<br>Determine critical characteristics | (5)<br>(3)<br>(4)<br>(5) | 25<br>15<br>20<br>25 |
| (3) | Service | Increase service response time<br>Increase service contacts | (3)<br>(4) | 9<br>12 |
| (5) | Process | Define 7-stage process<br>Establish 7-stage implementation team | (5)<br>(3) | 25<br>15 |
| (4) | Education | Determine education needs<br>Onsite curriculum plan<br>Establish minimum hours annual education | (4)<br>(5)<br>(4) | 16<br>20<br>16 |
| (4) | Commun-ication | Develop internal communication plan<br>Develop external communication plan | (2)<br>(3) | 8<br>12 |

**Figure 15.8**    Consider weights for the rows.

items. They then developed weights for the remaining items. A similar process was used to develop weights for each strategy. This is shown in the column entitled "Strategy weight." A composite weight was then developed by multiplying each strategy weight by its appropriate group weight. This is shown in the last column on the right.

## Objectives and Strategies

Figure 15.9 shows the next matrix. It lists the objectives from the prior matrix as inputs. The strategies related to these objectives are placed across the top of the matrix. The strategies are grouped as in the previous illustration.

- **Add any necessary targets**
- **Establish targets**

**Strategies**

**Objectives**

| Objectives \ Strategies | Reduce product faults/1000 | Increase MTBF | Add exciting quality | Determine critical characteristics | Increase service response time | Increase service contacts | Define 7-stage process | Establish 7-stage implementation team | Determine educational needs | Onsite curriculum plan | Minimum hours annual education | Develop internal communication plan | Develop external communication plan |
|---|---|---|---|---|---|---|---|---|---|---|---|---|---|
| | **Product quality/rel.** | | | | **Service** | | **Process** | | **Education** | | | **Communication** | |
| Improve product quality/rel. | ◉ | ◉ | | | | | ◉ | ○ | | | | | ○ |
| Improve customer service | | | | | ◉ | ◉ | ○ | | | | | | |
| Increase onsite education | | | | | | | | | ◉ | ○ | ◉ | | |
| Refine/improve communication | | | | ◉ | | | ○ | | | | | ◉ | ◉ |
| Refine/improve 7-stage process | | | | | | | ◉ | ◉ | | | | | |
| Establish technology group | | | ◉ | | | | | | | | | | |
| **Targets** | 0.5 per 1000 | 10% top five products | No. of ideas incorporated/year | Top five products by midyear | 24 hours top five products | 1 contact per quarter | Complete by midyear | Immediately | Complete by first quarter | Complete by midyear | 30 hours minimum yearly | For review in 60 days | For review in 90 days |

**Figure 15.9**   Develop a matrix for objectives versus strategies.

This illustration also shows the addition of targets for each strategy. Teams need to evaluate each strategy to make sure that (1) it is measurable, (2) the measure is meaningful, and (3) the measurements can be determined without establishing some new and elaborate measuring system. Some strategies, such as "Reduce product faults/1000," are easily measured by a target such as 0.5 defects per 1000 products. The second strategy could have several potential measures. If the mean time between failures is known for all the products, an average can be calculated. It is unlikely, however, that these values are known. They may require some data searches and testing. If they have to be determined, it is sometimes best to limit the size of the endeavor. The illustration shows that the task was limited to the top five volume products. A 10 percent goal was established for each. As indicated in the third column, an issue such as "Add exciting quality" can be handled by counting the "Number of ideas incorporated" in some time period. A few of the strategy targets are simply stated as dates for completing an action, such as "Define the seven-stage process."

The matrix showing objectives versus strategies should be developed and examined in the same manner as the prior matrix. Relationships should be determined and examined. Is there at least one strong symbol for each objective? Are there any strategies that appear to have only moderate or weak relationships to the objectives? If so, should they be reexamined for relevance? Also, the team can examine each objective and ask whether it will be satisfied by the accomplishment of the listed strategies. This would be similar to the action discussed for Figure 15.4.

## Strategies and Action Plans

Figure 15.10 shows the next probable level of deployment. The strategies from the prior matrix have been deployed (flowed down) to a new matrix. The grouped items are entered as inputs in the left side of the matrix. The weights for each strategy are also shown. These were developed earlier, as illustrated in Figure 15.8. A bar graph format is used here to provide a visual representation of the weight of each entry. For most people, graphics of this type and symbols such as those for strong, medium, and weak stand out more clearly than numerical weights.

The next level of detail—action plans—is entered across the top of the matrix. The same sequence of actions should then be followed on this matrix as on prior ones. Relationships and targets should be determined and placed in the matrix. The team should cross-check the relationships, examining them for inputs that have no strong action items and action items that have no strong relationship to inputs. Any questionable issues should be reexamined.

Teams may choose to reintroduce the idea of the customer benefit at this point to make sure it has not blurred. This is illustrated on the right side of Figure 15.10. The

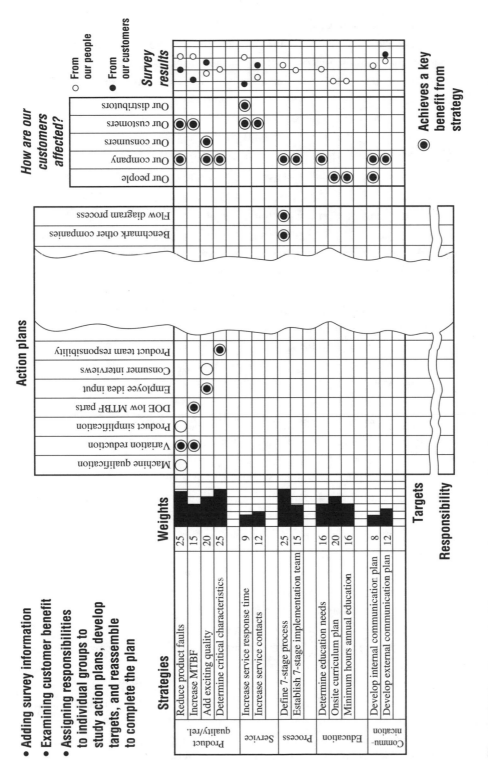

**Figure 15.10**   Cross-checking strategies versus action plans.

strong symbol was used as before to show that the customer gains a key benefit from the strategy. As noted in the prior discussion, the ultimate consumer and the distributor do not figure prominently in this plan. Had some additional objective been added at the point where this was first observed, stronger benefit would have been shown in this matrix for these customers.

## Surveying Customers and Employees

Survey results are shown on the far right side of this matrix (Figure 15.10). Surveys used for business planning purposes cannot be as definitive as those used in many product planning studies, for which an organization can usually obtain customer competitive evaluations through questionnaires. The hardest part of the challenge may be in determining to whom the questionnaire should be sent. This requires some knowledge of which customers use the company's products and which use the competitors' products. Once this is established, questionnaires can be sent out and results tallied.

The process is more difficult for nonproduct applications. For example, the first strategy is to reduce product faults. A company may have records defining the average number of faults per 1000 parts or per 100 shipments. It would be almost impossible to obtain a similar set of numbers for a comparable competitors' product. A survey might be sent to a company's customers asking for their evaluation of items such as performance for quality, on-time delivery, product durability, and response time. However, many customers are unwilling to share their evaluation of competitors for these same issues.

One technique that may be valuable is illustrated in Figure 15.10. A survey was sent to the company's customers asking for their evaluation of those issues pertinent to the business relationship. They were asked to rate only the surveying company, not its competitors. A five-point scale was used. Responses were tabulated and plotted. Similarly, a group of questions was sent out to people within the company seeking their evaluations.

The employees' evaluations and those of the company's customers can be compared on applicable items. For example, on the first strategy, "Reduce product faults," it is apparent that the employees believe the company is performing quite well. The customers, on the other hand, do not share this opinion. This highlights the need to share this information internally and to recalibrate employees' opinions so they agree more closely with those of the customers.

The data is reversed for the third strategy, "Add exciting quality." The customers feel this is being done well, whereas the employees do not. This warrants examination. Exciting quality, if properly introduced and marketed, can increase market share. The employees may understand this and desire more innovation to strengthen their company. In this case, employee response may well represent the voice that should be listened to.

The strategy "Increase service contacts" is rated higher by the customers than by those internal to the organization. It is possible that some additional discussion with the customers may reveal that this is being done better than originally believed. The importance level and real value of this strategy should be reexamined.

Once the organization reaches the action plan level matrix, the issues begin to materialize as specifics. They represent actionable challenges; they are measurable; and they probably require an additional level(s) of detail to enlarge on the specific actions required to make the strategies happen. This is frequently accomplished by having each department develop its specific action plans for accomplishing the action plans of the company. Some companies extend this further to develop action plans for individuals.

## Responsibilities and Reviews

At this point, it is usually desirable for the team to examine the action plans to determine responsibility. Each action plan should be examined. The team should determine which group within the organization is the one with the principal responsibility for carrying out the action and meeting its target. Thus, in the example (Figure 15.10), the first action plan, "Machine qualification," might become the responsibility of manufacturing. The second action plan, "Variation reduction," would likely be a manufacturing responsibility. "Product simplification" might be assigned to product engineering. "Conducting designed experiments" on the top five products to lower mean time between failure might become the domain of some cross-functional team that normally carries that responsibility. This determination can be placed on a new matrix similar to that shown in Chapter 14 in Figure 14.4.

Reviews should be conducted periodically, during the development of the business plan, to keep key members informed and to achieve consensus on the decisions. Responsibility will be discussed during these reviews. A responsibility matrix can be used to record the responsibility for each of the action plans. The matrix can also be used to record who lends support to the responsible party and to note key promise dates.

If desired, each responsible group can be requested to use the matrix format to develop an additional level of detail. This will describe the steps that a department or other organizational group will take to achieve the action shown on the strategy/action plan matrix (Figure 15.10). These lower-level actions are often called initiatives or departmental actions to distinguish them from company-level action plans.

In subsequent sessions, these initiatives can be reviewed and combined into a subsequent matrix detailing the specifics and providing traceable, measurable links between the original vision and the specific actions at the departmental level. This consolidation is not illustrated because it follows the flow-down sequence already described.

The following are key points from Chapters 14 and 15:

- The QFD matrix is an excellent tool to help organizations examine inputs, develop outputs and targets, and cross-check the strength of relationships. Therefore, it has potential for application in softer areas of planning as well as in product planning.
- The business planning illustration very clearly shows the flow-down or deployment concept of the QFD process. In each case, the "hows" from a matrix become the "whats" of the subsequent matrix. In each subsequent matrix, the level of detail increases. At the completion of the process, the items developed represent the actions that must be taken to respond to the initial inputs—the vision statements.
- The purpose of developing a QFD matrix is to help the organization effectively examine, relate, and track items. The matrix is not the objective! The objective is to help the team (1) organize its thought processes, (2) explore various ways to develop strong outputs for each of the inputs, and (3) strengthen the plan where weaknesses are observed.

# Other Possible Applications for the Matrix

*chapter sixteen*

Chapters 13 through 15 have discussed special applications of the QFD matrix. In Chapter 13, three examples were shown of matrices that could be used to augment the QFD process or to meet special challenges, such as those posed by continuous processing industries.

Chapters 14 and 15 discussed the use of the QFD matrix for business planning purposes. Business plans have a natural "flow-down" or "deployment" from broad levels of definition such as business goals to lower levels of detail such as departmental strategies. This is the same type of deployment seen in a product in which the "flow-down" goes from product planning to part, process, and manufacturing planning.

Thus, in Chapters 13 through 15, the concepts presented had significant links to the QFD process. This chapter deals with uses of the matrix concept that are not as strongly linked to the QFD process. The applications originated with teams that had used the QFD process for products and simply transferred the matrix concept to other applications. They are presented as examples and thought starters for readers who may find other applications within their companies.

## A Planning Matrix

The discussion and description of the product planning matrix in the text has been principally oriented to examples of physical products. In a general sense, they might be referred to as "hardware" or "hard" products. Many problems involving customers are of the "softer" type; that is, they involve systems or services that respond to customers' voices.

The example of the education and training survey presented in Chapter 12 is a typical "soft" application. After the second arrangement of the affinity diagram, there were 21 tertiary voices. A plan needs to be developed for how these 21 issues should be addressed. This can be done using a version of the planning matrix; an example is shown in Figure 16.1. Three typical tertiary headings are shown on the left. In the "how" section, the headings, such as "Develop process for workshop classes," represent a macrodefinition of the action required. Specific plans/responses are listed under each of these headings. Typically, in a product planning matrix, the "hows" answer the question of "how to measure" rather than "how to accomplish." In this matrix, there is a mixture. Some items, such as "Instruction/workshop ratio," "Use of preselected teams," and "Case study presentations," lend themselves to easy measurement. Others, such as those listed under the macroheading "Certification process plan," are

| | Develop process for workshop classes | | | | | | | Certification process plan | | | | | | Develop course preview process | | | | |
|---|---|---|---|---|---|---|---|---|---|---|---|---|---|---|---|---|---|---|
| | Instruction/workshop ratio | Room layout for team action | Team report-out process | Use of preselected teams | Postclass team projects | Case study presentations | Predeveloped worksheets | Establish certifying board | Instructor presentation to board | Instructor observation of class | Co-teaching period | Observation of solo performance | Board decision | Team selected from organization | Team members review course material | Review with course developer | Theory/pragmatic example ratio | Appraisals question pragmatism |
| Team orientation | √ | √ | √ | √ | √ | √ | √ | | | | | | | | | | √ | √ |
| Courses are pragmatic | | | | √ | √ | | | | | | | | | √ | √ | √ | √ | √ |
| Good quality instructors | | | | | | | | √ | √ | √ | √ | √ | √ | | | | √ | |
| | | | | | | | | | | | | | | | | | | |

**Figure 16.1**    Using the matrix format for recording proposed actions to respond to the education/training voices.

not as measurable. They represent the key elements of a process for certifying instructors. The process will have to be developed, and flowcharts and/or procedures will have to be generated. Once these are determined, methods can be developed for rating or auditing conformance to the process. The targets for these items are typically dates of completion rather than measures.

In the example shown, checkmarks rather than importance symbols are used. This is simply a matter of team judgment. If row weights or relationship symbols appear relevant, they should be used. As in the business plan, members of the organization can be surveyed for their evaluation of current levels of achievement for each of the 21 entries. These evaluations can be used as a basis for comparison as new plans are developed, implemented, and measured.

A somewhat similar situation existed in one company relative to its engineering change system. One subset of this system involved plant requests for changes. Plants experiencing problems with part manufacture or assembly often find that the problem can be resolved or mitigated by an engineering change. The company's system for processing plant requests was investigated as part of the overall investigation of the engineering change system. Interviews with people involved in the system revealed a number of issues, such as the following:

"Too much time getting the resident engineer (a product engineer assigned to work at the plant) to assess the plant request."

"Too much time lost between actions—too much waiting."

"The change request is not clear. Doesn't have proper description or signatures—need to send it back to the plant—lost time."

"Spend time assessing the change from an engineering viewpoint only to learn that the change time involved is so great or the inventory of related parts is so big that the change can't be accomplished during the current model."

"The plant's cost analysis of potential savings can't be trusted."

"The product engineers are too busy with other problems, like future models; they can't handle today's problems expeditiously."

These issues could be placed in a matrix, and solutions could be proposed, as in the previous example. Measures could be developed to respond to each voice, such as "Time for resident engineer's assessment," "Wait time," "Number of requests returned to plant," and "Number declined due to change time versus model time." These are good measures. A company could record and develop a tracking system for such measures.

However, a more obvious and immediate concern is to solve the bottlenecks in the engineering change process.

Where complex administrative problems are involved, the next most logical step is to review the process and to prepare a flowchart for examination. The flowchart provides an easily read graphic for examining the current business process. Discussion of the flowchart can lead to a number of innovative ideas for process simplification. A flowchart of this process in Figure 16.2 shows the requirement of a number of approvals. These contribute to the cumulative processing time because they usually involve mail time and wait time. For example, the request went from the plant to the change committee and then back to the resident engineer at the plant level. There are no parallel actions; everything is in a line sequence. Some immediate suggestions were as follows:

"Remove the plant manager's approval. Send him or her a copy."

"Involve the resident engineer immediately. Work as a team. Send the request in with both the plant and resident engineers' approvals. Include marked-up drawings denoting the proposal."

"Plant should call for a change committee number, put it on the change, and send copies to both the committee and the product engineer to avoid the sequential step."

This type of analysis is quick and effective. Proposed changes can be shown easily on a revised flow diagram. Following agreement, the team can complete a matrix, if desired. The measurements can be shown across the top, and action can be taken to develop appropriate tracking statistics.

## Problem Solution

Companies commonly use dozens of problem solving methodologies. They range from the simple scientific method approach or the "five why" method to complicated multi-step processes. It is not recommended that the matrix approach replace any of these problem solution methodologies. Many companies have invested a great deal of training time and expense to prepare employees for greater involvement and empowerment through the vehicle of problem solving. They should continue with the practices they selected and are utilizing effectively. However, they may wish to examine the use of a matrix in certain situations. The matrix helps them organize and analyze their thought processes.

Somewhere in the early stages of every problem-solving approach, there is period of examination to determine possible contributors to the problem. A common approach

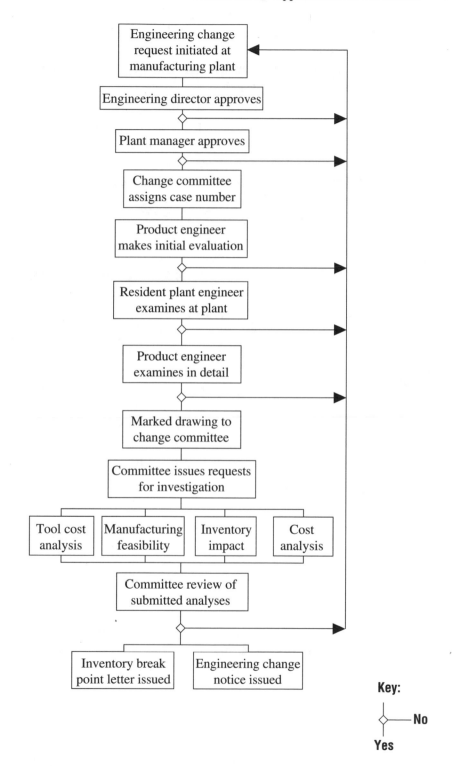

**Figure 16.2**    Developing a flowchart to examine the process.

is to assemble knowledgeable people and to discuss or brainstorm possible problem causes. This is followed by discussion to select the most likely causes. Facts are then gathered relative to these selected potential causes. Once the facts are known, discussion involves possible corrections or solutions.

The possible problem causes can be treated as inputs (whats) to a matrix. Possible solutions can be treated as "hows." Symbols can be used to examine the strength of the relationships. Examination of the presence and weight of the symbols can help prioritize the value of the various proposed solutions. Row and column weighting can also be used if desired. This use of the matrix has its best application in "soft" issues in which the solution involves a change in method or procedure. Harder issues, such as determination of changes to a machine, a process, or a material, will probably not benefit significantly from this type of matrix application.

Figure 16.3 shows an example of a problem involving machine repair. The plant had experienced a number of problems when machines were "down" and repairs were needed. In general, repairs were taking too long. When the repairs involved critical processes with minimal inventory, there was a significant ripple effect on many subsequent plant operations. A brainstorming session involving the repair personnel revealed a number of significant problems. These are shown on the left side of the matrix and involve such issues as "Out of spare parts," "Can't find the spare parts," "Spare parts for replacement are far away—in another factory or building," and "There are no flowcharts for quick diagnosis in troubleshooting." The results of the discussion were posted in the matrix. It was distributed to the team members and a subsequent session was held to discuss possible solutions.

The possible solutions are shown across the top of the matrix. The relationship symbols indicate the team's judgment about how much each proposal would contribute to the solution of the related problem. Row and column weights were used to help in the decision process.

One strong suggestion was to keep the most commonly needed repair parts at (or near) the machine. Further discussion indicated that this concept should be enhanced by using a kan ban card system for the replacement parts. In addition, any specialized tools required for the machine repair should be kept with the parts. The part storage containers were located close to the machines involved. The repair people could write the machine number, problem, and repair time on the kan ban card. The cards would be picked up daily and used for part reordering. The information about repairs would be entered into the proposed software maintenance system. One of the problems uncovered in the investigation was the frequent lack of parts due to poor understanding of the machine failure rates and replacement needs. The kan ban concept of replacement part management permitted both prompt reordering and development of a data base for managing maintenance. It was agreed that this could lead to some eventual preventive planning and use of vibration detectors and similar devices to indicate problems prior to breakdown.

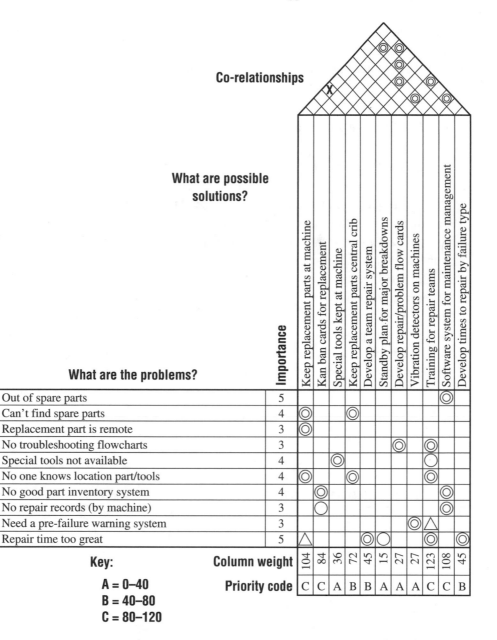

**Figure 16.3**    Using the matrix concept for problems and possible solutions.

The discussions revealed that many of the repair personnel had different experience levels and were following different approaches in diagnosis and repair. It was decided that a training program should be developed for these repair people. The idea of flowchart cards for diagnosis was determined to have a real value, and it was decided that these should be developed in conjunction with the training.

The final solution, in this case, became a composite of many of the proposals. Some of the proposals, such as a central crib and a standby plan, were not utilized because they did not represent the best solution potential.

## Service Sector Applications

The product planning matrix concept has excellent application to the service sector. The following two examples will help illustrate this potential.

Most software companies recognize the need to talk to their customers in the development of new software concepts. They recognize that these interviews are usually general rather than technical because it is difficult for people to comment on software that they have not used. However, designing a system without customer input could lead to disaster.

The most valuable use of customer input can be in the areas of updating and redesigning existing software. Once a piece of software has been marketed, the company knows who purchased its products. It may be possible to determine who has purchased competitors' products. Personal interviews can be conducted to generate customer wants and needs, and questionnaires can be developed to generate customer competitive evaluation data. Figure 16.4 shows a partial matrix for a software graphics program.

| What the customer wants | Importance | Customer's competitive evaluation 1 2 3 4 5 | Do we have this feature? | |
|---|---|---|---|---|
| Spell-checker | 6.8 | | N | Add feature |
| Able to type text directly in the work area | 8.1 | | Y | |
| Able to correct individual words in work area | 9.1 | | Y | |
| Can move individual lines of text in work area | 9.2 | | Y | |
| Can select and move any group of text lines | 8.8 | | Y | |
| Can evenly space any group of lines | 8.9 | | Y | |
| Align any selected group to right, left, center… | 8.7 | | Y | Look at competitor |
| Shrink any selected group horizontally and vertically | 8.9 | | Y | |
| Rotate any line or group to any angle | 6.3 | | N | Look at competitor |
| Fast use–Absolute minimum use of multiple menus | 9.1 | | | |
| Many type sizes available | 7.9 | | | Increase number |
| Provide set levels of magnification, i.e., 2x, 4x, 8x | 6.6 | | Y | |

**Key:**

■ = Our Company

**Figure 16.4**   The voice of the customer: "What do you want in a software graphics (drawing) program?"

Examination of this matrix very quickly indicates areas of great competitive opportunity and "catch-up" areas where the competition is a major leader. The first row indicates a major desire for a spell-checker that neither the surveying company nor its chief competitors are providing. Farther down the rows, it is apparent that the competitors are leading in the areas of rotating lines or groups to any desired angle and in the availability of type sizes. This type of survey can be invaluable for updating and redesign of a product.

In one instance, a company recognized that most of the changes being made to its software were based on responses to the "squeaking wheel." Once the change was made, it often received many calls from users who did not want the change and were angered by it. This created a need for subsequent changes to correct the earlier change, a very expensive process. Using a customer matrix gave knowledge of its competitive position and direction for needed actions involving a larger sampling of customers. The approach of a quick response to the squeaking wheel was dropped in favor of the matrix approach. The company experienced a significant decrease in the time spent in revisions after release of each software upgrade.

Figure 16.5 is an example of the application to a service industry. The customers' concerns are listed at left. They represent basic desires, such as "Quickly connect with the service representative," "Deal with a minimum number of people," "Have the installation and its connections explained," and "Have the service on time and completed with no site damage and no cleanup required."

Measures are shown across the top of the matrix. The competitive evaluation shown at right is for the surveying company only. In this case, there was no opportunity to survey a competitor. The matrix shows several areas in which the company needs to improve based on complaints, importance, and customer evaluations of service. The company had several measures in place for auditing its phone response times. These are shown in the performance data area of the matrix. *They can be compared to the customers' evaluations to determine if the perceptions agree with the internal measurements.* Targets or performance measurement goals can be established and placed in the lower section of the matrix.

For the most part, customers' reaction to a service is based on the contact they have with the people in the service organization. In stores, hotels, and restaurants, for example, the customers' level of satisfaction depends on how well they believe they were treated by the service representatives. Customers who are dissatisfied will usually take their business to another store, hotel, or restaurant the next time. Persons who buy a product that does not satisfy them have recourse through returns and warranty. Service situations are different. Unless a customer complains, the company may not even be aware of the problem. There is no real opportunity to redress the complaint of this type. The customer simply takes his or her business to another source, and the business is lost.

For this reason, service organizations should constantly survey their customers for wants, needs, and evaluations. They should have flowcharts of processes and

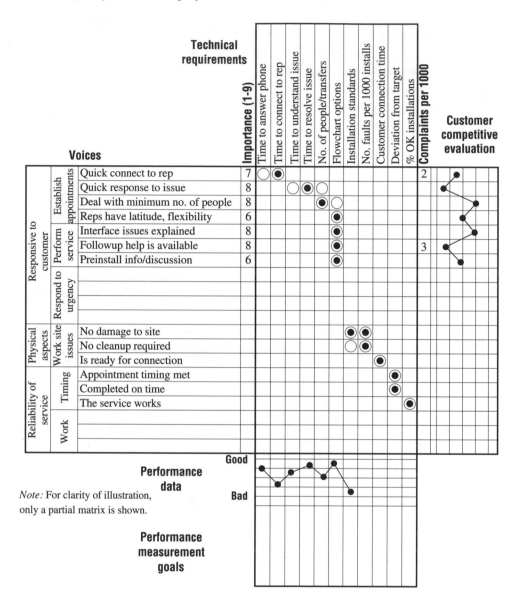

**Figure 16.5**    Translate the voices into technical operational requirements.

accompanying procedures for their operations. They should train their employees in these procedures and the expectations for standards of service. Frequent retraining is essential. Measurement through independent audits, phone monitoring, question-naires, and surveys must be ongoing. The partial matrix shown in Figure 16.5 is an example of the use of the matrix to organize the data in outline form for ease of analy-sis and selection of priority issues.

## The Matrix as a Checklist

Figure 16.6 is basically self-explanatory. It shows a partial matrix for a company that supplies packaging to various customers.

The entries at left represent the customers' lists of wants and needs. These can be generated by the individual sales representatives as they call on clients. As new problems

| What can we offer the customers to resolve their concerns?<br><br>Possible customer concerns | Bar codes | Reactive dyes | Holograms | Buried codes in microencapsulated tags | Time/temperature indicators | Molded styrofoam packaging | Pulp molded system packaging |
|---|---|---|---|---|---|---|---|
| Willfull tampering, e.g., of foods and medicine | | ◎ | | | | | |
| Traceability, e.g., of medicine, automobiles, parts | ◎ | | ◎ | | | | |
| Consumer confidence that contents are authentic | | | | ◎ | | | |
| Stock control for inventory purposes | ◎ | | ○ | | | | |
| Time/temperature concerns during storage and shipping | | | | | ◎ | | |
| Shelf-life concerns, e.g., of foods, medicines, chemicals | | | | | ◎ | | |
| No damage to contents | | | | | | ◎ | ◎ |
| No counterfeiting, e.g., of perfumes | | ○ | | ◎ | | | |

**Figure 16.6**   Using the matrix format as a checklist of solutions available for customer needs.

surface, the packaging specialists need to develop solutions. As these solutions are developed, they can be placed across the top of the matrix. Symbols can be used to indicate relationships. In this way, when a new solution or idea is developed, its potential for application to the customers' needs will be shown by the relationship symbols.

In response to a customer request, a sales representative can move down the left side of the matrix to find rows that represent similar requests. The potential solutions are then easily located by examining the columns denoted by the presence of relationship symbols. Documents of this type are living documents that need change as new requests and/or new solutions and devices are determined.

## A Matrix of Technical Requirements Versus Test Requirements

The product planning matrix is used to develop the technical requirements that respond to the customers' wants and needs. Companies recognize that they must have some system to verify that they meet these technical requirements. In many companies, this process of verification is called "qualification" or "validation." Companies that have a rigorous and well-defined product development program recognize that this validation process is a mandatory step in bringing their product to market. *Products that do not pass the tests that were established to verify that the technical requirements were met will not meet the customers' stated wants and needs.* Therefore, it is essential that a company examine its technical requirements carefully. If its test procedures are not designed to measure performance to the technical requirements and their targets, then the procedures should be revised. This is often evident in the product planning matrix. *If the customers' competitive evaluations differ from the competitive test assessments, this highlights the need to examine the test procedure and to revise it to more properly reflect customer evaluations.*

A matrix can be used effectively for this purpose. Figure 16.7 shows the technical requirements from the coffee example (Figure 5.18). The technical requirements are entered on the left side of the matrix. The targets for these requirements can be added on the far right side of the matrix, if desired. Furthermore, an action column can be added on the right side to record any special notes. For example, if a customer evaluation was in disagreement with the competitive assessment data, this would indicate a need to investigate the test. This type of comment can be noted in the action column. If the team had decided to measurably improve the performance of a technical requirement to increase customer satisfaction, it might note this because the range and type of test criteria could require changes to meet the new criteria.

Figure 16.7 shows the technical requirements for the cup compared to the test requirements. Relationships have been examined and noted by the typical symbols. The relationships indicate that certain tests are only moderately related to the technical

| | Test methods to verify requirements / Technical requirements | Cup temperature test | Fluid temperature test | Center of gravity test | Spill test | Indent/set test | Cup porosity/leak test | Environmental analysis | Place/remove force test | Tab standard test | |
|---|---|---|---|---|---|---|---|---|---|---|---|
| Cup | Temperature at hand | ○ | | | | | | | | | |
| Cup | Fluid temperature loss over time | | ○ | | | | | | | | |
| Cup | Tip force at top | | | ◎ | | | | | | | |
| Cup | Fluid loss vertical impact | | | | ◎ | | | | | | |
| Cup | Fluid loss horizontal impact | | | | ◎ | | | | | | |
| Cup | Indent/force relation | | | | | ◎ | | | | | |
| Cup | Force/set relation | | | | | ◎ | | | | | |
| Cup | Porosity | | | | | △ | ◎ | | | | |
| Lid | Material life cycle impact | | | | | | | ◎ | | | |
| Lid | Cup/lid interference | | | | | | | | ◎ | | |
| Lid | Retention force | | | | ○ | | | | ◎ | | |
| Lid | Depth drink well to rim | | | | ○ | | | | | ◎ | |
| Lid | Drink opening area | | | | | | | | | ◎ | |
| Lid | Evacuate angle | | | | | | | | | ◎ | |
| Lid | Tab remove force | | | | | | | | | ◎ | |
| | **Test method reference number** | TM 89-221 | TM 88-176 | TM 91-21 | TM 91-22 | TM 92-09 | TBD* | TBD | TM 87-52 | TM 87-53 | |

* TBD = To be determined

*Notes:*

1. TM 89-221 and TM 88-176 need revisions to include more current levels of serving temperatures.
2. Tests must be developed for cup porosity under conditions of time, temperature, and pressure.
3. Test procedure must be developed for evaluation of life cycle environmental impact.

**Figure 16.7** Comparing the test procedures against the technical requirements from the product planning matrix.

requirement. The blank columns show that tests need to be developed to respond to new issues, such as porosity and material life cycle impact. The notes at the bottom of the matrix record the team's determinations of the action necessary. Use of the matrix for this type of examination is similar to its use in business planning. It serves as an excellent device to cross-check one set of items against another and to highlight those areas where action is required.

# Organizing Teams and Planning QFD Projects

*chapter seventeen*

Over the last twenty years, we have witnessed major changes in the understanding and management of product and service quality. The challenge imposed by imports, particularly Japanese imports, elevated our consciousness about quality and the compelling need to take decisive action to improve it. Focus has changed from an inspect and correct approach to one of prevention, from engineering based requirements to requirements based on customer needs and expectations. Accompanying this has been a recognition that quality cannot be delegated as a management specialty; instead it must be a total organizational responsibility. Observations and benchmarking studies of companies with successful quality programs have improved our understanding of these organizations and their design, management, development, and renewal. It is apparent that such companies have organized systems and processes, encourage employee involvement, and continually work to improve both. Companies wishing to link themselves more closely with their customers recognize the need for a process to ensure that they understand customers' needs and factor them into their overall planning. QFD is an effective process which addresses this need. This awareness has been coupled with an increased understanding of the value of employee involvement, participative management, and leadership. It is the quality of the organization *in its totality* which defines the quality of its products and services.

The QFD process is a natural for employee involvement. It provides a rare opportunity for employees to listen to their customers and to work on cross-functional teams to translate customers' voices into action.

**Getting started:**

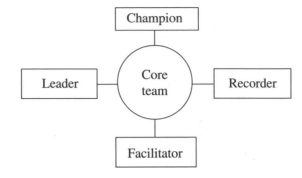

- **Core team**
  - Cross-functional
  - Changing leadership as project continues

- **Team guidelines**
  - How to operate as a team—team rules
  - Develop/hone skills as a team

- **Planning the QFD project**

- **Regular meetings/assignments**

- **Selection of the first project**

**Figure 17.1**    Managing the QFD process.

A wealth of information is available about the formation and operation of teams. It is not the intent of this text, therefore, to comment in detail on these issues. However, some concerns are specific to the QFD process. Therefore, a brief outline will be presented of the organization and planning necessary for a QFD project. Figure 17.1 shows the main topics for this discussion.

## Developing the Team and Team Guidelines

The first step is the formation of a team. The team should be cross-functional. A core team should include marketing, product design, process engineering, and manufacturing personnel. Depending on the organization, personnel from product planning, quality assurance, and other areas may also be involved. The total number of team members should be restricted to help the consensus process and to reduce time lost to extraneous conversations. Six is probably a good target number with a maximum of 10.

The number of representatives from each activity will change as the deployment process continues. Similarly, the leadership will change. In the product planning stage, marketing or product planning will normally assume leadership and have the most representatives, followed by product engineering. In product planning, the leadership role will switch to the product engineering group, and the number of marketing and planning people will diminish, being replaced by process and manufacturing people. As the QFD deployment moves to process and manufacturing planning, those activities will normally take on the team leadership.

It is highly advisable to have a facilitator work with the team throughout the process. This should be someone who has worked with the QFD process and can assist the team in its organization, planning, and actions. A recorder should be appointed to keep notes and make certain that any additions and changes to the developing matrix are recorded. Software for generation of QFD matrices is available from several sources: Using this software, any additions and other changes to the matrix can be made easily. Updated matrices containing the team decisions can be published for examination prior to the next meeting.

In most organizations, there is a champion or sponsor for most emerging methods. The team should recognize the existence of the champion(s) and plan periodic review sessions with him or her.

Once the team is formed, there should be a facilitated discussion on the team rules before QFD process begins. Even in organizations that have used teams extensively, each new team is a unique organization, and norms need to be established. As an absolute minimum, the team needs agreement on issues such as

- What is consensus? What is the test for consensus?
- What are the rules for operating meetings?
  - Start and stop times
  - Frequency
  - Length
  - Need to follow agenda and develop next meeting's agenda before termination of the current meeting
- What rules govern control of lengthy dissertations and "war stories"?
- What rules govern the response of people who missed the last meeting and want to be updated?
- What rules govern people who were not present when consensus was achieved and wish to reopen the discussion?

If time permits, some exercises to promote a team feeling and hone team skills are desirable.

## Planning the Project

Once the team is formed and norms are established, the next major step should be a review of the actual QFD project to be undertaken; this is a basic necessity. The better the original plan, the better each team member will understand his or her role and responsibility. Some of the key elements that should be discussed are as follows:

- What is the mission or objective of the QFD project? This should be a brief statement defining the overall objective.
- What are the steps for the QFD process? This should detail each of the major steps that the team plans for the project. The outline should be restricted to the major steps. Obviously, the precise steps will be related to the number of priority issues selected and the method selected for their investigation. A partial list of the major steps follows:
  - Determine market segment and demographics
  - Determine the chief competitors
  - Hold several focus groups to develop ideas about customer concerns
  - Conduct customer interviews to determine wants and needs
  - Review voice "verbatims"
  - Distribute "verbatims" to team members
  - Consolidate voices
  - Develop questionnaires to determine customer importance and competitive evaluations for company and chief competitors
  - Examine data and develop affinity diagram
  - Generate preplanning (customer matrix) chart; sort out any attributes, styling, and lower-level issues
  - Hold team meeting to review and discuss customer information matrix
  - Develop technical requirements
  - Determine required tests and initiate test requests
- Determine who is responsible for each of the steps and who will assist the process. Set target dates for completion of each step.
- Establish timetables for meetings and champion reviews

## Meetings, Assignments, and Project Selection

Anyone who has examined the QFD process recognizes that the data collection and team decision processes are time-consuming issues. The team should plan its meeting agendas and schedules with this in mind. Most teams meet once weekly for 2 or 3 hours. For major issues, such as determination of the technical requirements, action may be taken to use small teams outside the regular meetings or to double up meetings for several weeks. In most cases, there will be assignments for members outside the meetings, such as generation of test results, research on complaints, and followup on competitive assessment test results.

All of these issues of time must be considered in the original discussion of the scope of the project. It is better to start on a small project and restrict its scope than to become mired in a major project for which sufficient time has not been allocated.

The selection of the first project should be given serious consideration. To the extent possible, one should be chosen where there is a reasonably good chance of success. Much of this depends on the amount of customer information available. Many companies study QFD and want to use the process but have no depth of understanding of the customers' wants, needs, importance ratings, or competitive evaluations. There is a temptation to assemble a group of marketing people and pool ideas about what they think customers want based on conversations and dealings with them. This is an unscientific approach. It is not based on a statistically valid random sampling. The interview process was not based on a common set of questions. Verbatims were not recorded. *Teams have to avoid the temptation to generate this kind of data onsite. The final results will be no better than the inputs, and inputs generated in this manner usually are not representative of the customer.*

Finally, the team must constantly bear in mind that the objective is not to create QFD matrices; rather, it is to determine and execute those actions required to improve customer satisfaction.

## Making the QFD Process an Integral Part of the Product Development Process

Companies that have investigated new processes such as QFD and tools such as FTA and FMEA usually find that many of these mesh with their organizational needs and have good value. However, if these methodologies are not embedded in the company's product planning and development process, chances are strong that the processes and tools will seldom be used. Their absence from an approved process is tantamount to a declaration that they are not considered valuable requisites by the company.

The recent emergence of interest in the ideas of TQM represents another attempt to review the tools and processes that are accepted requisites for companies that wish to economically produce parts that satisfy their customers. A number of recent studies report that these programs are not achieving the expected results because they are not being embedded in the processes and culture of the organization. Success will not be achieved simply as a result of introducing the organization to new concepts and stating that they are endorsed by management. The effort needs to be accompanied by an investigation of the processes by which the company currently plans, designs, and manufactures a product. Flowcharts need to be developed for the existing processes and examined to determine how the new tools must be meshed with existing processes. The flow diagrams need to be examined for the most effective flow with a minimum of time lost due to approvals and nonvalue-added operations.

The new tools and processes should be meshed with existing processes in these flow diagrams. Once agreement is achieved that these represent the most efficient flow of the overall process from concept to delivery and service, they should become the established processes. People should be trained to follow them. Management tollgates should be established for reviews at critical points. Continual improvement of the processes should be an understood goal for everyone in the organization.

If QFD is made a formalized part of the product development cycle, it will help an organization accomplish the objective of understanding its customers and designing products and services that meet the customers' requirements in a superior, exciting way. Making it part of the process ensures that certain essential things occur:

1. The necessary customer surveys and interviews are funded.
2. The effort to get the voice of the customer is planned and is achieved early enough that it can be used to launch the product development process.
3. The QFD team is organized early in the process and plays an active part in the customer voice collection process.
4. The voice collection and development of the customer portion of the matrix precedes the development of a business plan for the proposed product. In this way, the plan will consider the customer priorities as stated by the customer.

To remain viable in a global economy, companies need to be in touch with their customers continually. Their planning needs to comprehend this voice through use of the QFD process. They need to use good engineering analysis tools, such as FMEA, value engineering analysis, Pugh concept selection, and designed experiments. The most effective way to ensure that the organization uses these processes and tools effectively is to embed them in the process for new product development and to audit the process sufficiently to ensure its efficacy.

# References

Barrier, Michael. "A New Sense of Service," *Nation's Business,* June 1991 (Vol. 79, No. 6): 16–21. Excerpted by permission, *Nation's Business,* June 1991. Copyright 1991, U.S. Chamber of Commerce.

Boehme, Christopher. "Nintendo Employees: Video Games Are Their Life," *Compass Readings,* December 1990: 22–30. Reprinted by permission of Skies America/Northwest Airlines.

Chandler, Colby H. "Beyond Customer Satisfaction," *Quality Progress,* February 1989: 30–32.

Garvin, David A. "Competing on the Eight Dimensions of Quality," *Harvard Business Review,* November/December 1987: 101–109. Reprinted by permission of *Harvard Business Review* Copyright © 1987 by the President and Fellows of Harvard College; all rights reserved.

Goodman, John. "The Nature of Customer Satisfaction," *Quality Progress,* February 1989: 37–40.

Hyatt, Joshua. "Ask and You Shall Receive," *Inc.,* September 1989: 90–101.

Kepner, Charles and Benjamin Tregoe. *The New Rational Manager,* Princeton, N.J.: Princeton Research Press, 1981: 83–102. Copyright © 1981 Kepner–Tregoe, Inc.; all rights reserved; reprinted with permission.

Kupfer, A. and A. Erdman. "An Outsider Fires Up a Railroad," *Fortune,* December 18, 1989: 133–146. © 1989 Time Inc.; all rights reserved.

Sharkey, Allen I. "Requirements Gathering Techniques Used with Quality Function Deployment," *Transactions from the Third Symposium on Quality Function Deployment,* Novi, Mich., June 24–25, 1991: 379–416.

Stipp, David. "Life-Cycle Analysis Measures Greenness, But Results May Not Be Black and White," *The Wall Street Journal,* February 28, 1991: B1, B4. Reprinted by permission of *The Wall Street Journal,* © 1989 Dow Jones & Company, Inc.; all rights reserved worldwide.

Swasy, Alicia. "P&G Gambles That Smaller Is Better with New Superconcentrated Detergent," *The Wall Street Journal,* October 16, 1989: B6. Reprinted by permission of *The Wall Street Journal,* © 1989 Dow Jones & Company, Inc.; all rights reserved worldwide.

Whitney, Daniel E. "Manufacturing by Design," *Harvard Business Review,* July/August 1988. Reprinted by permission of *Harvard Business Review,* N.J.: Copyright © 1987 by the President and Fellows of Harvard College; all rights reserved.

Wood, Robert Chapman. "Quality By Design," *Quality Review,* Spring 1988: 22–27.

# Index